Privacy Program Management

Tools for Managing Privacy Within Your Organization
Second Edition

Executive Editor and Contributor
Russell Densmore, CIPP/E, CIPP/US, CIPM, CIPT, FIP

Contributors
Susan Bandi, CIPP/US, CIPM, CIPT, FIP
João Torres Barreiro, CIPP/E, CIPP/US
Ron De Jesus, CIPP/A, CIPP/C, CIPP/E, CIPP/US, CIPM, CIPT, FIP
Jonathan Fox, CIPP/US, CIPM
Tracy Kosa
Jon Neiditz, CIPP/E, CIPP/US, CIPM
Chris Pahl, CIPP/C, CIPP/E, CIPP/G, CIPP/US, CIPM, CIPT, FIP
Tajma Rahimic
Liisa Thomas
Amanda Witt, CIPP/E, CIPP/US
Edward Yakabovicz, CIPP/G, CIPM, CIPT

An IAPP Publication

Copy editor and proofreader: Julia Homer

Indexer: Hyde Park Publishing Services

ISBN: 978-1-948771-23-8

Library of Congress Control Number: 2019931184

Contents

CHAPTER 1
Introduction to Privacy Program Management

CHAPTER 2
Privacy Governance

CHAPTER 3
Applicable Privacy Laws and Regulations

CHAPTER 4
Data Assessments

CHAPTER 5
Policies

CHAPTER 6
Data Subject Rights

CHAPTER 7
Training and Awareness

CHAPTER 8
Protecting Personal Information

About the IAPP

The International Association of Privacy Professionals (IAPP) is the largest and most comprehensive global information privacy community and resource, helping practitioners develop and advance their careers and organizations manage and protect their data.

The IAPP is a not-for-profit association founded in 2000 with a mission to define, support and improve the privacy profession globally. We are committed to providing a forum for privacy professionals to share best practices, track trends, advance privacy management issues, standardize the designations for privacy professionals and provide education and guidance on opportunities in the field of information privacy.

The IAPP is responsible for developing and launching the only globally recognized credentialing programs in information privacy: the Certified Information Privacy Professional (CIPP®), the Certified Information Privacy Manager (CIPM®) and the Certified Information Privacy Technologist (CIPT®). The CIPP, CIPM and CIPT are the leading privacy certifications for thousands of professionals around the world who serve the data protection, information auditing, information security, legal compliance and/or risk management needs of their organizations.

In addition, the IAPP offers a full suite of educational and professional development services and holds annual conferences that are recognized internationally as the leading forums for the discussion and debate of issues related to privacy policy and practice.

Preface

I am privileged to have worked with so many great privacy professionals on both the first edition of this textbook in 2013 and now on this second edition in 2019. The privacy landscape has changed remarkably in this five-year period. We have seen the first major, comprehensive privacy regulation implemented in the EU, with the General Data Protection Regulation (GDPR) impacting organizations and individuals around the globe. We have come to understand that individuals expect organizations to get it right when it comes to the protection of personal information. Demands for improved legislation to protect individuals and their rights have grown exponentially, giving regulators the power they need to ensure organizations comply. Organizations fear damage to their brand, loss of consumer confidence, and regulatory fines due to data breaches. There has never been a better time for organizations to demand well-trained, well-informed privacy professionals.

The privacy program manager is a critical component of every privacy program at any organization. We have seen this field develop over the last few years from a budding program management framework to an integrated and fully functioning multidisciplinary effort. Privacy program management is definitely a team sport. Subject matter expertise is needed in multiple areas ranging from regulatory compliance, policy implementation, training and awareness, data mapping and records of processing to third-party vendor management and contracting. It requires a holistic approach, with multiple skill sets to accomplish all the required aspects of privacy program management in every organization.

Over the last few years, I have come to believe that while a privacy program manager is responsible for bringing all the needed components of the privacy program to maturity, rarely does one person have expertise in all the different disciplines required. An individual skilled in the training and awareness domain may not excel at writing policies, and vice versa. A person who excels at managing data breaches may not do well at vendor management or contracting. I hope you see the point I am trying to make. Privacy is a complex topic with diverse skill sets, which are needed by the privacy organization to be successful. The privacy program manager should be able to understand all these areas but will most likely not be an expert in all of them. Who, then, should be the privacy program manager?

In the past, a legal expert (attorney) has often served as the chief privacy officer and the privacy program manager. Currently, I am seeing a division of duties among the chief privacy officer, the privacy program manager, and privacy engineers. The chief privacy officer may handle the legal and regulatory obligations for the organization while the privacy program manager oversees program compliance requirements, organizational functions, and execution of implementation and the privacy engineer manages the technical functions. There may be overlap, and certainly each of the different domains may serve multiple functions, but we are seeing these areas of expertise evolve.

The privacy program manager is responsible for proving to the organization that it has the proper controls in place and for helping demonstrate to regulators that the organization is handling personal data responsibly. There must be a data map showing what data the organization has and how that data is protected and processed. By definition, this is the privacy engineer's duty. The number of privacy engineers in the privacy profession is rising; in fact, the IAPP launched the Privacy Engineering Section in 2018. The value of such individuals is becoming clear. Perhaps this is the future, where the chief privacy officer, the privacy engineer, and the privacy program manager work together to cover all three roles. Certainly, the organization will need experts in each of these fields to be successful.

There appears to be no one-size-fits-all approach, especially in large multinational and complex organizations. I believe one individual may still be able to cover all of these functions for a small organization; however, I believe privacy program management has matured into a team sport and requires several teammates to be successful.

I would like to thank everyone who assisted with this textbook, especially the individual authors who contributed in their areas of expertise. They were all dedicated and supportive, proving we could work together as a holistic team to achieve success. Finally, I would also like to thank Mr. Edward Yakabovicz once again for assisting me with the final review of this text. His friendship and professional assistance are appreciated deeply.

Russell Densmore, CIPP/E, CIPP/US, CIPM, CIPT, FIP
January 2019

Acknowledgments

The IAPP is pleased to present this second edition of *Privacy Program Management: Tools for Managing Privacy Within Your Organization* in support of our Certified Information Privacy Manager (CIPM) program.

We rely on the expertise and support of privacy and data protection professionals from around the globe to provide our members with quality resources. Thank you to the many individuals who contributed their time and shared their knowledge for the revision of this textbook.

Our Training Advisory Board provides ongoing support and guidance. Thank you, members past and present, for your willingness to share your expertise. Current members include:

Francesco Banterle, CIPP/E
Punit Bhatia, CIPP/E, CIPM
Machiel Bolhuis, CIPP/E, CIPM, FIP
Michaela Buck
Duncan Campbell, CIPP/US
Ionela Cuciureanu
Evan Davies, CIPP/E
Karen Duffy, CIPP/E
Marjory Gentry, CIPP/E, CIPP/US, CIPM
Promila Gonsalves, CIPP/C
Ryan Hammer, CIPP/E, CIPP/G, CIPP/US, CIPM, CIPT, FIP
Missi Hart-Kothari, CIPP/US
Richard Ingle
Laura Kiviharju, CIPM
Henri Kujala, CIPP/E, CIPM, FIP
Viviane Maldonado
Ana Monteiro, CIPP/E, CIPM, CIPT, FIP
Michelle Muthiani, CIPP/E, CIPP/US

James Park, CIPP/E, CIPT
Anna Pateraki
Cassandra Porter, CIPP/US, CIPM, FIP
Stephen Ramey
Brandon Schneider, CIPP/G, CIPT, FIP
Thea Sogenbits
Tiina Suomela, CIPP/E, CIPM, FIP
Liisa Thomas
Maaike van Kampen - Duchateau, CIPP/E, CIPT, FIP
Emily Wall, CIPP/US, CIPM
Ben Westwood, CIPP/E, CIPP/US, CIPM, FIP
Christin Williams, CIPP/E, CIPP/US
Brett Wise, CIPP/US, CIPT, FIP
Matthew Woldin, CIPP/US, CIPM, FIP
Laurel Yancey, CIPP/E, CIPP/US, CIPM
Philip Yang, CIPM

The first edition of *Privacy Program Management* was published in 2013. I had the pleasure of working with Russell Densmore, CIPP/E, CIPP/US, CIPM, CIPT, FIP, who served as the executive editor for the project and led a team of highly respected privacy professionals including James M. Byrne; Elisa Choi, CIPT; Ozzie Fonseca, CIPP/US; Edward Yakabovicz, CIPP/G, CIPM, CIPT; and Amy E. Yates, CIPP/US. Their contributions ensured we had a strong foundation upon which to build this second edition.

We are very grateful that Russell Densmore agreed to serve as executive editor for the second edition of *Privacy Program Management*. Not only was he a pleasure to work with, he was also a very effective project manager, leading a team of privacy and data protection professionals from around the world through all stages of development, from draft outline to final manuscript, in addition to writing his own contribution. He generously provided his time, guidance and support to the whole team. Without him, this revision would not have been possible.

Thank you to Susan Bandi, CIPP/US, CIPM, CIPT, FIP; João Torres Barreiro, CIPP/E, CIPP/US; Ron De Jesus, CIPP/A, CIPP/C, CIPP/E, CIPP/US, CIPM, CIPT, FIP; Jonathan Fox, CIPP/US, CIPM; Tracy Kosa; Jon Neiditz, CIPP/E, CIPP/US, CIPM; Chris Pahl, CIPP/C, CIPP/E, CIPP/G, CIPP/US, CIPM, CIPT, FIP; Tajma Rahimic; Liisa Thomas; Amanda Witt, CIPP/E, CIPP/US; and Edward Yakabovicz, CIPP/G, CIPM, CIPT for your commitment and dedication to this project. We are grateful for your willingness to share your experience and knowledge in the pages of this book.

Many thanks to Pasha Steinburg and Shanna Pearce for their contributions to Chapter 9, and to Jyn Schultze-Melling for permission to include his chapter on the rights of data subjects from *European Data Protection: Law and Practice* as an excerpt in Chapter 6 of this book.

Grace Buckler, CIPP/E, CIPP/G, CIPP/US, CIPM, FIP; Anthony E. Stewart, CIPP/US, CIPM; Tiina Suomela, CIPP/E, CIPM, FIP; Matthew Woldin, CIPP/US, CIPM, FIP; David Wood, CIPP/E, CIPP/G, CIPP/US, CIPM, CIPT, FIP; and Laurel Yancey, CIPP/E, CIPP/US, CIPM reviewed the draft manuscript and provided insightful feedback that helped shape the final draft of the text.

We are grateful for the meticulous eye of Julia Homer, who both copyedited and proofread the manuscript. Thank you to Hyde Park Publishing Services for creating the book index.

We appreciate the hard work, expertise and dedication of the many professionals who contributed to the publication of this book. We hope you will find it to be both a useful tool for preparing for your CIPM certification and a practical resource for your professional career.

Marla Berry, CIPT
Training Director
International Association of Privacy Professionals

Introduction

In 2013, when we launched the Certified Information Privacy Manager (CIPM) program, the idea of operating a privacy program was still novel. Our profession largely evolved from law and compliance, and privacy was, in many ways, binary: The privacy pro gave the product or service a thumbs-up or thumbs-down.

Quickly, however, organizations with business models increasingly dependent on data came to realize that better management and customer trust were needed. Unless the privacy professional was involved at every step of product development, organizations faced too much risk. In public administrations, open data efforts and well-meaning attempts to unlock the value of public data were stymied. Work was wasted. Product leads were frustrated. Mistakes were made.

Further, with the passage of the EU's General Data Protection Regulation (GDPR), the idea of operational privacy, or "privacy by design," became law.

Now we see, through research conducted for our annual *IAPP-EY Privacy Governance Report*, that organizations with mature privacy operations not only have full teams of privacy professionals, they also have privacy pros embedded in various business operations and in administrative departments ranging from human resources to IT, marketing and sales. They provide privacy with multimillion-dollar budgets. They buy technology bespoke for privacy operations.

Nor is it any wonder. While the GDPR gets the headlines, there are any number of other privacy regulations around the world that require operational responses. These issues—from data subject access requests to requests for corrections or deletions and increasing requirements for data portability—require deliberate process, careful management and well-trained people.

In short, privacy program management is here to stay, and the need for sophisticated leaders who understand the complexities of the global digital marketplace will only increase. Thus, it's not surprising that the CIPM has become the IAPP's second-fastest-growing certification, behind only the CIPP/E, and that there is great demand for a new and improved textbook to support the certification program.

Yet again, Executive Editor Russell Densmore, CIPP/E, CIPP/US, CIPM, CIPT, FIP, has overseen a variety of valuable contributions in revamping *Privacy Program Management: Tools for Managing Privacy Within Your Organization*. There are more practical examples, more deep dives into the "how" of privacy management, and more information on the tools privacy professionals are using to create effective privacy programs.

For data protection officers, privacy program managers, global privacy leaders, and any number of other new titles emerging around the globe, the CIPM is the perfect tool for privacy professionals working in both the public and private sectors. This book helps unlock the benefits of CIPM and prepare those hoping to take the exam and get certified.

I am extremely pleased with the way the CIPM has been accepted around the globe as the new standard for how privacy is done on the ground and I hope you—and your organization—enjoy its benefits.

J. Trevor Hughes, CIPP
President and CEO
International Association of Privacy Professionals

CHAPTER 1

Introduction to Privacy Program Management

Russell Densmore, CIPP/E, CIPP/US, CIPM, CIPT, FIP

What is privacy program management? It is the structured approach of combining several disciplines into a framework that allows an organization to meet legal compliance requirements and the expectations of business clients or customers while reducing the risk of a data breach. The framework follows program management principles and considers privacy regulations from around the globe. It incorporates common privacy principles and implements concepts such as privacy by design and privacy by default.[1]

Businesses are motivated today, more than ever, to ensure they are compliant with regulations such as the General Data Protection Regulation (GDPR) and other laws and regulations implemented around the globe—in part, because they want to protect their brand name, reputation, and consumer trust. Large data breaches commonly make news headlines, and organizations have paid penalties and lost revenue or consumer trust. Millions of people have been affected by the sloppy data protection practices organizations have used in the past. These things must change.

It is time for the privacy profession to recognize the value of a holistic data privacy program and the ever-important privacy program manager. This chapter will delve into the requirements for becoming a privacy program manager. The Certified Information Privacy Manager (CIPM) certification indicates that a privacy program manager has the proper understanding of concepts, frameworks and regulations to hold the role of privacy program manager for their employer.[2]

1.1 Responsibilities of a Privacy Program Manager

The goals of a privacy program manager are to:

- Identify privacy obligations for the organization

- Identify business, employee and customer privacy risks

- Identify existing documentation, policies and procedures

- Create, revise and implement policies and procedures that effect positive practices and together comprise a privacy program

The goals of a privacy program (at a minimum) are to:

- Promote consumer trust and confidence

- Enhance the organization's reputation

- Facilitate privacy program awareness, where relevant, of employees, customers, partners and service providers

- Respond effectively to privacy breaches

- Continually monitor, maintain and improve the privacy program

The specific responsibilities of the privacy program manager include:

- Policies, procedures and governance

- Privacy-related awareness and training

- Incident response

- Communications

- Privacy controls

- Privacy issues with existing products and services

- Privacy-related monitoring

- Privacy impact assessments

- Development of privacy staff

- Privacy-related investigations

- Privacy-related data committees

- Privacy by design in product development

- Privacy-related vendor management

- Privacy audits

- Privacy metrics

- Cross-border data transfers

- Preparation for legislative and regulatory change

- Privacy-related subscriptions
- Privacy-related travel
- Redress and consumer outreach
- Privacy-specific or -enhancing software
- Privacy-related web certification seals
- Cross-functional collaboration with legal, information technology (IT), information security (sometimes referred to as IS or InfoSec), cybersecurity and ethics teams, among others
- Reporting to chief privacy officer (CPO), data protection officer (DPO), and/or data protection authority (DPA)

However, before starting the journey toward becoming a certified privacy program manager, you need to understand a few concepts. The first is accountability.

1.2 Accountability

What is accountability? Accountable organizations have the proper policies and procedures to promote proper handling of personal information and, generally, can demonstrate they have the capacity to comply with applicable privacy laws. They promote trust and confidence and make all parties aware of the importance of proper handling of personal information.

The concept of accountability is one of the most important concepts introduced by new data protection laws. It is about not only saying the organization is taking action, but actually being able to prove that it is. In other words, the organization is accountable for the actions it takes (or does not take) to protect personal data. The idea is that, when organizations collect and process information about people, they must be responsible for it. They need to take ownership and take care of it throughout the data lifecycle. By doing so, the organization can be held accountable.

If the evidence says the organization has a policy in place, the organization should follow that policy or document why it has deviated from policy.

Accountability as defined by laws can actually benefit organizations because, although it may impose obligations to take ownership and to explain how the organization is compliant, in exchange, it can give organizations a degree of flexibility about exactly how they will comply with their obligations. Privacy program managers are accountable for the safekeeping and responsible use of personal information—not just to investors and regulators, but also to everyday consumers and their fellow employees.

1.3 Beyond Law and Compliance

Numerous laws and requirements affect businesses today, and the topic of privacy is receiving extra attention from legislators and regulators. However, it is not just about laws and compliance. There are various motivators driving businesses to be more responsible with an individual's personal data.

One such motivator is consumer trust. Fines and fees from regulators are usually clearly defined and have a finite value to them. However, consumer trust can be broad, unbounded, and have much more severe repercussions. Loss of consumer trust can be ruinous to organizations. It is hard to obtain, and harder to get back once lost. Therefore, many organizations are motivated to have a mature privacy program to ensure they do not lose consumer trust.

Obviously, organizations that are business-to-consumer will be more interested in consumer trust than business-to-business (B2B) companies. However, all organizations have an interest in keeping trust with their partners, employees, contractors and customers. Proper handling of personal data is in every organization's best interest.

Alongside consumer trust is a company's branding. All organizations strive to keep their brands untarnished. To this extent, an organization needs to take the proper steps to ensure it:

- Meets regulatory compliance obligations

- Reduces the risk of data breach

- Meets expectations of clients

1.4 Why Does an Organization Need a Privacy Program?

The need for a privacy program may include any one or more of the following:

- Enhance the company's brand and public trust

- Meet regulatory compliance obligations

- Enable global operations and entry into new markets

- Reduce the risk of data breach

- Increase revenues from cross-selling and direct marketing

- Comply with the GDPR

- Provide a competitive differentiator

- Increase value and quality of data
- Reduce risk of employee and consumer lawsuits
- Be a good corporate citizen
- Meet expectations of business clients
- Meet consumer expectations/enhance trust

1.5 Privacy Across the Organization

Managing privacy within an organization requires the contribution and participation of many members of that organization. Because privacy should continue to develop and mature over time within an organization, functional groups must understand just how they contribute and support the overall privacy program as well as the privacy principles themselves. Importantly, individual groups must have a fundamental understanding of data privacy because, in addition to supporting the vision and plan of the privacy officer and the privacy organization, these groups may need to support independent initiatives and projects from other stakeholders. In some larger organizations, members of the privacy team may sit within other functional groups and have a dedicated privacy role— for example, marketing privacy managers may advise and sign off on new marketing initiatives and email campaigns from a privacy perspective. They may report to both the senior marketing manager and the head of privacy. Buy-in and a sense of ownership from key functions also assist with better acceptance of privacy and sharing of the responsibility across the organization rather than in one office. Based on the individual culture, politics and protocols of the organization, privacy professionals will need to determine the best methods, style and practices to work within the organization. Initially, this effort may be onerous, but afterward, the bonds and relationships will be much stronger and better understood.

Many functions directly support the various activities required by the privacy program. Among these activities are the adoption of privacy policies and procedures, development of privacy training and communications, deployment of privacy- and security-enhancing controls, contract development with and management of third parties who process the personal information of the organization, and the assessment of compliance with regulations and established control mechanisms.

As a rule, privacy policies and procedures are created and enforced at a functional level. Policies imposing general obligations on employees may reside with ethics, legal and compliance. Information technology may be responsible for human resource (HR) policies and procedures related to employee use of technical infrastructure. Policies that govern privacy requirements for providers of third-party services that have implications for personal data typically sit with procurement, while those concerning the use and disclosure of employee health information typically reside with HR.

Since activities that contribute to the protection of employee, customer and other data subjects' personal information span the entire organization, most groups within the organization should have some policies to address the appropriate use and protection of personal information specific to their own functional areas; all such policies will need to be produced in close consultation with the privacy office. There needs to be an awareness of the difference between having appropriate policies in place and actually using appropriate controls. Examples of the different functions involved in creating procedures related to privacy include:

- The **learning and development group** that manages activities related to employee training. (Training and awareness—with the intention of changing bad behaviors and reinforcing good ones—are integral to the success of the privacy program.) This function enables policies and procedures to be translated into teachable content and can help contextualize privacy principles into tangible operations and processes. In smaller companies, these responsibilities may fall on the privacy function. Whatever the size of the organization, the privacy team will always need to approve the training output that has been produced.

- The **communications group** can assist with publishing periodic intranet content, email communications, posters and other collateral that reinforce good privacy practices.

- The **information security group** is more closely aligned to the privacy group than any other function in the organization. Every security-enhancing technology that information security deploys—from encryption to parameter security controls and data loss prevention (DLP) tools—helps the privacy program meet its requirements for implementing security controls to protect personal information. As an example, EU data protection law incorporates security provisions into the law as one of its key principles. The information security group ensures that appropriate technological controls are employed (e.g., complex passwords, encryption, role-based access) and determines whether the various groups within an organization are aware of, and comply with, the organizational and technical controls that govern their activities and behaviors.

- The **IT group** supports and enhances the effectiveness of the privacy program by adding processes and controls that support privacy principles. For example, creating processes to develop and test software and applications in a manner that does not require the use of production data decreases the chances that the data will be compromised and that individuals who have no business need for the data will access it. Creating systems that support role-based access also supports the larger purposes of the privacy program by specifically identifying and limiting who can access the personal information in a particular database. The IT group should carry the mantle of privacy by design by implementing privacy principles into the realm of technology development, for instance, by limiting the data fields built into a tool or application to only those actually required to perform a process or action, or by building in functions that enable the user to easily delete data according to a retention schedule.

- An **internal audit group** can be considered an ally of the privacy program and, in a sense, a member of the privacy program, although it traditionally functions independently. This group assesses whether controls are in place to protect personal information and whether people and processes within the organization are abiding by these controls.

- **Procurement** plays an important role in ensuring that contracts are in place with third-party service providers who process personal information on behalf of the organization, and that the appropriate data privacy contractual language is imposed on these service providers. Most privacy laws require data controllers or other entities directly subject to data protection laws to ensure their privacy requirements are fulfilled. Procurement must perform due diligence, take action based on the results, and make sure contractual language reduces the organization's exposure. In smaller organizations, a legal department may create contract requirements if there is no procurement.

- Some of the other departments the organization should consider involving include:

  ◦ HR

  ◦ Ethics

  ◦ Marketing

  ◦ Business development

  ◦ Finance

- ° Legal
- ° Security
- ° Risk
- ° Governance
- ° Research and development

1.6 Awareness, Alignment and Involvement

Protecting personal data and building a program that drives privacy principles into the organization cannot be the exclusive job of the privacy officer or the privacy team, any more than playing a symphony is the exclusive responsibility of the conductor. As with an orchestra, many people, functions and talents will merge to execute on a vision.

Many organizations create a privacy committee or council composed of the stakeholders (or representatives of functions) that were identified at the start of the privacy program implementation process. These individuals and functions will launch the privacy program, and their expertise and involvement will continue to be tapped as remediation needs—some of which may sit within their areas of responsibility—are identified. They will be instrumental in making strategic decisions and driving them through their own departments.

Organizations with a global footprint often create a governance structure consisting of representatives from each geographic region and business function to ensure that proposed privacy policies, processes and solutions align with local laws (and to modify them where necessary).

Kirk M. Herath states this concept another way by saying the privacy professional must become part of the business solution, not an inhibitor. This involves interfacing closely with colleagues in many capacities across the organization as both an advisor and advocate. He states, "Expertise will help staff in other functions meet the privacy requirements of your organizational policy and applicable laws and regulations. Your ability to advocate and be proactive will help float privacy as an important, valuable, and ongoing consideration in many of the organization's internal groups."[3]

1.7 Summary

Privacy program managers are accountable for the safekeeping and responsible use of personal information—not just to investors and regulators, but also to everyday consumers and their fellow employees. Privacy program managers should be ready to demonstrate compliance with applicable data privacy laws, reduce risk, build trust and confidence in the brand, and enhance competitive and reputational advantages for the organization.

Endnotes

1 Ann Cavoukian, *Privacy by Design: The 7 Foundational Principles*, https://iab.org/wp-content/IAB-uploads/2011/03/fred_carter.pdf (accessed November 2018).

2 CIPM Certification, IAPP, https://iapp.org/certify/cipm/ (accessed November 2018).

3 Kirk M. Herath, *Building a Privacy Program: A Practitioner's Guide*, (Portsmouth, NH: IAPP, 2011).

CHAPTER 2

Privacy Governance

Ron De Jesus, CIPP/A, CIPP/C, CIPP/E, CIPP/US, CIPM, CIPT, FIP

Building a strong privacy program starts with establishing the appropriate governance of the program. The term *privacy governance* will be used here to generally refer to the components that guide a privacy function toward compliance with privacy laws and regulations and enable it to support the organization's broader business objectives and goals. These components include:

- Creating the organizational privacy vision and mission statement
- Defining the scope of the privacy program
- Selecting an appropriate privacy framework
- Developing the organizational privacy strategy
- Structuring the privacy team

> *Privacy professional* is a general term used to describe a member of the privacy team who may be responsible for privacy program framework development, management and reporting within an organization.

2.1 Create an Organizational Privacy Vision and Mission Statement

The privacy vision or mission statement of an organization is critically important and the key factor that lays the groundwork for the rest of the privacy program. The privacy vision should align with the organization's broader purpose and business objectives and be refined with feedback from key partners. It is typically composed of a few short sentences that succinctly describe the privacy function's raison d'être. Alternatively, privacy can be covered in an organization's overall mission statement or code of conduct.

> *A **privacy mission statement** describes the purpose and ideas in just a few sentences. It should take less than 30 seconds to read.*

As Herath states, "In just a few clear sentences, it communicates to stakeholders across all your different lines of business—from legal to human resources to sales and marketing—where the organization stands on privacy ... your customers and partners and the auditors and regulators with whom you deal need to feel confident that they understand how your privacy policies and procedures will affect them, that you are meeting any legal requirements and that you are protecting their interests."[1] The following examples illustrate some variations in privacy vision statements.

2.1.1 Stanford University

The Stanford University Privacy Office works to protect the privacy of university, employee, patient, and other confidential information. Our office helps to ensure the proper use and disclosure of such information, as well as, foster a culture that values privacy through awareness. The Privacy Office provides meaningful advice and guidance on privacy "Best Practices" and expectations for the University community.[2]

2.1.2 Microsoft

At Microsoft, our mission is to empower every person and every organization on the planet to achieve more. We are doing this by building an intelligent cloud, reinventing productivity and business processes and making computing more personal. In all of this, we will maintain the timeless value of privacy and preserve the ability for you to control your data.

This starts with making sure you get meaningful choices about how and why data is collected and used, and ensuring that you have the information you need to make the choices that are right for you across our products and services.

We are working to earn your trust every day by focusing on six key privacy principles:

- **Control**: *We will put you in control of your privacy with easy-to-use tools and clear choices.*

- **Transparency**: *We will be transparent about data collection and use so you can make informed decisions.*

- **Security**: *We will protect the data you entrust to us through strong security and encryption.*

- **Strong legal protections**: *We will respect your local privacy laws and fight for legal protection of your privacy as a fundamental human right.*

- **No content-based targeting**: *We will not use your email, chat, files or other personal content to target ads to you.*

- **Benefits to you**: *When we do collect data, we will use it to benefit you and to make your experiences better.*[3]

2.1.3 International Conference of Data Protection and Privacy Commissioners

The Conference's vision is an environment in which privacy and data protection authorities around the world are able effectively to fulfil their mandates, both individually and in concert, through diffusion of knowledge and supportive connections. This vision in part of a Conference strategic plan that also includes a mission statement, strategic priorities and an action plan.[4]

2.1.4 An Coimisiún um Chosaint Sonraí | Data Protection Commission

Protecting data privacy rights by driving compliance through guidance, supervision and enforcement.[5]

2.1.5 Information Commissioner's Office (ICO)

Mission: To uphold information rights for the UK public in the digital age.

Vision: To increase the confidence that the UK public have in organisations that process personal data and those which are responsible for making public information available.

Strategic Goals

1. *To increase the public's trust and confidence in how data is used and made available.*

2. *Improve standards of information rights practice through clear, inspiring and targeted engagement and influence.*

3. *Maintain and develop influence within the global information rights regulatory community.*

4. *Stay relevant, provide excellent public service and keep abreast of evolving technology.*

5. *Enforce the laws we help shape and oversee.*[6]

2.1.6 Data Protection Authority

The Authority's vision (Belgium)

In its reflections and activities the Authority aims to safeguard the balance between the right to privacy protection and other fundamental rights.[7]

2.2 Define Privacy Program Scope

After establishing a privacy mission statement and vision, you'll need to define the scope of the privacy program. Every organization has its own unique legal and regulatory compliance obligations, and you'll need to identify the specific privacy and data protection laws and regulations that apply to it. A typical approach to identifying scope includes the following two steps:

1. Identify the personal information collected and processed

2. Identify in-scope privacy and data protection laws and regulations

2.2.1 Identify the Personal Information Collected and Processed

The first step in gaining assurance that you are complying with your regulatory obligations is to know what personal information your organization collects, uses, stores and otherwise processes. There are several ways to ascertain this. Initially, you can take a less structured approach to identifying where data lives throughout the organization by setting up information-gathering interviews with the typical functions that usually collect, use, store and otherwise process personal information—human resources (HR), marketing, finance, and IT/information security. Taking a lighter touch can at least help you to determine the general categories and locations of personal information, which will be key pieces of data for the next step.

A more robust approach includes engaging an outside consultancy to assess where personal information is collected, stored, used and shared, or engaging other internal resources (e.g., internal audit) to assist the privacy team with the discovery. This more structured exercise of identifying data throughout the data lifecycle drives the development of more accurate and detailed data inventories, maps and other helpful documentation. Further, since maintaining written documentation about personal information (including information about how the organization processes the data, the categories of individuals impacted, and the recipients of data) has become formalized through Article 30 of the EU General Data Protection Regulation (GDPR), organizations that are subject to the GDPR should consider this more thorough, holistic approach to the initial personal information identification efforts. Chapter 4 covers developing data inventories, conducting data mapping and establishing these "records of processing" in further detail.

Some key questions that should be asked to help define the scope of the privacy program are:

- Who collects, uses and maintains personal information relating to individuals, customers and employees? In addition to your own legal entity, this group includes your service providers—so you need to understand these roles and obligations too.

- What types of personal information are collected and what is the purpose of collection?

- Where is the data stored physically?

- To whom is the data transferred?

- When (e.g., during a transaction or hiring process) and how (e.g., through an online form) is the data collected?

- How long is data retained and how is it deleted?

- What security controls are in place to protect the data?

2.2.2 Identify In-Scope Privacy and Data Protection Laws and Regulations

After you have identified key metadata about the personal information your organization collects (e.g., the specific data elements collected, from whom, where it's stored), the next step is to identify the organization's privacy obligations related to that data. Most global organizations are subject to many data protection and privacy laws—and some personal information collected and processed may be subject to more than one regulation. For example, a healthcare services company may be subject to domestic regulations governing the handling of personal health information. The company may also handle financial transactions and therefore be subject to financial reporting regulations as well. Even further, organizations that offer services to individuals located in other countries or that have locations overseas will likely be subject to global privacy obligations. Since no two entities are alike, you will need to determine the true scope for your situation.

> *If your organization plans to do business within a jurisdiction that has inadequate or no data protection regulations, institute your organization's requirements, policies and procedures instead of reducing them to the level of the country in which you are doing business. Choose the most restrictive policies—not the least restrictive.*

2.2.3 Scope Challenges

Determining the scope of your privacy program can be challenging, regardless of whether the program is domestic or global. Purely domestic privacy programs may need to monitor only state and/or regional laws, while global programs will need to be cognizant of cultural norms, differences and approaches to privacy protection. A key example is the U.S. versus EU approach. The former takes a limited sectoral approach, with laws that apply to specific industry sectors or categories of data, like the Health Insurance Portability and Accountability Act (HIPAA), the Gramm-Leach-Bliley Act (GLBA), and the Children's Online Privacy Protection Rule (COPPA). The latter takes a comprehensive approach (i.e., EU GDPR generally applies to all personal data, regardless of sector).

In addition to Europe, key Asian countries, the United States, Canada and Australia have either enacted some form of data protection legislation or are in the process of establishing their own laws, often modeling their laws on those established by the EU.

These laws may apply to your organization, whether it is located and operates in a particular country itself or just transfers personal information from that country to its home location. Determining the applicability of these laws to your organization is a key responsibility of the privacy professional, as is ensuring that relevant laws, regulations and other factors are considered from the start of the privacy program and throughout its lifecycle. Table 2-1 describes the different privacy approaches by jurisdiction, and Chapter 3 details, by jurisdiction, the specific privacy and data protection laws, regulations and frameworks you should understand.

Table 2-1: Sample Approaches to Privacy and Data Protection around the Globe

Country	Protection Models	Approach to Privacy Protection
United States	Sectoral Laws	Enactment of laws that specifically address a particular industry sector, such as: • Financial transactions • Credit records • Law enforcement • Medical records • Communications
EU member states, Canada	Comprehensive Laws	Govern the collection, use and dissemination of personal information in public and private sectors with an official oversight enforcement agency that: • Remedies past injustices • Promotes electronic commerce • Ensures consistency with pan-European laws
Australia	Co-Regulatory Model	Variant of the comprehensive model, where industry develops enforcement standards that are overseen by a privacy agency
United States, Japan, Singapore	Self-Regulated Model	Companies use a code of practice by a group of companies known as industry bodies. The Online Privacy Alliance (OPA), TrustArc (formerly TRUSTe), BBBOnline and WebTrust are examples of this type of model

Organizations operating in the United States face domestic privacy challenges that include determining whether your organization constitutes an entity that is subject to a law or industry standard that regulates data or the collection of data from certain individuals. "Financial institutions," as defined by the Gramm-Leach-Bliley Act, are subject to GLBA.[8] Certain types of organizations and entities known as "covered entities," such as healthcare providers (e.g., hospitals, clinics, pharmacies) and health plans (e.g., medical plans, organization benefit plans) are subject to HIPAA.[9] Websites collecting information from children under the age of 13 are required to comply with the Federal Trade Commission's (FTC's) COPPA.[10] A merchant of any size that handles cardholder information for debit, credit, prepaid, e-purse, and ATM and point of sale (POS) cards must follow the Payment Card Industry Data Security Standard (PCI DSS), which is a global standard.[11]

As the name suggests, PCI DSS is an industry security standard, not a law, but it still imposes certain data protection requirements on organizations, as well as certain notification obligations in the event of breaches; some U.S. states have adopted PCI DSS as part of legislated requirements.

Domestic U.S. privacy challenges also extend from federal laws and regulations to the states; up to 46 states now have data breach notification laws.[12] Accordingly, if you process the personal information of any resident of a state that has adopted a breach notification law, understand that to the extent that nonencrypted data has been compromised, your compliance obligations may include notifying the residents of the state as well as government bodies or state attorneys general offices.

Outside of the United States, many countries put more stringent privacy requirements on the government than on the private sector and impose separate requirements on certain industry sectors (e.g., telecommunications companies face stricter record-keeping requirements) or on data collected on employees.

Appropriately scoping your organization's privacy program is a challenging exercise. A successful approach requires:

- Understanding of the end-to-end personal information data lifecycle
- Consideration of the global perspective in order to meet legal, cultural and personal expectations
- Customizing of privacy approaches from both global and local perspectives
- Awareness of privacy challenges, including translations of laws and regulations and enforcement activities and processes
- Monitoring of all legal compliance factors for both local and global markets

2.3 Develop and Implement a Framework

Once you've determined which laws apply, you must design a manageable approach to operationalizing the controls needed to handle and protect personal information. Implementing and managing a program that addresses the various rights and obligations of each privacy regulation on a one-off basis is a nearly impossible task. Instead, using an appropriate privacy framework to build an effective privacy program can:

- Help achieve material compliance with the various privacy laws and regulations in-scope for your organization

- Serve as a competitive advantage by reflecting the value the organization places on the protection of personal information, thereby engendering trust

- Support business commitment and objectives to stakeholders, customers, partners and vendors

2.4 Frameworks

The term framework is used broadly for the various processes, templates, tools, laws and standards that may guide the privacy professional in privacy program management. Privacy frameworks began emerging in the 1970s. They can be broadly grouped into three categories: principles and standards; laws, regulations and programs; and privacy program management solutions. Examples include:

2.4.1 Principles and Standards

Fair Information Practices provide basic privacy principles central to several modern frameworks, laws and regulations.[13] Practices and definitions vary across codifications: rights of individuals (notice, choice and consent, data subject access), controls on information (information security, information quality), information lifecycle (collection, use and retention, disclosure), and management (management and administration, monitoring and enforcement).

The **Organisation for Economic Co-operation and Development (OECD) Guidelines on the Protection of Privacy and Transborder Flows of Personal Data** are the most widely accepted privacy principles; together with the Council of Europe's Convention 108, they are the basis for the EU Data Protection Directive and the GDPR.[14]

The American Institute of Certified Public Accountants (AICPA) and Canadian Institute of Chartered Accountants (CICA), which have formed the AICPA/CICA Privacy Task Force, developed the **Generally Accepted Privacy Principles (GAPP)** to guide organizations in developing, implementing and managing privacy programs in line with significant privacy laws and best practices.[15]

The **Canadian Standards Association (CSA) Privacy Code** became a national standard in 1996 and formed the basis for the Personal Information Protection and Electronic Documents Act (PIPEDA).[16]

The **Asia-Pacific Economic Cooperation (APEC) Privacy Framework** enables Asia-Pacific data transfers to benefit consumers, businesses and governments.[17]

Binding corporate rules (BCRs) are legally binding internal corporate privacy rules for transferring personal information within a corporate group. Article 47 of the GDPR lists requirements of BCRs (e.g., application of GDPR principles).[18] Under the GDPR, BCRs must be approved by the competent supervisory authority.

The **European Telecommunications Standards Institute (ETSI)** is an independent, not-for-profit, standardization organization in the telecommunications industry and produces globally applicable standards for information and communications technologies, including fixed, mobile, radio, converged, broadcast and internet technologies.[19]

2.4.2 Laws, Regulations and Programs

The **Canadian PIPEDA** provide well-developed and current examples of generic privacy principles implemented through national laws.[20]

EU data protection legislation includes the **GDPR**, which offers a new framework for data protection with increased obligations for organizations and far-reaching effects.[21]

The **EU-U.S. Privacy Shield** was officially adopted in 2016 by the European Commission and establishes a cross-border data transfer mechanism between the two regions that replaces the previous Safe Harbor Framework.[22]

HIPAA is a U.S. law passed to create national standards for electronic healthcare transactions, among other purposes.[23] HIPAA required the U.S. Department of Health and Human Services to promulgate regulations to protect the privacy and security of personal health information. The basic rule is that patients must opt in before their information can be shared with other organizations—although there are important exceptions, such as for treatment, payment and healthcare operations.

Local data protection authorities, such as France's Commission nationale de l'informatique et des libertés (CNIL), provide guidance on legal frameworks.[24]

2.4.3 Privacy Program Management Solutions

Privacy by design (PbD) calls for privacy to be taken into account throughout the whole product engineering process to ensure consideration of consumers' privacy protections.[25] This approach includes reasonable security for consumer data, limited collection and retention of such data, and reasonable procedures to promote data accuracy.

The **European Union Agency for Network and Information Security (ENISA)** provides recommendations on cybersecurity, supports policy development and its implementation, and collaborates with operational teams throughout Europe.[26]

The **National Institute of Standards and Technologies (NIST)** has published *An Introduction to Privacy Engineering and Risk Management in Federal Systems,* introducing concepts of privacy engineering and risk management for federal systems, including a common vocabulary to facilitate better understanding and communication of privacy risk within federal systems and effective implementation of privacy principles.[27] NIST also published the *Framework for Improving Critical Infrastructure Cybersecurity Version 1.1.*[28] The framework enables organizations—regardless of size, degree of cybersecurity risk, or cybersecurity sophistication—to apply the principles and best practices of risk management to improving security and resilience. It provides a common organizing structure for multiple approaches to cybersecurity by assembling standards, guidelines and practices that are working effectively today.

The different frameworks have varying objectives based on business needs, commercial grouping, legal/regulatory aspects, and government affiliations. The privacy questions most frameworks answer primarily include:

- Are privacy and the organization's privacy risks properly defined and identified in the organization?

- Has the organization assigned responsibility and accountability for managing a privacy program?

- Does the organization understand any gaps in privacy management?

- Does the organization monitor privacy management?

- Are employees properly trained?

- Does the organization follow industry best practices for data inventories, risk assessments and privacy impact assessments (PIAs)?

- Does the organization have an incident response plan?

- Does the organization communicate privacy-related matters and update that material as needed?

- Does the organization use a common language to address and manage cybersecurity risk based on business and organizational needs?

2.4.4 Rationalizing Requirements

Once an organization decides on a framework or frameworks, it will be easier to organize the approach for complying with the plethora of privacy requirements mandated by the laws and regulations that are applicable to it. One option is to rationalize requirements, which essentially means implementing a solution that materially addresses them. This activity is made simpler by several factors. First, at a high level, most data privacy legislation imposes many of the same types of obligations on regulated entities, and much of this regulation requires entities to offer similar types of rights to individuals. Among these shared obligations and rights, data protection regulations typically include: notice, choice, consent, purpose limitations, limits on retaining data, individual rights to access, correction and deletion of data, and the obligation to safeguard data—duties that are generally covered by the privacy frameworks previously identified. Further, there seems to be a growing consensus among data protection regulators and businesses on the actions and activities that meet these regulatory obligations.

Note that a rationalized approach to creating a privacy strategy also necessitates addressing requirements that fall outside of the common obligations (often termed *outliers*) on a case-by-case basis. Outliers result when countries' local laws exceed the requirements of national law, or when countries have industry- or data-specific requirements.

For example, rationalizing the common legal obligation of providing individuals with a right of access to their personal information means the organization must also identify the time frames within which data must be provided to individuals per applicable privacy law. In the EU, as a result of GDPR, prescribed time frames within which an organization must provide access to individuals (e.g., employees, consumers) now exist. In countries where no legal requirements exist (and the granting of access may be merely an organization policy), or where there is a generous amount of time extended to provide data, the organization can adopt a procedure that sets a common time period within which data must be provided. A rationalized approach that seeks to address both sets of requirements would result in the organization establishing a standard access process that generally meets the demands of many countries, with a local process that meets specific time frame requirements for individuals in EU countries only.

Another approach organizations employ, when possible, is to look to the strictest standard when seeking a solution, provided it does not violate any data privacy laws, exceed budgetary restrictions, or contradict organization goals and objectives. This approach is used more frequently than most organizations realize. In the example above, rather than responding to access requests of only EU-based individuals within a 30-day period, the organization would provide all individuals globally with access to their data within a prescribed, GDPR-compliant time frame. Other examples are shredding everything versus shredding only documents that contain personal or confidential information, or rolling out laptop encryption for the entire employee population as opposed to targeting only individuals who may perform functions that involve personal information.

2.5 Privacy Tech and Government, Risk and Compliance Vendors and Tools

Some organizations choose to use privacy tech vendors to help them achieve compliance within their selected privacy program framework. Privacy tech vendors offer a range of solutions, from assessment management to data mapping and de-identification and incident response. Note that a product or solution in and by itself is not compliant. When deployed as part of a properly thought-out privacy program, the solution is a tool that assists the organization with GDPR and multijurisdictional and regulatory compliance requirements.

2.5.1 Categories of Privacy Tech Vendors

Privacy tech vendors in the category of privacy program management typically work directly with the privacy office. Vendors may manage:

- Assessment
- Consent
- Data mapping
- Incident response
- Privacy information
- Website scanning/cookie compliance

Enterprise program management services require buy-in from the privacy office, IT and C-suite. Services include:

- Activity monitoring

- Data discovery

- De-identification/pseudonymization

- Enterprise communications[29]

2.5.2 Governance, Risk and Compliance Tools

According to a recent survey completed by the IAPP and EY, at least 35 percent of privacy professionals surveyed use governance, risk and compliance(GRC) tools as part of their privacy framework.[30] GRC is an umbrella term whose scope touches the privacy office as well as other departments, including HR, IT, compliance and the C-suite. GRC tools aim to synchronize various internal functions toward "principled performance"— integrating the governance, management and assurance of performance, risk and compliance activities. While many IT vendors provide capabilities to meet a single compliance requirement, true GRC vendors provide tools to oversee risk and compliance across the entire organization, helping to automate GRC initiatives that are mostly manual or beyond an organization's current capabilities.

GRC tools are generally used to:

- Create and distribute policies and controls and map them to regulations and internal compliance requirements

- Assess whether the controls are in place and working, and fix them if they are not

- Ease risk assessment and mitigation[31]

2.6 Develop a Privacy Strategy

Now that the framework through which the organization will organize its privacy requirements has been identified, the next consideration is the privacy strategy. Essentially, a privacy strategy is the organization's approach to communicating and obtaining support for the privacy program. Personal information may be collected and used across an organization, with many individuals responsible for protecting this information. No one solution mitigates all privacy risk, and there is no one-size-fits-all strategy that can be adopted. There are positive benefits to implementing a privacy strategy in today's environment, among them management's growing awareness of the importance of protecting personal information and the financial impact of mismanagement. With that said, getting buy-in at the appropriate levels can still be difficult.

Building a privacy strategy may mean changing the mindset and perspective of an entire organization. Everyone in an organization has a role to play in protecting the personal information an organization collects, uses and discloses. Management needs to approve funding to resource and equip the privacy team, fund important privacy-enhancing resources and technologies, support privacy initiatives such as training and awareness, and hold employees accountable for following privacy policies and procedures. Sales personnel must secure business contact data and respect the choices of these individuals. Developers and engineers must incorporate effective security controls, build safe websites, and create solutions that require the collection or use of only the data necessary to accomplish the purpose. All staff must understand and employ fundamental practices required to protect personal data—from secure methods of collecting, storing and transmitting personal data (both hard-copy and electronic) through secure methods of destruction. The adage "the chain is only as strong as its weakest link" truly reflects the way an organization must approach its privacy program. There are no shortcuts, and every individual within an organization contributes to the success of the privacy program.

Before an organization can embark on this journey, the management team will need to understand why their involvement and support is so critical. It is important to know the ultimate destination before beginning, and to have a roadmap for the journey. These factors and more must be contained in the privacy strategy to ensure success, buy-in and ownership from the widest possible pool of stakeholders.

2.6.1 Identify Stakeholders and Internal Partnerships

One of the most challenging aspects of building a privacy program and the necessary supporting strategy is gaining consensus from members of the organization's management on privacy as a business imperative. Building and gaining this consensus in stages is a must.

The first major step in building a coalition of supporters is to conduct informal one-on-one conversations with executives within the organization who have accountability for information management and/or security, risk, compliance or legal decisions. Internal partners, such as HR, legal, security, marketing, risk management and IT should also be included in conversations, as they too will have ownership of privacy activities, and their buy-in will be necessary. Depending on the organization's industry and corporate culture, the executives, managers and internal partners will each play a role in the development and implementation of the privacy strategy for the privacy program.

From these conversations, you should start to get a sense for which executive will serve as the program sponsor, or "champion" for the privacy program, or whether an executive is even necessary. The program sponsor should be someone who understands the importance of privacy and will act as an advocate for you and for the program. Effective program sponsors typically have experience with the organization, the respect of their colleagues, and access to or ownership of a budget. Final budgetary decision makers are the preferred program sponsors, but if they are unavailable, it is best to obtain approval from executive management closest to the organization's top executive. Frequently, sponsors function as risk or compliance executives within the organization. Sometimes chief operating officers (COOs) or chief information officers (CIOs) serve as program sponsors.

> *A privacy champion at the executive level acts as an advocate and sponsor to further foster privacy as a core organization concept.*

Most organizations, regardless of their size, industry and specific business, use personal information for roughly the same bundle of activities—for example, staff recruitment and ongoing employment administration, customer relationship management and marketing, and order fulfillment. Further, the use of this personal information is managed by a similar array of executives—regardless of the organization or its activities. It is common to refer to the individual executives who lead the relevant activities and own responsibility for them as stakeholders. Typically, in a larger organization, an executive privacy team will include some or all of the following individuals: senior security executive [e.g., chief security officer (CSO)]; senior risk executive [e.g., chief risk officer (CRO)]; senior compliance executive [(e.g., chief compliance officer (CCO)]; senior HR executive; senior legal executive (e.g., general counsel); senior information executive (e.g., CIO); senior physical security/business continuity executive; senior marketing executive (CMO); and a senior representative of the business.

Several best practices when developing internal partnerships include:

- Become aware of how others treat and view personal information
- Understand their use of the data in a business context

- Assist with building privacy requirements into their ongoing projects to help reduce risk

- Offer to help staff meet their objectives while offering solutions to reduce risk of personal information exposure

- Invite staff to be a part of the privacy advocate group to further privacy best practices

> *In smaller organizations, a legal department may create contract requirements if there is no procurement.*

2.6.2 Conduct a Privacy Workshop for Stakeholders

With the support of the privacy program sponsor, you should plan to conduct a workshop for the stakeholders who will support efforts to develop and launch a privacy program. Don't assume that all stakeholders have the same level of understanding about the regulatory environment or the complexity of the undertaking—there will invariably be different levels of privacy knowledge among the group. This is an opportunity to ensure everyone has the same baseline understanding of the risks and challenges the organization faces, the data privacy obligations that are imposed on it, and the increasing expectations in the marketplace regarding the protection of personal information.

> *Conduct a privacy workshop for stakeholders to level the privacy playing field by defining privacy for the organization, explaining the market expectations, answering questions, and reducing confusion.*

2.6.3 Keep a Record of Ownership

Once the importance of the privacy program has been established, key internal stakeholders may form a steering committee to ensure clear ownership of assets and responsibilities. Keep a record of these discussions as a tool for communication, and to ensure stakeholders can refer to what was decided. Such documentation also helps support accountability requirements of the GDPR and serves as the privacy program's due diligence in terms of which functions and individuals should be held accountable for privacy compliance.

2.7 Structure the Privacy Team

Structuring the privacy team is the last objective to formalizing the organization's approach to privacy. This section will focus on the many factors that should be considered to assist with the decisions involved in structuring the team and to ensure that the foundation for those decisions aligns with business objectives and goals. This final step aligns privacy governance for the organization with its privacy strategy.

2.8 Governance Models

There are different approaches and strategies for creating privacy office governance models. This text is not intended to educate thoroughly on the idiosyncrasies of various governance models, but to provide examples of types of governance models that should be examined when structuring your privacy program. Give thoughtful consideration to the models. They will be a basis for the making of decisions by your privacy team and the policies they will need to establish.

You should consider whether to apply the model only within a given geographical region(s) or globally depending on your operations. Many large organizations find they need to consider global implications when structuring privacy teams.

The positioning of the privacy team within an organization should rely on the authority it will receive under the governance model it follows. Positioning the privacy team under the corporate legal umbrella may be substantially different from aligning the team under the IT umbrella. Executive leadership support for the governance model will have a direct impact on the level of success when implementing privacy strategies.

No matter which model is chosen, there are some important steps to integrate into it:

- Involve senior leadership
- Involve stakeholders
- Develop internal partnerships
- Provide flexibility
- Leverage communications
- Leverage collaboration

Privacy governance models include centralized, local and hybrid versions, but are not limited to only these options. Governance models and the choice of the correct model objectives should ensure information is controlled and distributed to the right decision makers. Since decision making must be based on accurate and up-to-date management data, the allocation and design of the governance model will foster intelligent and more accurate decisions.

2.8.1 Centralized

Centralized governance is a common model that fits well in organizations used to utilizing single-channel functions (where the direction flows from a single source) with planning and decision making completed by one group. A centralized model will leave one team or person responsible for privacy-related affairs. All other persons or organizations will flow through this single point. Often this single point is the chief privacy officer (CPO) or corporate privacy office.

2.8.2 Local or Decentralized

Decentralization is the policy of delegating decision-making authority down to the lower levels in an organization, at a distance from and below a central authority. A decentralized organization has fewer tiers in the organizational structure, a wider span of control, and a bottom-to-top flow of decision making and ideas.

In a more decentralized organization, the top executives delegate much of their decision-making authority to lower tiers of the organizational structure. As a correlation, the organization is likely to run on less-rigid policies and wider spans of control among each officer of the organization. The wider spans of control also reduce the number of tiers within the organization, giving its structure a flat appearance. One advantage of this structure, if the correct controls are in place, will be the bottom-to-top flow of information, allowing decisions about lower-tier operations to be well-informed. For example, if an experienced technician at the lowest tier of an organization knows how to increase the efficiency of production, the bottom-to-top flow of information can allow this knowledge to pass up to the executive officers.

2.8.3 Hybrid

A hybrid governance model allows for a combination of centralized and local governance. This is most typically seen when a large organization assigns a main individual (or department) responsibility for privacy-related affairs and for issuing policies and directives to the rest of the organization. The local entities then fulfill and support the policies and directives from the central governing body. Members of the privacy team may also sit locally; for example, with regional compliance hubs in large multinationals. Each region may have a privacy manager who reports in to local management and/or the CPO at the global level.

2.8.4 Advantages and Disadvantages

Centralized management offers many advantages, with streamlined processes and procedures that allow the organization to create efficiency by using the same resources throughout the organization. Since decisions are made at the top layer, individual employees or groups cannot make their own decisions and must seek approval from a higher level.

With fewer layers of management, decentralized managers create and manage their own business practices. This may be inefficient, because each process may be reproduced many times instead of once. On the other hand, employees are also tasked with solving problems with which they are closest and most familiar.

The hybrid approach uses a decentralized decision-making process that tends to provide less outside influence for employees yet offers the advantage of the organizational resources of a larger, centralized organization. Typically, the hybrid model will dictate core values and let the employee decide which practice to use to obtain its goals. Working groups, individual offices and other groups are encouraged to make business decisions that consider revenue, operating costs and operations. Such models allow an organization to function in a global environment yet maintain common missions, values and goals.

Mixing centralized and decentralized management approaches into a hybrid approach enables the organization to achieve desired results that may span the globe or locations across town. Employees believe their contributions provide a sense of ownership, which encourages them to perform more efficiently and effectively, consistent with top management.

2.9 Establish the Organizational Model, Responsibilities and Reporting Structure

In establishing the overall organizational privacy model, one must consider the organizational structure as related to strategy, operations and management for responsibilities and reporting. The privacy professional should know how each major unit functions and should understand its privacy needs. The following is a short list of those roles for both large and small organizational structures, including:

- CPO
- Privacy manager
- Privacy analysts
- Business line privacy leaders

- First responders (i.e., incident response team members)

- Data protection officers (DPOs), including those for whom privacy is not their only responsibility, if applicable to the organization

Organizational structures function within a framework by which the organization communicates, develops goals and objectives, and operates daily. Companies can use one of several structures or switch from one to another based on need. Principles within that framework allow the organization to maintain the structure and develop the processes necessary to do so efficiently. Considerations include:

- **Hierarchy of command.** The authority of senior management, leaders and the executive team to establish the trail of responsibility.

- **Role definition.** Clear definition of the responsibilities to create individual expectations and performance.

- **Evaluation of outcomes.** Methods for determining strengths and weaknesses and correcting or amplifying as necessary.

- **Alteration of organizational structure.** Ability to remain dynamic and change as necessary to meet current objectives, adopt new technology or react to competition.

- **Significance.** Complex structure typical for large organizations; flat structures for smaller organizations.

- **Types of structures.** Product organizational structures, functional organizational structures and others.

- **Customers.** Consider the different needs depending on nature of products and services the organization offers.

- **Benefits.** To the organization, customers and stakeholders, as aligned to the objectives and goals.

2.9.1 Titles Used for Privacy Leaders

The titles an organization uses to denote its privacy leaders reveals much information about its approach to privacy, its reporting structure, and its industry. According to a recent survey completed by the IAPP and EY, the terms *privacy, chief* and *officer* are the most popular terms used in privacy management titles and are more often used than terms like *counsel, director* or *global.*[32] Further, a larger percentage of U.S.-headquartered organizations use the terms *privacy, vice president* and *director* for privacy management roles when compared with their European counterparts; similar roles in the EU are more likely to use the term *data* in such titles (likely a result of the "privacy" versus "data protection" divide between U.S. and EU-headquartered firms).

Some companies are asking their CPO to serve in the role of DPO (discussed in section 2.9.5), with or without adding the title. According to the survey, such companies are most likely in unregulated industries and those with business-to-business (B2B) models, suggesting these companies tend to appoint fewer but perhaps more educated or qualified personnel to privacy leadership roles and then ask more of them.[33]

2.9.2 Typical Educational and Professional Backgrounds of Privacy Leaders

Regardless of the title an organization chooses for its privacy leader, it's important that the individual possess the requisite skills and qualifications. While a legal background is a common requirement for most privacy positions, project management, controls implementation, audit, and information security experience have emerged as key qualities of privacy professionals. The company's specific industry, where the privacy leader is placed within the organization, and to whom the leader reports also influence the desired background and skills of privacy leaders. For example, a privacy leader reporting into the general counsel would likely be expected to possess legal qualifications, while a privacy leader reporting to the chief information security officer (CISO) may be expected to have a certain level of security and technical knowledge, in addition to privacy expertise.

As a relatively new field, and given the breadth of skills required outside of knowledge of privacy laws and regulations, privacy professionals have come from a diverse range of educational backgrounds. More recently, however, degree programs specializing in privacy law, cybersecurity, and privacy engineering have become available, including:

- Carnegie Mellon's Master of Science in Information Technology—Privacy Engineering (MSIT-PE)[34]

- Ryerson University's Certificate in Privacy, Access and Information Management[35]

- Brown University's Executive Master in Cybersecurity[36]

The emergence of these programs has further legitimized privacy as a distinct profession requiring increased attention, resourcing, executive support and credentialing.

2.9.3 Professional Certifications

Like other professional certifications, those offered by the IAPP provide a way for individuals in the industry to demonstrate that they possess a fundamental understanding of global privacy laws, concepts, best practices and technologies.[37] IAPP certifications, which are accredited by the American National Standards Institute (ANSI) under the International Organization for Standardization (ISO) standard 17024: 2012, are increasingly listed as minimum requirements in privacy job descriptions.

2.9.4 Conferences and Seminars

Conferences and seminars are rich resources for information and expert presentations on effective ways to build a privacy program and address privacy governance. Individuals learn from privacy experts about approaches to privacy management by attending sessions, working groups, and/or panel discussions that are assembled specifically to address this topic. Other topics include governance structures. Presentations on managing security incidents, creating a sustainable training and awareness program, and designing and implementing programs educate the audience on the subject matter itself while also providing industry insights into how an organization manages these issues and assigns accountability. Information is also obtained through informal exchanges of ideas among privacy professionals and those interested in this industry. Learning from experts and peers is an incredibly valuable method for acquiring information about privacy approaches.

2.9.5 The DPO Role

Designation of a DPO is a new requirement under Article 37 of the GDPR. The concept of designating an individual accountable for an organization's privacy compliance, however, is not new. For example, Canada's PIPEDA requires that an organization appoint someone to be accountable for its compliance with the act's fair information principles; South Korea's Data Protection Act mandates the appointment of a DPO with specific responsibilities;[38] and Germany, under its implementation of EU Data Protection Directive (95/46/EC), required organizations to appoint a DPO under certain circumstances (e.g., if the company employed more than nine persons). With the GDPR, this requirement is formalized, and so are key criteria with respect to the need, reporting position and qualifications of the DPO.

2.9.5.1 When is a DPO Required?

Article 37 of the GDPR establishes the specific criteria triggering the requirement for an organization to designate a DPO.[39]

Subject to some exceptions, designation of a DPO is required:

- By public authorities or bodies

- Where the organization's "core" activities consist of processing operations that require "regular and systematic monitoring of data subjects on a large scale"

- Where the organization's "core" activities consist of processing "special" categories of data on a large scale[40]

Even if it's determined that a DPO is not required, the organization may choose to voluntarily appoint one. Keep in mind that formally appointing a DPO will subject the organization to the following DPO requirements:

- **Reporting structure and independence.** The position of the DPO is formally elevated by Article 38, whereby the DPO is required to "report to the highest management level of the controller or the processor." While "highest management level" is not further defined by the GDPR, its literal interpretation would be at the level of C-level management or the board of directors.[41] In practice, such a reporting line may not be feasible or practical, depending on several factors such as the size of the company, the accessibility of CEO, and the likelihood of the reporting line to affect the DPO's independence. Organizations should consider these key factors when deciding the DPO's reporting lines.

- **Qualifications and Responsibilities.** Article 37 mandates several requirements for the DPO's qualifications and position, including that the DPO possess "expert knowledge of data protection law and practices." Quantifying "expert knowledge" is subjective—a reasonable interpretation of someone possessing expert knowledge in the field would be the privacy professional who has spent most of their career practicing privacy law or operationalizing privacy programs, for example.[42] Such expertise is likely required as a result of Article 39, which requires the DPO to perform certain activities, including monitoring the company's compliance with the GDPR, providing advice during data protection impact assessments (DPIAs) and cooperating with supervisory authorities.[43]

Designating a DPO is no trivial task given the role's specific qualifications, responsibilities and organizational visibility. It's important to create a position that is "fit for purpose," in other words, one that considers the company's unique requirements in light of the criteria expected of DPOs by the GDPR.

2.10 Summary

Defining the appropriate governance of a privacy program is complex and challenging. Once adopted and implemented, proper governance ensures that an organization's approach to privacy adequately supports its compliance with legal obligations, aligns with broader business objectives and goals, is fully supported at all levels across the company, and culminates in the protection of personal information.

Endnotes

1 Kirk M. Herath, *Building a Privacy Program: A Practitioner's Guide*, p. 75, (Portsmouth, NH: IAPP, 2011).

2 Mission Statement, University Privacy Office, Stanford University, https://privacy.stanford.edu/about-us/mission-statement (accessed November 2018).

3 Privacy at Microsoft, Microsoft, https://privacy.microsoft.com/en-US/ (accessed November 2018).

4 Mission and Vision, International Conference of Data Protection and Privacy Commissioners, https://icdppc.org/the-conference-and-executive-committee/strategic-direction-mission-and-vision/ (accessed November 2018).

5 Mission Statement, An Coimisiún um Chosaint Sonraí | Data Protection Commission, https://www.dataprotection.ie/docs/Mission-Statement/a/7.htm (accessed November 2018).

6 Mission, vision ad goal, ICO, https://ico.org.uk/about-the-ico/our-information/mission-and-vision/ (accessed November 2018).

7 The Authority's vision and mission, Data Protection Authority, https://www.dataprotectionauthority.be/vision-and-mission (accessed November 2018).

8 GLBA, 15 U.S.C, Subchapter I, § 6809 (1999).

9 HIPAA of 1996, 45 C.F.R. §§ 160.102, 160.103.

10 COPPA of 1998, 15 U.S.C. 6501–6505.

11 PCI DSS, PCI Security Standards Council, https://www.pcisecuritystandards.org/documents/PCI_DSS_v3-2-1.pdf (accessed November 2018).

12 National Conference of State Legislatures, *State Security Breach Notification Laws*, www.ncsl.org/research/telecommunications-and-information-technology/security-breach-notification-laws.aspx (accessed November 2018).

13 The Code of Fair Information Practices, Epic.org, https://epic.org/privacy/consumer/code_fair_info.html (accessed November 2018).

14 OECD Guidelines on the Protection of Privacy and Transborder Flows of Personal Data, OECD, http://www.oecd.org/internet/ieconomy/oecdguidelinesontheprotectionofprivacyandtransborderflowsofpersonaldata.htm (accessed November 2018).

15 *Generally Accepted Privacy Principles: CPA and CA Practitioner Version*, August 2009, IAPP, https://iapp.org/media/presentations/11Summit/DeathofSASHO2.pdf (accessed November 2018).

16 Principles Set Out in the National Standard of Canada Entitled Model Code for the Protection of Personal Information, CAN/CSA-Q830-96, Government of Canada, Justice Laws website, https://laws-lois.justice.gc.ca/eng/acts/P-8.6/page-11.html#h-26 (accessed November 2018).

17 APEC Privacy Framework (2015), APEC, https://www.apec.org/Publications/2017/08/APEC-Privacy-Framework-(2015) (accessed November 2018).

18 GDPR, Article 47, http://www.privacy-regulation.eu/en/article-47-binding-corporate-rules-GDPR.htm (accessed November 2018).

19 ETSI, https://www.etsi.org/standards (accessed November 2018).

20 Personal Information Protection and Electronic Documents Act, (S.C. 2000, C.5), Government of Canada, Justice Laws website, laws-lois.justice.gc.ca/eng/acts/P-8.6/index.htm (accessed November 2018).

21 GDPR, http://www.privacy-regulation.eu/en/index.htm (accessed November 2018).

22 Privacy Shield Framework, https://www.privacyshield.gov/EU-US-Framework (accessed November 2018).

23 HIPAA of 1996, 45 C.F.R. §§ 160.102, 160.103.

24 CNIL, https://www.cnil.fr/en/home (accessed November 2018).

25 Ann Cavoukian, "Privacy by Design: The 7 Foundational Principles," https://iab.org/wp-content/IAB-uploads/2011/03/fred_carter.pdf (accessed November 2018).

26 ENISA, https://www.enisa.europa.eu/ (accessed November 2018).

27 Sean Brooks, Michael Garcia, Naomi Lefkovitz, Suzanne Lightman, Ellen Nadeau, "An Introduction to Privacy Engineering and Risk Management in Federal Information Systems," NIST), U.S. Department of Commerce (DOC), https://nvlpubs.nist.gov/nistpubs/ir/2017/NIST.IR.8062.pdf (accessed November 2018).

28 Framework for Improving Critical Infrastructure Cybersecurity Version 1.1, April 16, 2018, NIST, U.S. DOC, https://nvlpubs.nist.gov/nistpubs/CSWP/NIST.CSWP.04162018.pdf (accessed November 2018).

29 *2018 Privacy Tech Vendor Report*, IAPP, https://iapp.org/resources/article/2018-privacy-tech-vendor-report/ (accessed November 2018).

30 *IAPP-EY Annual Privacy Governance Report of 2016*, IAPP, https://iapp.org/resources/article/iapp-ey-annual-governance-report-2017/ (accessed November 2018); to see the *IAPP-EY Annual Privacy Governance Report of 2018*, visit, https://iapp.org/resources/article/iapp-ey-annual-governance-report-2018/ (accessed November 2018).

31 Neil Roiter, "IT GRC tools: Control your environment," *CSO from IDG*, https://www.csoonline.com/article/2127514/compliance/it-grc-tools--control-your-environment.html (accessed November 2018).

32 *IAPP-EY Annual Privacy Governance Report of 2017*, IAPP, https://iapp.org/resources/article/iapp-ey-annual-governance-report-2017/ (accessed November 2018); To see the *IAPP-EY Annual Privacy Governance Report of 2018*, visit https://iapp.org/resources/article/iapp-ey-annual-governance-report-2018/ (accessed November 2018).

33 *IAPP-EY Annual Privacy Governance Report of 2017*, IAPP, https://iapp.org/resources/article/iapp-ey-annual-governance-report-2017/ (accessed November 2018); To see the *IAPP-EY Annual Privacy Governance Report of 2018*, visit, https://iapp.org/resources/article/iapp-ey-annual-governance-report-2018/ (accessed November 2018).

34 MSIT—Privacy Engineering, Carnegie Mellon University, http://privacy.cs.cmu.edu/ (accessed November 2018).

35 Privacy, Access and Information Management, Ryerson University, https://ce-online.ryerson.ca/ce/default.aspx?id=3778 (accessed November 2018).

36 Executive Master in Cybersecurity, Brown University, https://professional.brown.edu/cybersecurity/ (accessed November 2018).

37 IAPP, https://iapp.org/ (accessed November 2018).

38 Cynthia Rich, "Privacy and Security Law Report," Bloomberg BNA, https://media2.mofo.com/documents/150518privacylawsinasia.pdf, accessed November 2018.

39 Thomas J. Shaw, Esq., *The DPO Handbook: Data Protection Officers under the GDPR*, (Portsmouth, NH: IAPP, 2018).

40 GDPR, Article 37, www.privacy-regulation.eu/en/article-37-designation-of-the-data-protection-officer-GDPR.htm (accessed November 2018).

41 GDPR, Article 38, www.privacy-regulation.eu/en/article-38-position-of-the-data-protection-officer-GDPR.htm (accessed November 2018).

42 GDPR, Article 37.

43 GDPR, Article 39, www.privacy-regulation.eu/en/article-39-tasks-of-the-data-protection-officer-GDPR.htm (accessed November 2018).

CHAPTER 3

Applicable Privacy Laws and Regulations

Susan Bandi, CIPP/US, CIPM, CIPT, FIP

Compliance with data protection laws and regulations is a major driver for many organization's privacy programs. This chapter describes some of the most commonly encountered data privacy laws, regulations and statutes around the world.

As there are numerous global privacy laws and regulations, privacy professionals should seek assistance from their organization's legal office, outside counsel or a third-party research firm to ensure all relevant laws and regulations have been captured.

> *A roadmap or crosswalk of the organization's privacy requirements is as simple or complex as the organization desires. For some, a simple spreadsheet with tabs for applicable law, audit protocol and specific contract language is sufficient.*[1]

Elements of these global laws and regulations overlap in requirements. So it's a sound practice to capture this information in a spreadsheet or by another tracking method to note the similarities. These include notice, choice and consent, purpose limitation, individual rights, data retention limits, and data transfers.

Understanding the scope of data collected and processed by the organization will guide the privacy professional in the task of researching and compiling applicable laws, regulations and statutes. The privacy professional and/or the organization's legal office must understand applicable national laws and regulations as well as local laws and regulations. Laws are typically grouped into the following categories:

- General privacy laws [e.g., the EU's General Data Protection Regulation (GDPR); national privacy laws in countries including Australia, New Zealand, Argentina, Israel and Uruguay]

- Federal privacy laws, such as those in the United States, that apply to only a specific market sector

- State laws and provincial laws

- Health privacy laws

- Financial privacy laws

- Online privacy laws

- Communication privacy laws

- Information privacy laws

- Education

- Privacy in one's home

3.1 U.S. Federal Government Privacy Laws

Table 3-1 lists the primary privacy-related laws enforced by the U.S. federal government.[2] The United States is relatively unique in the way it crafts its privacy law-making, with no omnibus, far-reaching legislation that covers personal data collection and use in a comprehensive way.

Table 3-1: Privacy-Related Laws Enforced by the U.S. Federal Government

U.S. Federal Legislation	Enforcement	Focused Concern
Federal Privacy Act of 1974, as amended at 5 U.S.C. 552a[3]	Individual private right of action	Government-held records about individuals retrieved by personal identifiers (name, Social Security number, other identifying number or symbol)
Gramm-Leach-Bliley Act of 1999 (GLBA)[4]	Consumer Financial Protection Bureau (CFPB); state departments of insurance; state attorneys general (see next table for more details)	Anti-money laundering laws
Health Insurance Portability and Accountability Act (HIPAA) of 1996[5]	Department of Health and Human Services (DHHS) Office of Civil Rights; state attorneys general	Medical records, protected health information (PHI), specific category data (GDPR), medical research
Controlling the Assault of Non-Solicited Pornography and Marketing Act (CAN-SPAM) of 2003[6]	Federal Trade Commission (FTC)	Commercial electronic mail messages, sexually oriented material

U.S. Federal Legislation	Enforcement	Focused Concern
Children's Online Privacy Protection Act (COPPA) of 1998[7]	FTC	Collection of information from children under 13 by operators of websites and online services
Fair and Accurate Credit Transactions Act (FACTA) of 2003[8]	FTC, Board of Governors Federal Reserve System, Federal Deposit Insurance Corporation (FDIC), National Credit Union Administration, Office of the Comptroller of the Currency, and Office of Thrift Supervision	Identity theft through handling of consumer account information
Fair Credit Reporting Act (FCRA) of 1970[9]	FTC and Consumer Financial Protection Bureau (CFPB)	Accuracy and fairness of credit reporting; credit-reporting agencies adopt reasonable procedures, credit information, collection, access to credit reports
National Do Not Call Registry[10]	FTC	Telemarketing calls at home
Telephone Consumer Protection Act (TCPA) of 1991[11]	FTC, Federal Communications Commission (FCC) and states	Telemarketing calls and use of automatic telephone-dialing systems
Driver's Privacy Protection Act (DPPA) of 1994[12]	Individual private right of action	Privacy and disclosure of personal information gathered by state departments of motor vehicles (DMVs)
Electronic Communications Privacy Act (ECPA) of 1986[13]	State or law enforcement agency	Federal wiretapping and electronic eavesdropping; unauthorized government access to electronic communication
Video Privacy Protection Act (VPPA) of 1988[14]	Individual private right of action	Wrongful disclosure of video tape rental or sale records
Family Educational Rights and Privacy Act (FERPA)[15]	U.S. Department of Education, Family Policy Compliance Office	Improper disclosure of personally identifiable information (PII) derived from education records; unfair and deceptive trade practices
Federal Trade Commission Act (Section 5) of 1914[16]	FTC	Unfair or deceptive acts or practices in or affecting commerce

3.1.1 U.S. Industry-Specific Concerns

Each of these industries have privacy-related concerns with implications for consumers:

- **Healthcare.** HIPAA and Health Information Technology for Economic and Clinical Health (HITECH) cover healthcare facilities as well as researchers and anyone doing business with healthcare operations.

- **Financial.** Organizations must monitor confidentiality, financial, (particularly GLBA) and terrorism (anti-money laundering, specifically) laws.

- **Telecom.** Not just the content of communications is important for protection, but also metadata and location information, to which law enforcement often wants access.

- **Online.** Watch out for issues presented by online transactions, the lure of detailed information (to law enforcement, marketers and criminals) available on the web for scraping and collection, and the global nature of online privacy concepts.

- **Government.** The courts are constantly re-evaluating definitions of "public records" and governments have specific obligations regarding transparency that often conflict with privacy.

- **Education.** Laws are focused on educational agencies and institutions (e.g., public schools) receiving funding under any program administered by the U.S. Department of Education and private post-secondary schools.

- **Video.** Originally designed to protect renters and purchasers of goods from videotape rental stores, laws have now been interpreted to apply to online streaming services.

- **Marketing.** This has become one of the most complicated areas of privacy. Professionals must understand not just law, but rapidly evolving technology, self-regulatory schemes, and new data marketplaces.

- **Energy.** An emerging privacy arena due to the emergence of smart grid technology and so-called smart houses.

- **HR.** Standard ideas of confidentiality in this area are running up against technology in the work environment, where efficiency often means monitoring.

3.1.2 Self-Regulation: Industry Standards and Codes of Conduct

In addition to U.S. laws, there are also sector-specific voluntary and contractual initiatives that establish codes of conduct for the communities of interest. Table 3-2 highlights some of the more notable self-regulatory programs.

Table 3-2: Notable Self-Regulatory Programs

Self-Regulation (Voluntary)	Sector Affected
Payment Card Industry Data Security Standard (PCI DSS)[17]	Any organization, regardless of size or number of transactions, that accepts, transmits or stores any cardholder data branded with one of the five card association/brand logos
DMA Guidelines for Ethical Business Practices[18]	Individuals and entities involved in data-driven marketing in all media[19]
VeriSign, TrustArc, McAfee, PayPal trust marks[20]	Online vendors' ecommerce sites[21]
Children's Advertising Review Unit (CARU) guidelines[22]	National advertising primarily directed to children under the age of 12 in any medium
Network Advertising Initiative (NAI) Code of Conduct[23]	NAI members' approach to privacy and data governance in connection with the collection and use of data for interest-based advertising

3.2 Global Privacy Laws

In large part, the rest of the globe's countries have privacy and data protection legislation that covers the collection and use of personal data in general, with perhaps increasing protection and sensitivity required for certain categories of data, such as health data or data regarding sexual orientation. These laws generally apply based on where the company does business, serving customers and the industry. As a rule of thumb, anyone actively trying to solicit business in a country is subject to its privacy and data protection laws. It is important, therefore, to recognize this and understand all laws and regulations that apply to your business operation. As outlined in Table 3-3, for example, if a U.S.-based organization is operating or serving customers in the EU, the GDPR will apply. If an EU company does business in Canada, the Personal Information and Electronic Documents Act (PIPEDA) and other various provincial privacy laws may apply.

Table 3-3: Global Privacy Laws

Country/Region	International Guidelines/Legislation	Responsible Authority
	Organisation for Economic Co-operation and Development (OECD) Guidelines on the Protection of Privacy and Transborder Flows of Personal Data[24]	
EU	GDPR[25]	Member state supervisory authority/Lead supervisory authority
Asia-Pacific Economic Cooperation (APEC)	APEC privacy framework[26]	Member economies undertake commitments on a voluntary basis
Angola	Data Protection Law (Law no. 22/11 of 17 June 2011)[27]	Agência de Proteção de Dados (APD)
Argentina	Personal Data Protection Law No. 25,326 (PDPL)[28]	Dirección Nacional de Protección de Datos Personales (DNPDP)
Australia	Privacy Act 1988[29]	Office of the Australian Information Commissioner
Belarus	Law on Information, Informatisation and Information Protection of 10 November 2008 No. 455 Z[30]	Operational and Analytical Centre under the President of the Republic of Belarus and the Ministry of Communications and Informatisation of the Republic of Belarus
Bermuda	Personal Information Protection Act 2016 (PIPA)[31]	Privacy commissioner
Bosnia and Herzegovina	Law on Protection of Personal Data ("Official Gazette of Bosnia and Herzegovina," no. 49/06)[32]	Personal Data Protection Agency
Brazil	General Data Protection Law, Law No. 13.709/2018 (LGPD)[33]	Not yet established
Canada	PIPEDA[34]	Office of the Privacy Commissioner of Canada (Note: Canadian provinces have their own, often stricter, privacy laws)
Cape Verde	Data Protection Law (Law 133/V/2001 of 22 January 2001)[35]	Comissão Nacional de Proteção de Dados Pessoais
Chile	Law 19,628 on the Protection of Private Life (Personal Data Protection Act)[36]	There is no national regulator overseeing data protection issues

Country/Region	International Guidelines/Legislation	Responsible Authority
China	Cybersecurity Law of the People's Republic of China[37]	Cyberspace Administration of China (CAC) (Note: sector-specific regulators may also monitor and enforce data protection issues)
Colombia	Law 1266 of 2008 (Habeas Data Act)[38] Law 1581 of 2012[39]	Deputy Superintendence for the Protection of Personal Data of the Superintendence of Industry and Commerce
Costa Rica	Law No. 8968, Protection in the Handling of the Personal Data of Individuals[40]	Agencia de Protección de Datos de los Habitantes (PRODHAB)
Ghana	Data Protection Act, 2012 (Act 843)[41]	Data Protection Commission
Hong Kong	Personal Data (Privacy) Ordinance (Cap. 486)[42]	Office of the Privacy Commissioner for Personal Data
India	Information Technology Act, 2000[43]	Ministry of Electronics and Information Technology
Israel	Protection of Privacy Law, 5741-1981 (PPL)[44]	Privacy Protection Authority
Japan	Act on Protection of Personal Information (APPI)[45]	Personal Information Protection Commission (PPC)
Malaysia	Personal Data Protection Act 2010 (PDPA)[46]	Personal Data Protection Commissioner
Mexico	Federal Law on the Protection of Personal Data Held by Private Parties[47]	National Institute for Transparency, Access to Information and Personal Data Protection
Monaco	Data Protection Law n° 1.165 of 23 December 1993[48]	Commission de Contrôle des Informations Nominatives (CCIN)
Morocco	Law n° 09-08 of 18 February 2009 relating to the protection of individuals with respect to the processing of personal data[49]	Commission Nationale de Protection des Données Personnelles (CNDP)
New Zealand	Privacy Act 1993[50]	Office of the Privacy Commissioner
Peru	Personal Data Protection Law (PDPL)[51]	General Agency on Data Protection
Philippines	Data Privacy Act of 2012[52]	National Privacy Commission
Qatar	Law No. 13 of 2016 Concerning Personal Data Protection[53]	Qatar Ministry of Transport and Communications (MoTC)

Country/Region	International Guidelines/Legislation	Responsible Authority
Russia	Data Protection Act No. 152 FZ dated 27 July 2006[54]	Federal Service for Supervision of Communications, Information Technologies and Mass Media (Roskomnadzor)
Singapore	Personal Data Protection Act 2012 (No. 26 of 2012)[55]	Personal Data Protection Commission
South Africa	Protection of Personal Information Act 4 of 2013 (POPIA)[56]	Information Regulator
South Korea	Personal Information Protection Act (PIPA)[57]	Ministry of the Interior and Safety (MOIS)
Taiwan	Personal Data Protection Law (PDPL)[58]	Ministries and city/county governments act as competent authorities
Turkey	Law on the Protection of Personal Data No. 6698 dated 7 April 2016 (LPPD)[59]	Kişisel Verileri Koruma Kurumu [Personal Data Protection Authority(DPA)]
UAE- Dubai (DIFC)	DIFC Law No. 1 of 2007 Data Protection Law (amended by DIFC Law No. 5 of 2012 Data Protection Law Amendment Law)[60]	Commissioner of Data Protection (CDP)
Uruguay	Data Protection Act Law No. 18.331 (11 August 2008)[61]	Unidad Reguladora y de Control de Datos Personales (URCDP)
Vietnam	Law on Cybersecurity[62]	Not yet established

3.3 General Data Protection Regulation Overview

In December 2016, the EU Parliament and Council finally agreed upon the GDPR, a regulation first proposed in 2012, and, as of May 25, 2018, is now enforceable.[63] The GDPR offers a new framework for data protection with increased accountability for organizations, and its reach is extraterritorial. Given the size and scope of the EU economy, the GDPR has rapidly become a global standard for data protection that every working privacy professional must understand on some level. Below are the general provisions of the GDPR the privacy professional is most likely to encounter. (This is not intended to be a thorough review of all the articles.[64])

3.3.1 Article 1: Subject-Matter and Objectives

1. *This Regulation lays down rules relating to the protection of natural persons with regard to the processing of personal data and rules relating to the free movement of personal data.*

2. *This Regulation protects fundamental rights and freedoms of natural persons and their right to the protection of personal data.*

3. *The free movement of personal data within the Union shall be neither restricted nor prohibited for reasons connected with the protection of natural persons with regard to the processing of personal data.*[65]

3.3.2 Article 2: Material Scope

1. *This Regulation applies to the processing of personal data wholly or partly by automated means and to the processing other than by automated means of personal data which form part of a filing system or are intended to form part of a filing system.*

2. *This Regulation does not apply to the processing of personal data:*

    a. *in the course of an activity which falls outside the scope of Union law;*

    b. *by the Member States when carrying out activities which fall within the scope of Chapter 2 of Title V of the TEU;*

    c. *by a natural person in the course of a purely personal or household activity;*

    d. *by competent authorities for the purposes of the prevention, investigation, detection or prosecution of criminal offences, the execution of criminal penalties, including the safeguarding against and the prevention of threats to public security.*

3. *For the processing of personal data by the Union institutions, bodies, offices and agencies, Regulation (EC) No 45/2001 applies. Regulation (EC) No 45/2001 and other Union legal acts applicable to such processing of personal data shall be adapted to the principles and rules of this Regulation in accordance with Article 98.*

4. *This Regulation shall be without prejudice to the application of Directive 2000/31/EC, in particular of the liability rules of intermediary service providers in Articles 12 to 15 of that Directive.*[66]

3.3.3 Article 3: Territorial Scope

1. *This Regulation applies to the processing of personal data in the context of the activities of an establishment of a controller or a processor in the Union, regardless of whether the processing takes place in the Union or not.*

2. *This Regulation applies to the processing of personal data of data subjects who are in the Union by a controller or processor not established in the Union, where the processing activities are related to:*

   a. *the offering of goods or services, irrespective of whether a payment of the data subject is required, to such data subjects in the Union; or*

   b. *the monitoring of their behavior as far as their behavior takes place within the Union.*

3. *This Regulation applies to the processing of personal data by a controller not established in the Union, but in a place where Member State law applies by virtue of public international law.*[67]

The GDPR sets out specific requirements for organizations collecting or processing the personal data of individuals (data subjects) in the EU, what rights it grants to individuals, and what consequences exist for noncompliance. The privacy professional should clearly understand what consumers can do, what organizations must do, and what regulators can do. Table 3-4 identifies some of these items.[68]

Table 3-4: What Consumers Can Do, What Organizations Must Do, What Regulators Can Do

What Consumers Can Do	<ul><li>Withdraw consent for processing.</li><li>Request a copy of all their data.</li><li>Request to move their data to a different organization in a machine-readable format.</li><li>Request that you delete information they consider no longer relevant.</li><li>Object to automated decision-making processes, including profiling.</li></ul>

What Organizations Must Do	• Implement privacy by default and privacy by design. • Implement processes for data subject requests. Provide mechanisms such as contact information, email or link where individuals can contact the organization to exercise their privacy rights. • Maintain appropriate data security. • Notify data subjects and regulators of data breaches (in some circumstances). • Follow special rules for directly processing children's data. • Provide notice of intention to process personal information. • Appoint a data protection officer (DPO) (in some circumstances). • Take responsibility for processing activities of third-party vendors. • Conduct data protection impact assessments (DPIAs) in some circumstances. • Ensure adequacy or appropriate safeguards for data transfers. • Consult with regulators before processing (in some circumstances). • Keep records (in most circumstances) and demonstrate compliance.
What Regulators Can Do	• Ask for records of processing activities and proof of steps taken to comply with GDPR. • Impose temporary data processing bans, require data breach notification, or order erasure of personal data. • Suspend cross-border data flows. • Enforce penalties of up to €20 million or 4 percent annual revenues for noncompliance.

3.4 Commonalities of International Privacy Laws

As stated earlier, there are commonalities among provisions in global privacy and data protection laws, regulations and standards. Privacy managers must know and understand the common legal elements to avoid duplication of compliance efforts when a jurisdiction-by-jurisdiction approach is taken.

3.4.1 Similarities across jurisdiction

Requirements for ensuring individual rights (i.e., access, correction and deletion), and obligations (safeguarding data) are common. Other similarities include contractual requirements, audit protocol, self-regulatory regimes and marketplace expectations.

3.5 Cross-Border Transfers

An organization sharing personal information across borders [e.g., human resource (HR) data that is moved to a centralized headquarters] may be subject to various national and local privacy/data protection laws and regulations (e.g., GDPR, APEC). There are several approved options for exercising these cross-border data transfers in various jurisdictions. The EU is perhaps best-known for its cross-border transfer rules, but some jurisdictions, including Russia, essentially don't allow the transfer of personal data outside borders at all.

As an example of how organizations may have to address these so-called data localization requirements, Table 3-5 outlines options for transferring personal data outside of the EU.

Table 3-5: Cross-Border Data Transfer Approved Options

Adequacy Decision	Adequacy is based on the concept of essential equivalence: There must be an adequate level of protection of personal data essentially equivalent to the protection of personal data in the EU for data to freely travel from the EU to another jurisdiction. (Article 45)
Appropriate safeguards (if no adequacy) are mechanisms the company can adopt to protect personal data and facilitate ongoing and systematic cross-border personal data transfers. Examples include: • Binding corporate rules (BCRs) • Standard contractual clauses (SCCs) • Codes of conduct or certification mechanisms • Ad hoc contractual clauses authorized by supervisory authorities	 • Allow large multinational companies to adopt a policy suite with binding rules for handling personal data. (Articles 46(b), 47) • SSCs, [Articles 46(c); Model contracts (Recital 109)] • Approved codes of conduct (Article 40) and certification mechanisms (Article 42) with binding and enforceable commitments (Articles 40-43) • Required supervisory authority authorization • Individual tailoring to a company's needs • Differences at the member-state level

Not every jurisdiction is as strict with cross-border data transfer as the EU, and even the EU has certain derogations for when none of the previous mechanisms fit your needs, especially in employment situations or where law enforcement is involved.

In general, the transparency principle applies here in large part, along with what may be called *surprise minimization*: Is the country to which you're transferring personal data likely roughly equivalent in terms of privacy protections? Would a person who has entrusted you with personal data be likely to object to their data traveling to that country?

An example from the Office of the Privacy Commissioner of Canada: "Individuals should expect that their personal information is protected, regardless of where it is processed. Organizations transferring personal information to third parties are ultimately responsible for safeguarding that information. Individuals should expect transparency on the part of organizations when it comes to transferring to foreign jurisdictions."[69]

Pay particular attention to personal information access by national security agencies, law enforcement and foreign courts. As a rule of thumb, adjust the privacy program to the most stringent legal requirements to which the data processing is subject. While particularly sophisticated data governance operations may with confidence know exactly where each piece of personal data was collected and is traveling and follows the rules for those cross-border data transfers, many organizations play it safe and err on the side of caution.

Also, note that definitions of key terms (e.g., *controller, processor, sensitive data, processing, data transfer*) may differ from one jurisdiction to another. You must know the implications of doing business with countries that have inadequate or no privacy laws. In many cases, the risks may outweigh the benefits.

3.6 Organizational Balance and Support

Ensuring the privacy program aligns with business initiatives is very important. Business units must know and understand the goals and objectives of the privacy program and be part of the solution:

- Compliance should be the baseline

- Privacy by design, plus strategizing with business colleagues, will further the organization's goals and help strike a balance

- Compliance creates an opportunity to simultaneously re-evaluate and improve data management practices, such as data inventory and data access controls

- Compliance should be achieved with the least amount of business disruption, as business disruption is another form of penalty that should be considered in addition to potential fines for noncompliance[70]

3.7 Understanding Penalties for Noncompliance with Laws and Regulations

Legal and regulatory penalties are typically imposed by an industry to enforce behavior modifications due to previous neglect and improper protection of data. Privacy is not different; organizations are held accountable to protect the privacy of the data with which they have been entrusted. As penalties for violation of privacy laws and regulations become more pervasive and serious, the privacy professional must be prepared to address, track and understand penalties that could affect the organization. For example, as shown in Table 3-6, per the HITECH Act, which amended the HIPAA privacy and security rules, the maximum penalty for breach of protected health information per year is now $1.5 million.[71]

Table 3-6: HIPAA Violation Penalties[72]

Violation	Penalties
Unaware of violation	$100-$50,000/violation Up to $1.5 million/year
Reasonable cause	$1,000-$50,000/violation Up to $1.5 million/year
Willful neglect	$10,000-$50,000/violation Up to $1.5 million/year
Willful neglect–no effort to correct	$50,000/violation Up to $1.5 million/year

In the EU, the GDPR creates two tiers of maximum fines depending on whether the controller or processor committed any previous violations and the nature of violation. Fines depend on several factors, with the higher fine threshold being 4 percent of an undertaking's worldwide annual turnover or €20 million, whichever is higher. Some examples of noncompliance in the following areas will fall under this tier: data subjects' rights, cross-border data transfers, obligations of member state law, and noncompliance with a supervisory authority's order. (Infringements tend to be more substantive.) The lower fine threshold is 2 percent of an undertaking's worldwide annual turnover or €10 million, whichever is higher. Most noncompliance obligations fall under this tier.

For many organizations, however, the level of fines and enforcement activity in a given jurisdiction will often guide the organization in making the priorities for remediation of its data protection compliance following a gap analysis. Therefore, it may be important to also link this activity to the business case development at the outset.

> *One possible strategy is to use examples of high-profile breaches suffered by other organizations to gain management buy-in for the budget to support and mature the privacy program.*

3.8 Understanding the Scope and Authority of Oversight Agencies

Oversight typically relates to the "watchful care, management or supervision" of something. Specific to the previous section, oversight agencies can fine or impose penalties, civil and criminal, based on laws and regulations. Knowledge of these oversight organizations will help you understand when involvement is warranted or unwarranted, whom to call or contact, and when those actions are necessary by law. Table 3-8 lists some of the oversight organizations around the world.

Table 3-8: Oversight Organizations around the World

Country and Regulatory Authority	Enforcement Powers
China Cyberspace Administration of China (CAC) and other sector-specific regulators	The PRC currently lacks a centralized enforcement mechanism for data protection. The DPAs typically have the power to: • Issue warnings and orders to comply • Impose fines up to approximately RMB 500,000 • Revoke license to operate • Suspend or prohibit violators from engaging in similar businesses • Refer cases for criminal proceedings[73]
Japan Personal Information Protection Commission (PPC)	• Issue warnings and orders to comply • Issue orders to suspend the act of violation • Conduct investigation[74]
South Korea Ministry of the Interior and Safety (MOIS)	• Conduct investigation • Impose administrative sanctions for violations of the law • Refer cases for criminal proceedings[75]

Country and Regulatory Authority	Enforcement Powers
Singapore Personal Data Protection Commission	• Conduct investigation upon suspicion or receipt of complaints • Impose fines for violation of Do Not Call provisions of the Personal Data Protection Act up to SGD 10,000 • Provide direction to entities to help achieve compliance with the law • Refer cases for criminal proceedings[76]
Hong Kong Office of the Privacy Commissioner for Personal Data	• Issue warnings • Impose fines up to HK$50,000 • Refer cases for criminal proceedings[77]
Thailand	• Bill pending approval by the Council of State[78]
Indonesia Minister of Communication and Informatics	• Issue warnings • Suspend part or all components and other activities of a violator for temporary periods • Revoke license to operate • Impose criminal penalties under the Electronic Information Law[79]
Malaysia Department of Personal Data Protection	• Conduct investigation of any offense under the Personal Data Protection Act • Conduct search and seizure when approved by a magistrate • Issue orders for production of evidence • Refer cases for criminal proceedings[80]
Philippines National Privacy Commission	• Conduct investigation • Facilitate or enable settlement of complaints through alternative dispute resolution processes • Adjudicate, award indemnity on matters affecting any personal information • Issue cease and desist orders • Impose a temporary or permanent ban on the processing of personal information • Refer cases for criminal proceedings[81]
New Zealand Office of the Privacy Commissioner	• Conduct audit to determine compliance with the law • Inquire into any matter that appears or may appear to be infringing privacy of an individual • Conduct investigation • Refer the commissioner's opinion to director of human rights[82]

Country and Regulatory Authority	Enforcement Powers
Australia Office of the Australian Information Commissioner (OAIC)	• Investigate upon suspicion or referral • Impose contractual obligations through enforceable undertaking • File injunction against violators • Impose fines up to AUS $420,000 according to the seriousness of a violation[83]
India Data Protection Authority of India (not established yet)	• Issue warnings, reprimands, and cease and desist orders • Provide direction to entities to help achieve compliance with the law • Suspend business activity for violations
Turkey Kişisel Verileri Koruma Kurumu [Personal Data Protection Authority (DPA)]	• Organize inspections *ex officio* or following a complaint • Impose administrative fines • Refer cases for criminal proceedings[84]
Russia Federal Service for Supervision of Communications, Information Technologies and Mass Media (Roskomnadzor)	• Conduct inspection and investigation • Request information relating to compliance with the law • Revoke license for noncompliance • File civil actions on behalf of harmed data subjects • Impose administrative fines and civil penalties of up to ₽50,000 according to the seriousness of the violation • Refer cases for criminal proceedings[85]
EU Member state supervisory authority/Lead supervisory authority	• Investigate and adjudicate individual complaints • Conduct inquiries upon suspicion of or on the basis of a complaint • Provide directions to controllers for remedying a breach and for improving protection of the data subjects • Issue warnings and reprimands • Order to rectify, block, erase or destroy data when processed in violation of the law • Impose temporary or definite ban on processing • Conduct search and seizure when there are reasonable grounds for doing so • Refer matters to community institutions, European Parliament, Council and Commission of the European Union, the Court of Justice of the European Communities and other relevant institutions[86]

Country and Regulatory Authority	Enforcement Powers
Iceland The Icelandic Data Protection Authority	• Conduct investigation upon suspicion and charge entity the cost of audit and investigation • Order a data processor or controller to take action • Issue warnings • Revoke certification of compliance • Charge daily fines and administrative fines, up to 2 percent or 4 percent of companies' annual global revenue for violations of the act • Refer cases for criminal proceedings[87]
Canada Office of the Privacy Commissioner of Canada	• Investigate complaints • Conduct audits and enforce court orders under federal laws • Issue reprimands[88]
Mexico National Institute for Transparency, Access to Information and Personal Data Protection	• Resolve data protection disputes • Conduct verification procedures • Enforce penalty application proceedings and impose sanctions for infringements of the Federal Personal Data Law[89]
Argentina Dirección Nacional de Protección de Datos Personales (DNPDP)	• Conduct investigation upon suspicion or complaints filed by data subjects, national ombudsman or consumer association • Give warnings • Impose fines between ARS $1,000 to ARS $100,000 • Revoke permission to operate[90]
Uruguay Unidad Reguladora y de Control de Datos Personales (URCDP)	• Conduct audit, inspection and investigation • Issue subpoena • Conduct search and seizure • Impose fine up to USD $60,000 • Suspend activities of the violator • Revoke license to operate[91]
Brazil	• DPA not yet established
Colombia Deputy Superintendence for the Protection of Personal Data of the Superintendence of Industry and Commerce	• Issue injunction against processing of personal data of an individual • Impose penalties of up to COP $2,000 minimum monthly legal wages (approximately USD $430,000) for each case • Suspend profession or commercial activities of the violator for a temporary period or permanently • Issue orders for production of evidence of compliance with the applicable law • Refer cases for criminal proceedings[92]

Country and Regulatory Authority	Enforcement Powers
Morocco Commission Nationale de Protection des Données Personnelles (CNDP)	• Conduct investigation of individual complaints • Conduct investigation to monitor and verify processing of personal data is carried out in accordance with the law • Impose penalties • Refer cases for criminal proceedings[93]
Egypt	• Data protection draft law pending parliamentary approval
Kenya The Communications Authority of Kenya	• Impose penalties of up to KES 300,000 for violations of Kenya Information and Communications Act (KCIA) • Refer cases for criminal proceedings for violations of KCIA • Impose fine of up to KES 5 million for violations of the Sim Card Regulations (SCR) by telecommunication operators • Refer cases for criminal proceedings for violations of the HIV and AIDS Prevention and Control Act (HAPCA)[94]
South Africa Information Regulator	• Conduct investigation • Facilitate or enable settlement of complaints through alternative dispute resolution processes[95]

3.9 Other Privacy-Related Matters to Consider

The frameworks presented in these chapters cover many of the main privacy laws and regulations but do not cover every detail for every country, state or local government. Instead, frameworks provide the high-level detail necessary to manage and keep informed on privacy-relevant matters that concern any organization. Other privacy matters to consider include the geographical location, global privacy functions and organizations, and international data sharing.

3.10 Monitoring Laws and Regulations

Methods to track the changes include using many resources, such as the internet, printed and online journals, automated online services and third-party vendors. Each organization should investigate the best methods based on cost, requirements and industry to ensure issue customization, easy access, professional support, reliability rating and complete, accurate coverage. Regardless of an organization's size and complexity, the privacy professional may wish to consider some form of third-party support because of the number of new laws, changing regulations and other complex factors influencing privacy today.

3.11 Third-Party External Privacy Resources

If an organization is small, or the privacy office staffing is limited, the privacy professional and organization could consider third-party solutions to track and monitor privacy laws relating to the business. These third parties include legal and consultancy services that can assign people to the organization and use automated online services that allow research on privacy law, news and business tools. Privacy professionals from large and small firms can also take advantage of a growing number of free resources to help them to keep up to date with developments in privacy. These include the IAPP's e-newsletter, the *Daily Dashboard*, and its many other publications, including the *Privacy Tracker*, which is dedicated to following changes in privacy law around the world. Most law firms with privacy practices also regularly produce updates and often host free-to-attend seminars or webinars. In addition, several independent organizations share sound privacy practices based on privacy issues that continue to arise worldwide.

3.12 Summary

As a part of privacy program management, the privacy policy framework begins with an understanding of the organization's operations and its compliance with privacy laws and regulations in various jurisdictions. This approach will identify the tasks involved in developing organizational privacy policies, standards and/or guidelines.

With the abundance of data privacy concerns, changing regulatory environments, social media networking, increased sharing of personal data, and advancements in the use of technology in everyday life, the privacy professional's responsibilities will continue to evolve. Vigilance is required.

As privacy management becomes more complex, the privacy professional needs flexible and reusable best practices to create solid privacy programs. Programs must conform with cultural, technological and legal changes, otherwise, gaps will form between internal privacy management practices and the expectations of society.

Frameworks, in the form of reusable structures, checklists, templates, processes and procedures, prompt and remind the privacy professional of the details necessary to inform all privacy-relevant decisions in the organization. Having this framework and a blueprint provides clear guidance on protecting data privacy to align with the expectations, requirements, laws and public demands for handling personal information safely and properly.

There is no one-size-fits-all standard for a privacy program. Establishing and implementing the program with the necessary inputs and protocols is critical to effective management and compliance. An adaptable and flexible approach will assist the organization in making strategic business decisions when selecting models, strategies and technologies for the protection and privacy of data handling and usage.

Privacy laws and regulations comprise a complex regulatory environment. They change and are becoming much more specific and detailed in order to meet shifting consumers' expectations regarding their privacy. It is the organization's role, and that of the privacy professional, to meet those expectations. Implementing the framework is the first cornerstone to protecting privacy in the organization and to providing the foundation for effective privacy management.

Endnotes

1 Diedre Rodriquez, "10 Steps to a Quality Privacy Program: Part One," *The Privacy Advisor*, IAPP June 24, 2013, https://iapp.org/news/a/10-steps-to-a-quality-privacy-program-part-one/ (accessed November 2018).

2 Kirk M. Herath. *Building a Privacy Program: A Practitioner's Guide*, p. 22, (Portsmouth, NH: IAPP, 2011).

3 Privacy Act of 1974, 5 U.S.C. § 552a, https://www.gpo.gov/fdsys/pkg/USCODE-2012-title5/pdf/USCODE-2012-title5-partI-chap5-subchapII-sec552a.pdf (accessed November 2018).

4 GLBA, https://www.gpo.gov/fdsys/pkg/PLAW-106publ102/pdf/PLAW-106publ102.pdf (accessed November 2018).

5 HIPAA of 1996, https://www.gpo.gov/fdsys/pkg/PLAW-104publ191/pdf/PLAW-104publ191.pdf (accessed November 2018).

6 CAN-SPAM of 2003, https://www.ftc.gov/sites/default/files/documents/cases/2007/11/canspam.pdf (accessed November 2018).

7 COPPA of 1998, https://www.ftc.gov/enforcement/rules/rulemaking-regulatory-reform-proceedings/childrens-online-privacy-protection-rule (accessed November 2018).

8 FACTA of 2003, https://www.ftc.gov/enforcement/statutes/fair-accurate-credit-transactions-act-2003 (accessed November 2018).

9 FCRA of 1970, https://www.ftc.gov/enforcement/rules/rulemaking-regulatory-reform-proceedings/fair-credit-reporting-act (accessed January 2019).

10 National Do Not Call Registry, https://www.donotcall.gov/ (accessed November 2018).

11 TCPA of 1991, https://transition.fcc.gov/cgb/policy/TCPA-Rules.pdf (accessed November 2018).

12 DPPA of 1994, https://dmv.ny.gov/forms/mv15dppa.pdf (accessed November 2018).

13 ECPA of 1986, https://it.ojp.gov/PrivacyLiberty/authorities/statutes/1285 (accessed November 2018).

14 VPPA of 1988, https://www.gpo.gov/fdsys/pkg/STATUTE-102/pdf/STATUTE-102-Pg3195.pdf (accessed November 2018).

15 FERPA, https://www2.ed.gov/policy/gen/guid/fpco/ferpa/index.html (accessed November 2018).

16 Federal Trade Commission Act (Section 5: Privacy and Security) of 1914, https://www.ftc.gov/enforcement/statutes/federal-trade-commission-act (accessed November 2018).

17 PCI DSS, https://www.pcisecuritystandards.org/ (accessed November 2018).

18 DMA Guidelines for Ethical Business Practices (formally the Direct Marketing Association), DMA, https://thedma.org/accountability/ethics-and-compliance/dma-ethical-guidelines/ (accessed November 2018).

19 DMA Member Principles, DMA, https://thedma.org/accountability/ethics-and-compliance/dma-ethical-guidelines/#member-principles (accessed November 2018).

20 VeriSign, https://www.verisign.com/ (accessed November 2018); TrustArc (the new TRUSTe), https://www.trustarc.com/ (accessed November 2018); McAfee, https://www.mcafee.com (accessed November 2018); PayPal, https://www.paypal.com (accessed November 2018).

21 Trust marks, https://ecommerceguide.com/guides/ecommerce-store-trust-marks/ (accessed November 2018).

22 CARU guidelines, www.caru.org/guidelines/index.aspx (accessed November 2018).

23 NAI Code of Conduct, www.networkadvertising.org/code-enforcement/code/ (accessed November 2018).

24 OECD Guidelines on the Protection of Privacy and Transborder Flows of Personal Data, www.oecd.org/sti/ieconomy/oecdguidelinesontheprotectionofprivacyandtransborderflowsofpersonaldata.htm (accessed November 2018).

25 GDPR, https://eur-lex.europa.eu/legal-content/EN/TXT/?qid=1528874672298&uri=CELEX%3A32016R0679 (accessed November 2018).

26 APEC privacy framework, https://www.apec.org/Publications/2005/12/APEC-Privacy-Framework (accessed November 2018).

27 Lei No. 22/11 da Protecção de Dados Pessoais de 17 de Junho (in Portuguese), http://files.mwe.com/info/pubs/Law_22_11_Data_Privacy_Law.pdf (accessed November 2018).

28 Ley 25.326 de Protección de los Datos Personales (in Spanish), http://servicios.infoleg.gob.ar/infolegInternet/anexos/60000-64999/64790/norma.htm (accessed November 2018).

29 Privacy Act 1988, https://www.oaic.gov.au/privacy-law/privacy-act/ (accessed November 2018).

30 Law on Information, Informatisation and Information Protection of 10 November 2008 No. 455 Z (in Russian), https://portal.gov.by/i/portalgovby/download/zakon-455-3.pdf (accessed November 2018).

31 Personal Information Protection Act 2016, www.bermudalaws.bm/laws/Annual%20Laws/2016/Acts/Personal%20Information%20Protection%20Act%202016.pdf (accessed November 2018).

32 Personal Data Protection Agency in Bosnia and Herzegovina, www.azlp.gov.ba/propisi/Default.aspx?id=5&pageIndex=1&langTag=en-US (accessed November 2018).

33 Lei Geral de Proteção dos Dados Pessoais (in Portuguese), www.planalto.gov.br/ccivil_03/_Ato2015-2018/2018/Lei/L13709.htm (accessed November 2018).

34 PIPEDA of 2000, https://www.priv.gc.ca/en/privacy-topics/privacy-laws-in-canada/the-personal-information-protection-and-electronic-documents-act-pipeda/ (accessed November 2018).

35 Lei n° 133/V/2001 of 22 January 2001 (in Portuguese), https://www.afapdp.org/wp-content/uploads/2018/05/Cap-vert-Lei-n%C2%B0133-V-2001-do-22-janeiro-2001.pdf (accessed November 2018).

36 Sobre Protección de La Vida Privada (in Spanish), https://www.leychile.cl/Navegar?idNorma=141599 (accessed November 2018).

37 People's Republic of China Cyber Security Law (in Chinese), www.npc.gov.cn/npc/xinwen/2016-11/07/content_2001605.htm (accessed November 2018).

38 Ley Estatutaria 1266 de 2008 - Habeas Data Act (in Spanish), www.alcaldiabogota.gov.co/sisjur/normas/Norma1.jsp?i=34488 (accessed November 2018).

39 Ley Estatutaria 1581 de 2012 (in Spanish), www.defensoria.gov.co/public/Normograma%202013_html/Normas/Ley_1581_2012.pdf (accessed November 2018).

40 Ley de Protección de la Persona frente al tratamiento de sus datos personales, N° 8968 (in Spanish), www.archivonacional.go.cr/pdf/ley_8968_proteccion_datos_personales.pdf (accessed November 2018).

41 Data Protection Act, 2012, https://www.dataprotection.org.gh/sites/default/files/Data%20Protection%20Act%20%2C%202012%20%28Act%20843%29.pdf (accessed November 2018).

42 Cap. 486 Personal Data (Privacy) Ordinance, https://www.elegislation.gov.hk/hk/cap486 (accessed November 2018).

43 Information Technology Act, 2000, www.wipo.int/wipolex/en/text.jsp?file_id=185998 (accessed November 2018).

44 Protection of Privacy Law, 5741-1981, www.wipo.int/wipolex/en/text.jsp?file_id=347462 (accessed November 2018).

45 APPI, https://www.ppc.go.jp (accessed November 2018).

46 Personal Data Protection Act 2010, https://www.kkmm.gov.my/pdf/Personal%20Data%20Protection%20Act%202010.pdf (accessed November 2018).

47 Ley Federal de Protección de Datos Personales en Posesión de los Particulares, 2010 (in Spanish), www.diputados.gob.mx/LeyesBiblio/pdf/LFPDPPP.pdf (accessed November 2018).

48 Loi n° 1.165 du 23/12/1993 relative à la protection des informations nominatives (in French), https://www.legimonaco.mc/305/legismclois.nsf/db3b0488a44ebcf9c12574c7002a8e84/28a1a1d90812e249c125773f003beebb!OpenDocument (accessed November 2018).

49 Loi n° 09-08 relative à la protection des personnes physiques à l'égard du traitement des données à caractère personnel (in French), https://www.cndp.ma/images/lois/Loi-09-08-Fr.pdf (accessed November 2018).

50 Privacy Act 1993, www.legislation.govt.nz/act/public/1993/0028/latest/DLM296639.html (accessed November 2018).

51 Ley N° 29733 - Ley de Protección de Datos Personales (in Spanish), www.leyes.congreso.gob.pe/Documentos/Leyes/29733.pdf (accessed November 2018).

52 Republic Act 10173 – Data Privacy Act of 2012, https://www.privacy.gov.ph/data-privacy-act/ (accessed November 2018).

53 Law No. 13 of 2016 Concerning Personal Data Protection, https://www.dlapiperdataprotection.com/system/modules/za.co.heliosdesign.dla.lotw.data_protection/functions/handbook.pdf?country-1=QA (accessed January 2018).

54 Federal Law on Personal Data No. 152-FZ, https://iapp.org/resources/article/english-translation-of-the-russian-federal-law-on-personal-data/ (accessed November 2018).

55 Personal Data Protection Act 2012, https://sso.agc.gov.sg/Act/PDPA2012 (accessed November 2018).

56 Protection of Personal Information Act 4 of 2013, https://www.gov.za/sites/default/files/37067_26-11_Act4of2013ProtectionOfPersonalInfor_correct.pdf (accessed November 2018).

57 Personal Information Protection Act, http://koreanlii.or.kr/w/images/a/a3/PIPAct_1308en.pdf (accessed November 2018).

58 Personal Data Protection Law (PDPL), https://www.dlapiperdataprotection.com/index.html?c=TW&c2=&go-button=GO&t=law (accessed January 2019).

59 Law on the Protection of Personal Data No. 6698 (in Turkish), www.mevzuat.gov.tr/MevzuatMetin/1.5.6698.pdf (accessed November 2018).

60 Data Protection Law DIFC Law No. 1 of 2007, https://www.difc.ae/files/7814/5517/4119/Data_Protection_Law_DIFC_Law_No._1_of_2007.pdf (accessed November 2018).

61 La Ley 18331 Protección de Datos Personales y Acción de Habeas Data del 11 agosto del año 2008 y el Decreto reglamentario 414/2009 (in Spanish), http://agesic.gub.uy/innovaportal/file/302/1/Ley_N_18331.pdf (accessed November 2018).

62 Law on Cybersecurity. At the time of the writing of this book, a copy of the law had not been officially published; however you can view a copy of the draft here: https://auschamvn.org/wp-content/uploads/2018/06/Draft-Cyber-Security-Law-Version-20-ENG.docx (accessed January 2019).

63 GDPR, https://eur-lex.europa.eu/legal-content/EN/TXT/?qid=1528874672298&uri=CELEX%3A32016R0679 (accessed November 2018).

64 For a more thorough review, see European Data Protection: Law and Practice (Portsmouth, NH: IAPP).

65 GDPR, Article 1, https://eur-lex.europa.eu/legal-content/EN/TXT/?qid=1528874672298&uri=CELEX%3A32016R0679 (accessed November 2018).

66 GDPR, Article 2, https://eur-lex.europa.eu/legal-content/EN/TXT/?qid=1528874672298&uri=CELEX%3A32016R0679 (accessed November 2018).

67 GDPR, Article 3, https://eur-lex.europa.eu/legal-content/EN/TXT/?qid=1528874672298&uri=CELEX%3A32016R0679 (accessed November 2018).

68 "GPDR Awareness Guide," IAPP, https://iapp.org/resources/article/gdpr-awareness-guide/ (accessed November 2018).

69 "Guidelines for Processing Personal Data Across Borders," Office of the Privacy Commissioner, January 2009, https://www.priv.gc.ca/en/privacytopics/personal-information-transferred-across-borders/gl_dab_090127/ (accessed November 2018).

70 Siegel, Bob, "For a Successful Privacy Program, Use These Three As." The Privacy Advisor, IAPP, February 22, 2016, https://iapp.org/resources/article/for-a-successful-privacy-program-use-these-three-as-three-part-series/ (accessed November 2018).

71 "What are the Penalties for HIPAA Violations?" June 25, 2015, HIPAA Journal, https://www.hipaajournal.com/what-are-the-penalties-for-hipaa-violations-7096/ (accessed November 2018).

72 Id.

73 Data Protection Laws of the World, DLA Piper, China, https://www.dlapiperdataprotection.com/index.html?t=authority&c=CN (accessed November 2018).

74 Amended Act on the Protection of Personal Information (tentative translation), Personal Information Protection Commission, Japan, https://www.ppc.go.jp/files/pdf/Act_on_the_ Protection_of_Personal_Information.pdf (accessed November 2018).

75 Kwang Bae Park and Sunghee Chae, "Data protection in South Korea: Overview," Thomson Reuters, Practical Law, https://uk.practicallaw.thomsonreuters.com/Document/ I1d81ec834f2711e498db8b09b4f043e0/View/FullText.html?transitionType=SearchItem&context Data=(sc.Default) (accessed November 2018).

76 Legislation and Guidelines, Personal Data Protection Commission, Singapore, https://www.pdpc .gov.sg/Legislation-and-Guidelines/Enforcement-of-the-Act (accessed November 2018).

77 Data Privacy Law: The Ordinance at a Glance, Privacy Commissioner for Personal Data, Hong Kong, https://www.pcpd.org.hk/english/data_privacy_law/ordinance_at_a_Glance/ordinance.html (accessed November 2018).

78 Haruethai Boonklomjit , Natpakal Rerknithi , Anna Gamvros and Ruby Kwok, "Overview of Thailand Draft Personal Data Protection Act," Norton, Rose, Fulbright, https://www .dataprotectionreport.com/2018/08/overview-of-thailand-draft-personal-data-protection-act/ (accessed November 2018).

79 Denny Rahmansyah and Saprita Tahir, "Data Protection in Indonesia: overview," Thomson Reuters, Practical Law, https://uk.practicallaw.thomsonreuters.com/Document/ Ic7ba28fe5f0811e498db8b09b4f043e0/View/FullText.html?transitionType=SearchItem&context Data=(sc.Default) (accessed November 2018).

80 Personal Data Protection Act 2010, https://www.kkmm.gov.my/pdf/Personal%20Data%20 Protection%20Act%202010.pdf (accessed November 2018).

81 Republic Act 10173 – Data Privacy Act of 2012, National Privacy Commission, https://www.privacy. gov.ph/data-privacy-act/ (accessed November 2018).

82 Privacy Act 1993, New Zealand legislation, www.legislation.govt.nz/act/public/1993/0028/latest/ DLM296639.html (accessed November 2018); Data Protection in New Zealand: overview, Thomson Reuters, Practical Law, https://www.dlapiperdataprotection.com/index.html?t=enforcement&c=NZ (accessed November 2018).

83 Guide to Privacy Regulation Action, Australian Government, Office of the Australian Information Commissioner, https://www.oaic.gov.au/about-us/our-regulatory-approach/guide-to-privacy- regulatory-action/ (accessed November 2018).

84 Burak Özdağıstanli, "Data Protection in Turkey: overview," Thomson Reuters, Practical Law, https:// uk.practicallaw.thomsonreuters.com/Document/I02064fb01cb611e38578f7ccc38dcbee/View/ FullText.html?transitionType=SearchItem&contextData=(sc.Search) (accessed November 2018).

85 Sergey Medvedev, "Privacy in the Russian federation: overview," Thomson Reuters, Practical Law, https://uk.practicallaw.thomsonreuters.com/Document/I0e929cf2091911e598db8b09b4f043e0/ View/FullText.html?transitionType=SearchItem&contextData=(sc.Search) (accessed November 2018).

86 Regulation (EC) No 45/2001 of the European Parliament and the Council of 18 December 2009, Official Journal of the European Communities, https://edps.europa.eu/sites/edp/files/publication/ reg_45-2001_en.pdf (accessed November 2018).

87 Data Protection Laws of the World, DLA Piper, Iceland, https://www.dlapiperdataprotection.com/ index.html?t=authority&c=IS (accessed November 2018).

88 "What we do," Office of the Privacy Commissioner of Canada, https://www.priv.gc.ca/en/about-the-opc/what-we-do/ (accessed November 2018).

89 Begoña Cancino, "Data Protection in Mexico: overview," Thomson Reuters, Practical Law, https://uk.practicallaw.thomsonreuters.com/8-502-5162?transitionType=Default&contextData=(sc.Default) (accessed November 2018).

90 Data Protection Laws of the World, DLA Piper, Argentina, https://www.dlapiperdataprotection.com/index.html?t=enforcement&c=AR (accessed November 2018).

91 Data Protection Laws of the World, DLA Piper, Uruguay, https://www.dlapiperdataprotection.com/index.html?t=enforcement&c=UY (accessed November 2018).

92 Deputy Superintendence for the Protection of Personal Data, Industria y Comercio Superintendcia, www.sic.gov.co/en/deputy-superintendence-for-the-protection-of-personal-data (accessed November 2018).

93 Missiona, Royaume Du Moaroc, https://www.cndp.ma/fr/cndp/missions.html (accessed November 2018).

94 Nzilani Mweu, "Data Protection in Kenya: overview," Thomson Reuters, Practical Law, https://uk.practicallaw.thomsonreuters.com/Document/Ia70843cf38c111e89bf099c0ee06c731/View/FullText.html?transitionType=SearchItem&contextData=(sc.Default) (accessed November 2018).

95 Rohan Isaacs and Kerri Crawford, "Privacy in South Africa: overview," Thomson Reuters, Practical Law, https://uk.practicallaw.thomsonreuters.com/Document/I86a475b3ccd211e498db8b09b4f043e0/View/FullText.html?transitionType=SearchItem&contextData=(sc.Search) (accessed November 2018).

CHAPTER 4

Data Assessments

João Torres Barreiro, CIPP/E, CIPP/US

A successful privacy program cannot be built and maintained without a comprehensive view of the data organizations store and process. Data assessments can help to inventory and track personal information as well as determine the impact organizational systems and processes will have on privacy. Data assessments are tools that can help organizations identify privacy risks to individuals in advance and deal with them effectively at the beginning of any project that involves the processing of personal data. Addressing potential problems early will help to achieve a more robust compliance regime and ultimately reduce costs.

In this chapter, we will examine different types and functions of data assessments, including two key types, privacy impact assessments (PIAs) and data protection impact assessments (DPIAs). Performing periodic privacy risk assessments is a key activity for the implementation of a Three Lines of Defence model in terms of enterprise risk management.[1]

4.1 Inventories and Records

How do you know where your personal data resides, how it is used in the organization, and why it is important? The data inventory, also known as a data map, provides answers to these questions by identifying the data as it moves across various systems, and thus indicating how it is shared and organized and where it is located. That data is then categorized by subject area, which identifies inconsistent data versions, enabling identification and mitigation of data disparities, which in turn serves to identify the most and least valuable data and reveal how it is accessed, used and stored.

Data inventories are legally required for some institutions, such as those covered by the Gramm-Leach-Bliley Act (GLBA) Safeguards Rule. Creating and maintaining them may be the responsibility of the privacy function, the information technology (IT) function, or both—always with input from all business functions that require, own or make decisions about the use of the data.[2] Most often, the budget for this undertaking is shared across these departments.

Questions can be used to determine the data assets of an organization. They should be specific to the organization's line of business and may be organized around the data lifecycle—collection, usage, transfers, retention and destruction. Internal policies and procedures, laws, regulations and standards may also be used to compose the questions. Based on these aspects, the data inventory offers a good starting point for the privacy team to prioritize resources, efforts, risk assessments and current policy in response to incidents. A data inventory should include the items in Table 4-1.

Table 4-1: Elements of a Data Inventory

Element	Explanation
The nature of a repository of privacy-related information	What is the context and purpose of the repository?
The owner of the repository	What is the starting point for further investigation into the repository?
Location of the repository	Where is the data moving from and to?
The volume of information in this repository	How much data is in the repository?
The format of the information	Is this a paper or electronic repository? Is it structured or unstructured?
The use of the information	How is the information being used?
Type (or types) of privacy-related information in the repository	What kinds of information are in the repository (e.g., physical or email addresses, government-issued identification numbers, health information, salary information)?
Where the data is stored	In which country or countries is the data stored?
Where the data is accessed	From which country or countries is the data accessed?
International transfers	Where will the data flow (from country to country)?
With whom the data is shared	Is the data shared with third parties? Are they controllers or processors?

Once the data inventory has been completed and documented, the information can be used when necessary to address both incidents and standard risk assessments. This process will help set the organizational priorities for privacy initiatives by providing data locations, data use, data storage and data access, which allows the privacy team to justify priorities and understand the scope of data usage in the organization.

When building your data inventory, select the tool that will enable your organization to most easily update it. Options may include spreadsheets, a governance, risk and compliance (GRC) software system, an internally developed system or another product. Updating data inventories is often a manual process involving multiple departments. Remember that changes in the organization may trigger the need to update data inventories.

In addition to creating a data inventory, the privacy professional may want to establish an inventory of applicable laws and regulations.[3] Conducting a gap analysis can help. This task requires effort and resources, especially when the privacy program is first being established. Consider international, local and industry-specific standards and laws, and then map gaps against them. Most laws have some overlap, so be sure to involve the legal team in the process. Although not always necessary, some organizations may decide to use a privacy compliance tool.[4]

4.2 Records of Processing Activities Under the General Data Protection Regulation

One of the more onerous new requirements under the General Data Protection Regulation (GDPR) is the obligation under Article 30 for controllers and processors to maintain a detailed record of their processing activities.[5] A prescriptive list of the contents of this record includes:

- The name and contact details of the controller or processor, data protection officer (DPO), and/or data protection representative
- The purposes for the processing (for controllers)
- A description of the categories of personal data and categories of data subjects (for controllers) or the categories of processing (for processors)
- The categories of recipients (for controllers)
- Any international transfers to third countries
- Where possible, the retention periods for the various categories of personal data (for controllers)
- A general description of the safeguards implemented

It is important to note that this detailed record of processing must be disclosed to a data protection authority (DPA) upon request. The only exemption from the requirement to maintain a detailed record of processing is when the controller or processor employs fewer than 250 people, provided that the processing it undertakes is occasional, does not include sensitive personal data, and is not likely to result in a risk for the rights and freedoms of the individual. For example, processing may result in a risk of this nature when a controller or processor is carrying out profiling activities.[6] To meet the requirement to maintain a detailed record of processing activities, a business should carry out and maintain a data flow analysis report identifying the different categories of personal data, the purposes for which the personal data is processed, the recipients, and the way the data flows around the business and externally through different systems.[7]

To begin to tackle the data and processing inventory project, the DPO, working with the controller and processor teams, would look to identify several starting points and then move forward on each. One starting point would be to identify and interview all known data owners. An organization should have someone located in each business unit who is responsible for each type of data collected. If the organization has a records or data team, they should also be consulted, as data custodians may be separate from data owners. The digital marketing teams would know what information they gather and use to reach new customers. The corporate counsel teams may have information on data types as well, as they need to know how to freeze such data for litigation purposes.[8]

The IT organization should have database administrators who should have schemas of the databases of varying kinds. The team responsible for backups and business continuity should also know what data is retained and what needs to be restored. The software team should have lists of all software used by the organization. The process owner of each can be queried for the personal data of which they are aware. The compliance team would have details of personal data, including some applicable to compliance with non-GDPR privacy statutes (e.g., ePrivacy Directive/Regulation). And the administrator who currently answers data subject access requests would have more information about personal data sources.[9]

Information from these sources and others identified as the interview process progresses can be used to begin to put together a current data inventory. Not all this data will be personal data. Nonpersonal data, which is outside the scope of the GDPR, needs to be identified. Implementing a new process means that revised or new apps or systems must thoroughly document the personal data they are processing, which will help to keep the data inventory from becoming outdated.[10]

While gathering information about personal data, the team should also be gaining an understanding of how that data is being processed.[11] Additional information to discover includes the type of security used to protect the data (e.g., encryption), the retention periods for the data, who has access to it, who is it disclosed to, and the legal basis for processing the data. If done correctly, a data and processing inventory will begin to emerge that builds a foundation upon which to address many of the controller's or processor's obligations. Many iterations will be required, but from this data and processing inventory, the DPO will understand in some depth the GDPR compliance situation of their organization and be able to begin formulating gap plans to remediate any noncompliance.[12]

4.3 Assessments and Impact Assessments

Three types of assessments and impact assessments are of concern at this point: privacy assessments, PIAs and DPIAs. Although these terms are often used in other contexts to refer to the same concept, you can also differentiate them.

4.3.1 Privacy Assessment: Measuring Compliance

Privacy assessments measure an organization's compliance with laws, regulations, adopted standards and internal policies and procedures. Their scope includes education and awareness; monitoring and responding to the regulatory environment; data, systems and process assessments; risk assessments; incident response; contracts; remediation; and program assurance, including audits.

Privacy assessments are conducted internally by the audit function, the DPO or a business function, or externally by a third party. They can happen at a predefined time period or be conducted in response to a security or privacy event or at a request of an enforcement authority. The standards used can be subjective, such as employee interviews, or objective, such as information system logs.

4.3.2 Privacy Impact Assessment

A PIA is an analysis of the privacy risks associated with processing personal information in relation to a project, product or service. To be an effective tool, a PIA also should suggest or provide remedial actions or mitigations necessary to avoid or reduce/minimize those risks. Requirements regarding PIAs emanate from industry codes, organizational policy, laws, regulations or supervisory authorities.

PIAs can help facilitate privacy by design, which is the concept of building privacy directly into technology, systems and practices at the design phase. It helps ensure privacy is considered from the outset, and not as an afterthought. Privacy by design will be covered in greater detail in Chapter 8.

To be an effective tool, a PIA should be accomplished early, in other words:

- Prior to deployment of a project, product or service that involves the collection of personal information

- When there are new or revised industry standards, organizational policies, or laws and regulations

- When the organization creates new privacy risks through changes to methods by which personal information is handled

Below are some of the events that may trigger the need for a PIA:

- Conversion of information from anonymous to identifiable format

- Conversion of records from paper-based to electronic format

- Significant merging, matching and manipulation of multiple databases containing personal information

- Application of user-authentication technology to a publicly accessible system

- System management changes involving significant new uses and/or application of new technologies

- Retiring of systems that held or processed personal data

- Incorporation of personal information obtained from commercial or public sources into existing databases

- Significant new interagency exchanges or uses of personal information

- Alteration of a business process resulting in significant new collection, use and disclosure of personal information

- Alteration of the character of personal information due to addition of qualitatively new types

- Implementation of projects using third-party service providers

Regardless of the geographical location or the requirements based in law, regulation or guideline, the PIA is a risk management tool used to identify and reduce the privacy/data protection risks to individuals and organizations and aimed at ensuring a more holistic risk management strategy. Details of PIAs, how they are used, and formats, methodologies and processes around the assessments will vary depending on industry, private- or public-sector orientation, geographical location or regional requirements, and sensitivity or type of data. The privacy professional should identify the appropriate methodology and approaches based on these various factors and tailor the model to the specific needs of the organization.

One of the biggest challenges for privacy professionals is to prioritize the projects, products or services that should be submitted to a PIA. To identify the data-processing activities that represent a higher privacy risk, some organizations first conduct an express PIA, which consists of a small questionnaire that assesses the need for a full and more comprehensive PIA. This approach enables all stakeholders to dedicate their resources to the areas where the risks and potential harms for individuals are most significant and to mitigate these risks, creating better outcomes and more effective protection for individuals.[13]

4.3.3 PIAs in the United States

The U.S. government, under the E-Government Act of 2002, required PIAs from government agencies when developing or procuring IT systems containing personally identifiable information (PII) of the public or when initiating an electronic collection of PII.[14] This requirement is preceded by a privacy threshold analysis (PTA) to determine if a PIA is needed. The PTA would seek to determine from whom data is collected, what types of personal data are collected, how such data is shared, whether the data has been merged, and whether any determinations have been made as to the information security aspects of the system.[15] The Privacy Act requirements include the rights to receive timely notice of location, routine use, storage, retrievability, access controls, retention and disposal; rights of access and change to personal information; consent to disclosure; and maintenance of accurate, relevant, timely and complete records.[16] As such, the PIA will describe in the detail the information collected or maintained, the sources of that information, the uses and possible disclosures, and potential threats to the information.

The uses to which the information is put by the system are described next, including the legal authority for collecting the data, the retention periods and eventual destruction, and any potential threats based on use of the data. Also included are any information dissemination and the controls used, the rights listed above, the information security program used, and compliance with the Privacy Act.[17] Under implementation guidance, the following were reasons for initiating a PIA:

- Collection of new information about individuals, whether compelled or voluntary

- Conversion of records from paper-based to electronic format

- Conversion of information from anonymous to identifiable format

- System management changes involving significant new uses and/or application of new technologies

- Significant merging, matching or other manipulation of multiple databases containing PII

- Application of user-authentication technology to a publicly accessible system

- Incorporation into existing databases of PII obtained from commercial or public sources

- Significant new interagency exchanges or uses of PII

- Alteration of a business process resulting in significant new collection, use and/or disclosure of PII

- Alteration of the character of PII due to the addition of qualitatively new types of PII

- Implementation of projects using third-party service providers[18]

4.3.4 International Organization for Standardization (ISO)

ISO 29134 is a set of guidelines for the process of running a PIA and the structure of the resulting report.[19] It is not a standard for PIAs, unlike, say, a standard for information security. These guidelines define a PIA as a process for identifying and treating, in consultation with stakeholders, risks to PII in a process, system, application or device. They reiterate that PIAs are important not only for controllers and their processors but also for the suppliers of digitally connected devices. They also specify that the PIA should start at the earliest design phase and continue until after implementation. The process first involves conducting a threshold analysis to determine whether a PIA is needed, then preparing for a PIA, performing a PIA and following up on the PIA. The performing phase consists of five steps:

1. Identifying information flows of PII

2. Analyzing the implications of the use case

3. Determining the relevant privacy-safeguarding requirements

4. Assessing privacy risk using steps of risk identification, risk analysis and risk evaluation

5. Preparing to treat privacy risk by choosing the privacy risk treatment option; determining the controls using control sets such as those available in ISO/IEC 27002 and ISO/IEC 29151, and creating privacy risk treatment plans

The follow-up phase consists of:

- Preparing and publishing the PIA report

- Implementing the privacy risk treatment plan

- Reviewing the PIA and reflecting changes to the process

The structure of the PIA report should include sections on the scope of the assessment, privacy requirements, the risk assessment, the risk treatment plan, and conclusions and decisions. The risk assessment includes discussion of the risk sources, threats and their likelihood, consequences and their level of impact, risk evaluation, and compliance analysis. There should also be a summary that can be made public.[20]

4.3.5 Data Protection Impact Assessments

When an organization collects, stores or uses personal data, the individuals whose data is being processed are exposed to risks. These risks range from personal data being stolen or inadvertently released and used by criminals to impersonate the individual, to worry being caused to individuals that their data will be used by the organization for unknown purposes. A DPIA describes a process designed to identify risks arising out of the processing of personal data and to minimize these risks as much and as early as possible. DPIAs are important tools for negating risk and for demonstrating compliance with the GDPR.[21]

Under the GDPR, noncompliance with DPIA requirements can lead to fines imposed by the competent supervisory authority. Failure to carry out a DPIA when the processing is subject to a DPIA, carrying out a DPIA in an incorrect way, or failing to consult the competent supervisory authority where required can result in an administrative fine of up to €10 thousand, or in the case of an undertaking, up to 2 percent of the total worldwide annual revenue of the preceding financial year, whichever is higher.[22]

DPIAs are required only when an organization is subject to the GDPR and although the term PIA is often used in other contexts to refer to the same concept, a DPIA has specific triggers and requirements under the GDPR.

4.3.6 When is a DPIA Required?

In case the processing is "likely to result in a high risk to the rights and freedoms of natural persons," the controller shall, prior to processing, carry out a DPIA.[23] The nature, scope, context, purpose, type of processing, and use of new technologies should, however, be considered. The use of new technologies, in particular, whose consequences and risks are less understood, may increase the likelihood that a DPIA should be conducted. Article 35 provides some examples when a processing operation is "likely to result in high risks:"

    a. *Systematic and extensive evaluation of personal aspects relating to natural persons which is based on automated processing, including profiling, and on which decisions are based that produce legal effects concerning the natural person or similarly significantly affect the natural person;*

    b. *Processing on a large scale of special categories of data, or of personal data relating to criminal convictions and offences; or*

    c. *A systematic monitoring of a publicly accessible area on a large scale.*[24]

This abovementioned list is nonexhaustive and the Article 29 Working Party (WP29)[25] provides a more concrete set of processing operations that require a DPIA due to their inherent high risk:[26]

- **Evaluation or scoring:** includes profiling and predicting, especially from aspects concerning the data subject's performance at work, economic situation, health, personal preferences or interests, reliability or behavior, and location or movements.

- **Automated decision-making with legal or similar significant effect:** processing that aims at taking decisions on data subjects producing "legal effects concerning the natural person" or that "similarly significantly affects the natural person."

- **Systematic monitoring:** processing used to observe, monitor or control data subjects, including data collected through networks or a systematic monitoring of a publicly accessible area.

- **Sensitive data or data of a highly personal nature:** this includes special categories of personal data, as well as personal data relating to criminal convictions or offences.

- **Data processed on a large scale:** the WP29 recommends that the following factors, in particular, be considered when determining whether the processing is carried out on a large scale: (1) the number of data subjects concerned, either as a specific number or as a proportion of the relevant population; (2) the volume of data and/or the range of different data items being processed; (3) the duration, or permanence, of the data processing activity; and (4) the geographical extent of the processing activity.

- **Matching or combining datasets:** for example, originating from two or more data processing operations performed for different purposes and/or by different data controllers in a way that would exceed the reasonable expectations of the data subject.

- **Data concerning vulnerable data subjects:** the processing of this type of data is a criterion because of the increased power imbalance between the data subjects and the data controller, meaning the individuals may be unable to easily consent to, or oppose, the processing of their data, or exercise their rights. Vulnerable data subjects may include children, employees and more vulnerable segments of the population requiring special protection (e.g., persons with mental health concerns, asylum seekers, the elderly).

- **Innovative use or application of new technological or organizational solutions**, such as the combined use of fingerprints and face recognition for improved physical access control.

- When the processing in itself **prevents data subjects from exercising a right or using a service or a contract.**[27]

In most cases, a data controller can consider that a processing that meets two criteria would require a DPIA to be carried out. In general, the WP29 considers that the more criteria are met by the processing, the more likely it is to present a high risk to the rights and freedoms of data subjects, and therefore to require a DPIA, regardless of the measures the controller envisions adopting.

However, in some cases, a data controller can consider that a processing meeting only one of these criteria requires a DPIA. In cases where it is not clear whether a DPIA is required, the WP29 recommends that a DPIA be carried out.[28] A DPIA is a useful tool to help controllers build and demonstrate compliance with data protection law.[29]

Conversely, a processing operation may still be considered by the controller not to be "likely to result in a high risk." In such cases, the controller should justify and document the reasons for not carrying out a DPIA and include/record the views of the data protection officer.

In addition, as part of the accountability principle, every data controller *"shall maintain a record of processing activities under its responsibility"* including inter alia the purposes of processing, a description of the categories of data and recipients of the data and *"where possible, a general description of the technical and organizational security measures referred to in Article 32(11)"* (Article 30(1)) and must assess whether a high risk is likely, even if they ultimately decide not to carry out a DPIA.[30]

4.3.6.1 What Should a DPIA Include?

The GDPR sets out the minimum features of a DPIA:

- A description of the processing, including its purpose and the legitimate interest being pursued

- The necessity of the processing, its proportionality and the risks that it poses to data subjects

- Measures to address the risks identified[31]

Figure 4-1: Generic Iterative Process for Carrying Out a DPIA[32]

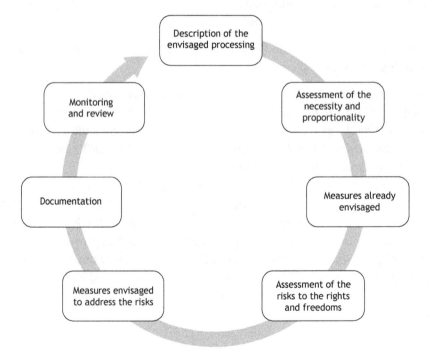

The Information Commissioner's Office (ICO) in the UK has available on its website several guidelines on DPIAs.[33] Similarly, the Commission nationale de l'informatique et des libertés (CNIL) in France has updated its PIA guides as well as its PIA tool.[34] The method is consistent with the WP29 guidelines and with risk management international standards. CNIL's PIA method is composed of three guides:

1. **The method** explains how to carry out a PIA

2. **The models** help to formalize a PIA by detailing how to handle the different sections introduced in the method

3. **The knowledge base** is a code of practice that lists measures to be used to treat the risks[35]

4.3.6.2 When Must the Supervisory Authority be Contacted?

Whenever the data controller cannot find sufficient measures to reduce the risks to an acceptable level (i.e., the residual risks are still high), consultation with the supervisory authority will be necessary.[36]

Scenarios that should lead to contact with a supervisory authority include:

- An illegitimate access to data leading to a threat on the life of the data subjects, a layoff or a financial jeopardy

- Inability to reduce the number of people accessing the data because of its sharing, use or distribution modes, or when a well-known vulnerability is not patched

Moreover, the controller will have to consult the supervisory authority whenever Member State law requires controllers to consult with, and/or obtain prior authorization from, the supervisory authority in relation to processing by a controller for the performance of a task carried out by the controller in the public interest, including processing in relation to social protection and public health.[37]

4.3.6.3 Components of a DPIA

Different methodologies could be used to assist in the implementation of the basic requirements set out in the GDPR. Annex 1 of the WP29's *Guidelines on Data Protection Impact Assessment* lists several examples of data protection and privacy impact assessment methodologies. To allow these different approaches to exist while allowing controllers to comply with the GDPR, common criteria have been identified on

Annex 2 of the same guidelines. They clarify the basic requirements of the Regulation but provide enough scope for different forms of implementation. These criteria can be used to show that a particular DPIA methodology meets the standards required by the GDPR. It is up to the data controller to choose a methodology, but this methodology should be compliant with the criteria provided in Annex 2 of the guidelines mentioned earlier in this paragraph.[38]

4.3.7 Attestation: A Form of Self-Assessment

Attestation is a tool for ensuring functions outside the privacy team are held accountable for privacy-related responsibilities. Once you have determined the privacy responsibilities of each department and the relevant privacy principles against which their personal information practices will be assessed, you can use this information to craft questions related to each responsibility. The designated department is required to answer the questions and, potentially, provide evidence. Attestation questions should be specific and easy to answer, usually with yes or no responses. Regular self-assessments can form part of an organization's privacy management systems and demonstrate a responsible privacy management culture.

In the United States, one example of attestation involves NIST 800-60, a guide from the National Institute of Standards and Technology (NIST) and the U.S. Department of Commerce (DOC).[39] The guide maps types of information and information systems to security categories. For example:

- **Task**—classify data.

- **Owner**—IT.

- **Questions**—Has the NIST 800-60 classification system been reviewed to ensure understanding of each category? Has each type of data within the information system been mapped to a category? Have data types that cannot be easily categorized been flagged, analyzed and classified by the chief information security officer (CISO)?

- **Evidence**—spreadsheet with data inventory, categories and classifications.

The Irish Office of the Data Protection Commission (DPC) has published a guide to such audits with helpful appendices for self-assessment.[40]

4.4 Physical and Environmental Assessment

Information security is the protection of information for the purpose of preventing loss, unauthorized access or misuse. Information security requires ongoing assessments of threats and risks to information and of the procedures and controls to preserve the information, consistent with three key attributes:

1. **Confidentiality:** access to data is limited to authorized parties

2. **Integrity:** assurance that the data is authentic and complete

3. **Availability:** knowledge that the data is accessible, as needed, by those who are authorized to use it

Information security is achieved by implementing security controls, which need to be monitored and reviewed to ensure that organizational security objectives are met. It is vital to both public and private sector organizations.

Security controls are mechanisms put in place to prevent, detect or correct a security incident. The three types of security controls are physical controls, administrative controls and technical controls.[41] For now, we are going to focus on the assessment of physical and environmental controls. The other information security practices will be covered in greater detail in Chapter 8.

Physical and environmental security refers to methods and controls used to proactively protect an organization from natural or manmade threats to physical facilities and buildings as well as to the physical locations where IT equipment is located or work is performed (e.g., computer rooms, work locations). Physical and environmental security protects an organization's personnel, electronic equipment and data/information. Key terms and concepts found in this competency include:

- Access cards
- Access control
- Alarms
- Assessment
- Asset disposal, including document destruction, media sanitization (e.g., hard drives, USB drives)
- Biometrics
- Defense-in-depth

- Environmental threats

- Identification and authentication

- Inventory

- Manmade threats

- Natural threats

- Perimeter defense

- Risk management

- Threat and vulnerability

- Video surveillance

4.5 Assessing Vendors

A procuring organization may have specific standards and processes for vendor selection. A prospective vendor should be evaluated against these standards through questionnaires, privacy impact assessments and other checklists. Standards for selecting vendors may include:

- **Reputation.** A vendor's reputation with other companies can be a valuable gauge of the vendor's appropriate collection and use of personal data. Requesting and contacting references can help determine a vendor's reputation.

- **Financial condition and insurance.** The vendor's finances should be reviewed to ensure the vendor has sufficient resources in case of a security breach and subsequent litigation. A current and sufficient insurance policy can also protect the procuring organization in the event of a breach.

- **Information security controls.** A service provider should have sufficient security controls in place to ensure the data is not lost or stolen.

- **Point of transfer.** The point of transfer between the procuring organization and the vendor is a potential security vulnerability. Mechanisms of secure transfer should be developed and maintained.

- **Disposal of information.** Appropriate destruction of data and/or information in any format or media is a key component of information management—for both the contracting organization and its vendors. The Disposal Rule under the Fair and Accurate Credit Transactions Act of 2003 (FACTA) sets forth required disposal protections for financial institutions. The Disposal Rule requirements provide a good baseline for disposal of personal information more generally.

- **Employee training and user awareness.** The vendor should have an established system for training its employees about its responsibilities in managing personal or sensitive information.

- **Vendor incident response.** Because of the potentially significant costs associated with a data breach, the vendor should clearly explain in advance its provisions for responding to any such breach with the cooperation needed to meet the organization's business and legal needs.

- **Audit rights.** Organizations should be able to monitor the vendor's activities to ensure it is complying with contractual obligations. Audit needs can sometimes be satisfied through periodic assessments or reports by independent trusted parties regarding the vendor's practices.[42]

Evaluating vendors should involve all relevant internal and external stakeholders, including internal audit, information security, physical security and regulators. Results may indicate improvement areas that may be fixed or identify higher-level risk that may limit the ability of that vendor to properly perform privacy protections. Once risk is determined, organization best practices may also be leveraged to assist a vendor too small or with limited resources by offering help with security engineering, risk management, training through awareness and education, auditing, and other tasks.

Contract language should be written to call out privacy protections and regulatory requirements within the statement of work and then mapped to service-level agreements to ensure there are no questions about the data privacy responsibilities, breach response, incident response, media press releases on breaches, possible fines, and other considerations, as if the vendor were part of the organization. The following list gives a few examples of the kind of information you may want to consider, including:

- Specifics regarding the type of personal information to which the vendor will have access at remote locations

- Vendor plans to protect personal information

- Vendor responsibilities in the event of a data breach

- Disposal of data upon contract termination

- Limitations on the use of data that ensure it will be used only for specified purposes

- Rights of audit and investigation

- Liability for data breach

The purpose of the vendor contract is to make certain all vendors are in compliance with the requirements of your organization's privacy program.

4.5.1 Assessing Vendors under the GDPR

Article 28 of the GDPR uses the device of limiting the controller's use of processors to those who can provide "sufficient guarantees" about the implementation of appropriate technical and organizational measures for compliance with the Regulation and for the protection of the rights of data subjects. This idea of sufficient guarantees encompasses much more than the creation of contracts, but the use of contracts is a key control mechanism. The focus is on obtaining proof of the processor's competence.

To make any sense and to be truly effective, the idea of sufficient guarantees must encompass assurance mechanisms. There must be appropriate checking and vetting of the processor by the supplier via a third-party assessment or certification validation, both before a contract is created and afterward. In appropriate circumstances, the processes of assurance must include audit processes, which are made clear in Article 28(3)(h). If the controller is unable to establish proof of the processor's competence, it must walk away; otherwise, it will be in automatic breach of Article 28. All this must work in a commercial context. The defining feature of the controller-processor relationship is that the processor can act only on the instructions of the controller. As can be seen from Article 28(10), if the processor steps outside the boundaries of its instructions, it risks being defined as a controller, with all the attendant obligations.

None of these provisions are new to European data protection law from the previous directive to the GDPR. What is new to legislation is the duty to assist the controller with achieving compliance and reducing risk, which includes assisting the controller with the handling of the personal data breach notification requirements (Article 28(3)(f)). Given this more practical application, it is clear that the controller and the processor will need to work closely to ensure effective incident detection and response. Arguably, Article 28 poses many challenges for the established order of things, particularly when there is an imbalance between the controller and processor in the market. When the processor is a technology giant, there may be a risk that it may use its more powerful position in a way that the GDPR says triggers controllership under Article 28(10). Thus, for the processor industry, there are very good incentives to behave flexibly during contract formation and procurement.[43]

4.6 Mergers, Acquisitions and Divestitures: Privacy Checkpoints

Mergers, acquisitions and divestitures contain many legal and compliance aspects, with their own sets of concerns related to privacy. Mergers form one organization from others, while acquisitions involve one organization buying one or many others; in divestitures, companies sell one division of an organization for reasons that may include the parent company's desire to rid itself of divisions not integral to its core business.

An organization can be exposed to corporate risk by merging with or acquiring companies that have different regulatory concerns. Merger and acquisition processes should include a privacy checkpoint that evaluates:

- Applicable new compliance requirements

- Sector-specific laws [e.g., Health Insurance Portability and Accountability Act (HIPAA) in the United States]

- Standards [e.g., the Payment Card Industry Data Security Standards (PCI DSS)]

- Jurisdictional laws/regulations [e.g., the Personal Information Protection and Electronic Documents Act (PIPEDA), GDPR]

- Existing client agreements

- New resources, technologies and processes to identify all actions that are required to bring them into alignment with privacy and security policies before they are integrated into the existing system

With respect to both partial and total divestitures, the organization should conduct a thorough assessment of the infrastructure of all, or any part of, the entity being divested prior to the conclusion of the divestiture. These activities are performed to confirm that no unauthorized information, including personal information, remains on the organization's infrastructure as part of the divestiture, with the exception of any preapproved proprietary data.

4.7 Summary

In recent years, with the proliferation of information communication technologies and the complex data protection problems they raise, data assessments and risk management have taken an even more prominent role in various privacy law regimes. The risk-based approach, which is now fully enacted by the GDPR, confirms this trend. Nevertheless, the necessity of conducting data assessments goes beyond compliance with certain legal requirements. They are an important risk management tool with clear financial benefits. Identifying a problem early will generally require a simpler and less costly solution. Moreover, data assessments allow organizations to reduce the ongoing costs of a project by minimizing the amount of information being collected or used and devising more straightforward processes for staff. Finally, data assessments improve transparency and accountability, making it easier for data subjects and supervisory authorities to understand how and why the personal data is being used.

Endnotes

1 For more information about the Three Lines of Defence model, please see Ken Doughty, "The Three Lines of Defence Related to Risk Governance," *ISACA Journal Volume 5* (2011), https://www.isaca .org/Journal/archives/2011/Volume-5/Documents/11v5-The-Three-Lines-of-Defence-Related-to-Risk-Governance.pdf (accessed November 2018). More detailed information on how to deploy this model for privacy governance can be found in "Privacy Governance and Controls: How do you know you are doing it right?" IAPP Practical Privacy Series 2014, New York City, https://iapp. org/media/presentations/14PPS/PPSNY14_Privacy_Governance_Controls_PPT.pdf (accessed November 2018).

2 Peter Swire, DeBrae Kennedy-Mayo, *U.S. Private-Sector Privacy: Law and Practice for Information Privacy Professionals*, Second Edition (Portsmouth, NH: IAPP, 2018).

3 *Data Protection Laws of the World*, DLA Piper, https://www.dlapiperdataprotection.com/index .html#handbook/world-map-section (accessed August 2018); *Global Privacy Handbook*, 2018 Edition, Baker McKenzie, https://tmt.bakermckenzie.com/-/media/minisites/tmt/files/global_ privacy_handbook-_2018.pdf?la=en (accessed November 2018).

4 For a list of technology solutions on the market, *see 2018 Privacy Tech Vendor Report*, IAPP, https://iapp.org/media/pdf/resource_center/2018-Privacy-Tech-Vendor-Report.pdf (accessed August 2018).

5 GDPR, Article 30, www.privacy-regulation.eu/en/article-30-records-of-processing-activities-GDPR.htm (accessed November 2018).

6 The GDPR defines profiling in Article 4(4) as "any form of automated processing of personal data consisting of the use of personal data to evaluate certain personal aspects relating to a natural person, in particular to analyze or predict aspects concerning that natural person's performance at work, economic situation, health, personal preferences, interests, reliability, behavior, location or movements." For more information about profiling, *see* "Guidelines on Automated Individual Decision-making and Profiling for the Purposes of Regulation 2016/679," October 2017, http:// ec.europa.eu/newsroom/article29/document.cfm?doc_id=49826 (accessed November 2018).

7 William RM Long, Geraldine Scali, Francesca Blythe, *Privacy & Data Security Practice Portfolio Series, Portfolio No. 550, EU General Data Protection Regulation* (Arlington: Bloomberg BNA, 2016).

8 Thomas J. Shaw, *DPO Handbook: Data Protection Officers under the GDPR* (Portsmouth, NH: IAPP, 2018).

9 *Id.*

10 *Id.*

11 As explained by Peter Swire, DeBrae Kennedy-Mayo, *U.S. Private-Sector Privacy: Law and Practice for Information Privacy Professionals,* Second Edition, almost anything that someone may do with personal information might constitute processing under privacy and data protection laws. The term *processing* refers to the collection, recording, organization, storage, updating or modification, retrieval, consultation and use of personal information. It also includes the disclosure by transmission, dissemination or making available in any other form, linking, alignment or combination, blocking, erasure, or destruction of personal information.

12 *Id.*

13 For more information about this phase-based approach, please see the interview "Thought Leaders in Privacy: João Torres Barreiro," Data Guidance 2018, https://www.dataguidance.com/thought-leaders-in-privacy-joao-torres-barreiro/ (accessed August 2018).

14 Public Law 107-347 (December 2002).

15 *See,* e.g., Privacy Threshold Analysis, U.S. Department of Homeland Security (DHS), https://www.dhs.gov/xlibrary/assets/privacy/DHS_PTA_Template.pdf (accessed November 2018).

16 5 U.S.C. § 552a(d)–(e).

17 *See,* e.g., Privacy Impact Assessment for ECS, DHS, (January 2013), https://www.hsdl.org/?abstract&did=731572 (accessed November 2018).

18 Thomas J. Shaw, *DPO Handbook Data Protection Officers under the GDPR*; OMB Mem. M-03-22, "Guidance for Implementing the Privacy Provisions of the E-Government Act," (September 2003), https://www.whitehouse.gov/wp-content/uploads/2017/11/203-M-03-22-OMB-Guidance-for-Implementing-the-Privacy-Provisions-of-the-E-Government-Act-of-2002-1.pdf (accessed November 2018).

19 ISO/IEC 29134:2017, Information technology—Security techniques—Guidelines for privacy impact assessment, International Organization for Standardization, (June 2017), https://www.iso.org/standard/62289.html.

20 Thomas J. Shaw, *DPO Handbook: Data Protection Officers under the GDPR.*

21 "Data Protection Impact Assessments (DPIA)," Data Protection Commission, http://gdprandyou.ie/data-protection-impact-assessments-dpia/#what-is-a-data-protection-impact-assessment (accessed November 2018).

22 GDPR, Article 35(1) and (3)–(4), www.privacy-regulation.eu/en/article-35-data-protection-impact-assessment-GDPR.htm (accessed November 2018); GDPR, Article 35(2) and (7)–(9), www.privacy-regulation.eu/en/article-35-data-protection-impact-assessment-GDPR.htm (accessed November 2018); GDPR, Article 36 (3)(e), www.privacy-regulation.eu/en/article-36-prior-consultation-GDPR.htm (accessed November 2018); "Guidelines on Data Protection Impact Assessment (DPIA) and determining whether processing is 'likely to result in a high risk' for the purposes of Regulation 2016/679," April 2017, https://ec.europa.eu/newsroom/document.cfm?doc_id=44137 (accessed November 2018).

23 GDPR, Article 35, www.privacy-regulation.eu/en/article-35-data-protection-impact-assessment-GDPR.htm (accessed November 2018).

24 GDPR, Article 35(3); www.privacy-regulation.eu/en/article-35-data-protection-impact-assessment-GDPR.htm (accessed November 2018).

25 Upon enactment of the GDPR, May 25, 2018, the Article 29 Working Party has been replaced by the European Data Protection Board. However, the opinions from the Working Party are still valid.

26 The GDPR does not define the concept of *risk*. However, a definition of risk that has been used in the privacy community and proposed for the application of the GDPR is as follows: "privacy risk equals the probability that a data processing activity will result in an impact, threat to or loss of (in varying degrees of severity) a valued outcome (e.g. rights and freedoms). An unacceptable privacy risk, therefore, would be a threat to, or loss of, a valued outcome that cannot be mitigated through the implementation of effective controls and/or that is unreasonable in relation to the intended benefits." For more information about what constitutes risk, see "Risk, High Risk, Risk Assessments and Data Protection Impact Assessments under the GDPR", Centre for Information Policy Leadership, Hunton & Williams LLP, 21 December 2016, https://www.informationpolicycentre .com/uploads/5/7/1/0/57104281/cipl_gdpr_project_risk_white_paper_21_december_2016.pdf (accessed August 2018).

27 "Guidelines on Data Protection Impact Assessment (DPIA) and determining whether processing is "likely to result in a high risk" for the purposes of Regulation 2016/679."

28 *Id.*

29 *Id.*

30 *Id.*

31 GDPR, Article 35(7) and recitals 84 and 90.

32 "Guidelines on Data Protection Impact Assessment (DPIA) and determining whether processing is 'likely to result in a high risk' for the purposes of Regulation 2016/679."

33 For more information, access the ICO website, https://ico.org.uk/for-organisations/guide-to-the-general-data-protection-regulation-gdpr/data-protection-impact-assessments-dpias/ (accessed November 2018).

34 For more information, access the CNIL website on https://www.cnil.fr/en/cnil-publishes-update-its-pia-guides (accessed November 2018).

35 "CNIL's PIA method updated and adapted to the GDPR," CNIL, https://www.cnil.fr/en/cnil-publishes-update-its-pia-guides (accessed December 2018).

36 Pseudonymization and encryption of personal data (as well as data minimization and oversight mechanisms, among others) are not necessarily appropriate measures for reducing risks to an acceptable level. They are only examples. Appropriate measures depend on the context and the risks specific to the processing operations.

37 "Guidelines on Data Protection Impact Assessment (DPIA) and determining whether processing is 'likely to result in a high risk' for the purposes of Regulation 2016/679."

38 *Id.*

39 *Volume I: Guide for Mapping Types of Information and Information Systems to Security Challenges,* NIST, DOC, August 2008, https://nvlpubs.nist.gov/nistpubs/Legacy/SP/nistspecialpublication800-60v1r1.pdf (accessed November 2018).

40 "Guide to Audit Process, Version 2.0," Office of the Data Protection Commissioner, August 2014, https://www.dataprotection.ie/docimages/documents/GuidetoAuditProcessAug2014.pdf (accessed November 2018).

41 Peter Swire, DeBrae Kennedy-Mayo, *U.S. Private-Sector Privacy: Law and Practice for Information Privacy Professionals, Second Edition.*

42 *Id.*

43 Stewart Room, *European Data Protection: Law and Practice*, p. 175-176 (Portsmouth, NH: IAPP, 2018).

CHAPTER 5

Policies

Edward Yakabovicz, CIPP/G, CIPM, CIPT

Policies provide a deliberate system of principles to guide decisions by dictating a course of action and providing clear instructions for implementation through procedures, protocols or guidance documents. The objective of this chapter is to review the basic construct of an organizational policy specific to privacy management. It will define the components of a privacy policy and the practices necessary to make that policy successful by discussing the importance of communication and the way other organizational policies support and reinforce the privacy policy. As Bob Siegel, the founder and president of Privacy Ref, Inc., explains:[1]

> *It is not enough for a business to create a privacy policy and place it on its website; a business must define policies and practices, verify that their employees are following the practices and complying with policies, and confirm that third-party service providers are adequately protecting any shared information as well. As customer demands and regulatory requirements change, the business' privacy practices and policies must be reviewed and revised to meet this changing business environment.*

5.1 What is a Privacy Policy?

A privacy policy governs the privacy goals and strategic direction of the organization's privacy office. As discussed in Chapter 2, it is important that the organization first develop a privacy vision or mission statement that aligns with its overall strategy and objectives. This statement helps guide management of the privacy program and allocation of resources to support the program. It also serves as the foundation for developing effective privacy policies. Depending on the industry and organization's customers, the privacy policy could also be dictated by law and regulations or by industry standard.

Policies become difficult to create if there is no definition of how they influence and can be used by an organization. They should be considered at the highest level of governance for any organization. In addition, they should be clear and easy to understand, accessible to all employees, comprehensive yet concise, action-oriented, and measurable and testable. Policies should align to organizational standards for format, structure and intent to meet organizational goals.

The privacy policy is a high-level policy that supports documents such as standards and guidelines that focus on technology and methodologies for meeting policy goals through manuals, handbooks and/or directives. Examples of documents supported by the privacy policy include:

- Organization standards, such as uniforms, identification badges and physical building systems

- Guidelines on such topics as the use of antivirus software, firewalls and email security

- Procedures to define and then describe the detailed steps employees should follow to accomplish tasks, such as hiring practices and the creation of new user accounts[2]

The privacy policy also supports a variety of documents communicated internally and externally that:

- Explain to customers how the organization handles their personal information

- Explain to employees how the organization handles personal information

- Describe steps for employees handling personal information

- Outline how personal data will be processed

5.2 Privacy Policy Components

Although policy formats will differ from organization to organization, a privacy policy should include the following components:

Purpose. This component explains why the policy exists as well as the goals of the privacy policy and program, which could be used to meet a privacy standard based on national, regional or local laws. This component could also meet other nonbinding standards or frameworks that answer the needs of the organization.

Scope. Scope defines which resources (e.g., facilities, hardware and software, information, personnel) the policy protects.

Risk and responsibilities. This section assigns privacy responsibilities to roles throughout the organization, typically overseen by a privacy program office or manager.

The responsibilities of leaders, managers, employees, contractors, vendors and all users of the data at the operations, management and use levels are delineated. Most importantly, this component serves as the basis for establishing all employee and data user accountability.

Compliance. Compliance issues are a main topic in privacy policy. Sometimes they are found in the relevant standard—such as the applicable data protection law—and are not written into the organization's privacy policy document. Potential compliance factors include the following:

- **General organization compliance** to ensure the privacy policy assigns roles and responsibilities at the proper level in the organization to create an oversight group. This group has responsibility for monitoring compliance with the policy, conducting enforcement activities, and aligning with the organization's priorities.

- The **ability to apply penalties and disciplinary actions** with authorization for the creation of compliance structures that may include disciplinary actions for specific violations.

- **Understanding of the penalties for noncompliance** with laws and regulations. Legal and regulatory penalties are typically imposed within any industry to enforce behavior modification needed to rectify previous neglect and lack of proper data protection. Privacy is no different; organizations are now held accountable for protecting the privacy of the data with which they have been entrusted. As penalties for violation of privacy laws and regulations become more serious, the privacy professional must be prepared to address, track and understand any penalty that could affect the organization.

The privacy policy should not be confused with detailed process manuals and practices that are typically outlined in standards, guidelines, handbooks and procedures documents. Remember, the privacy policy is the high-level governance that aligns with the privacy vision or mission statement of the organization.

5.2.1 Privacy Notice versus Privacy Policy

A **privacy policy** is an internal document addressed to employees and data users. This document clearly states how personal information will be handled, stored and transmitted to meet organizational needs as well as any laws or regulations. It will define all aspects of data privacy for the organization, including how the privacy notice will be formed, if necessary, and what it will contain.

A **privacy notice** is an external communication to individuals, customers or data subjects that describes how the organization collects, uses, shares, retains and discloses its personal information based on the organization's privacy policy. This is discussed in more detail in Chapter 6.

5.3 Interfacing and Communicating with an Organization

Protecting personal information and building a program that drives privacy principles into the organization cannot be the exclusive job of the privacy officer or the privacy team, any more than playing a symphony is the exclusive responsibility of the conductor. As with an orchestra, many people, functions and talents will merge to execute the privacy vision or mission of the organization.

Many organizations create a privacy committee or council composed of stakeholders (or representatives of functions). These individuals may launch the privacy program and manage it throughout the privacy policy lifecycle. They can be instrumental in making strategic decisions that may affect the vision, change key concepts, or determine when alterations are needed. Because of their experience and knowledge, they play a critical role in communicating the privacy policy, which is almost as important as having a solid privacy policy; without informed communications, the policy will simply sit on a shelf or hard drive.

Organizations with a global footprint often create a governance structure composed of representatives from each business function and from every geographic region in which the organization has a presence to ensure that proposed privacy policies, processes and solutions align with local laws and are tailored to them as necessary. This governance structure also provides a communication chain, both formally and informally, that the privacy professional should continue to use in performing key data protection activities.

5.4 Communicating the Privacy Policy within the Organization

The privacy program management team should answer the following questions when developing an effective internal communications plan:

- What is the purpose of the communication? For example, does it simply communicate the existence of a policy or spread knowledge about the policy, or is it intended to train employees and cause behavior modification concerning privacy?

- How will the privacy team work with the communications team? What methods—such as meetings, phone calls, and conference calls—will be used?

- Who is the audience for the communication relating to policy? Are there different potential user groups such as production or administrative staff, managers, and vendors?

- What existing communication modes—such as a company intranet—can be employed? What assets, such as posters, flyers, mouse pads and other awareness tools, will be needed?

- Which functional areas most align with the privacy program, and how should one best communicate with each? For example, production, administrative, information assurance, cybersecurity (sometimes called information security) and human resources (HR) may all need to be in close coordination.

- What is the best way to motivate training and awareness for the organization? Which metrics are best for tracking effectiveness and demonstrating the return on investment?

- Has the privacy team conducted a privacy workshop for stakeholders to define privacy for the organization, explain the market expectations, answer questions, and reduce confusion?

Communications should include the formal privacy policy to help ensure that everyone (including third-party service providers) in an organization receives the same guidance and adheres to the same privacy mission and vision.

5.5 Policy Cost Considerations

Several potential costs are associated with developing, implementing and maintaining policies. The most significant are related to implementing the policy and addressing the impacts on the organization that potentially limit, reduce, remove or change the way data is protected. Historically, privacy has been governed by information security, but it now requires resources assigned directly to privacy management. The establishment and upkeep of a privacy management program does not come at a negligible cost to the organization or impact on its people. Limiting any business function has a direct and sometimes measurable impact on employees' or data users' ability to perform certain tasks. The privacy professional should be cognizant that all changes made to any policy affect the organization.[3]

Other costs are incurred through the policy development and management process. Administrative and management functions are required to draft, develop, finalize and then update the policy. Beyond that, the policy must be disseminated and then communicated through training and awareness activities. Although the cost is unavoidable for policy management, in most cases due to regulations, there must be a balance between practical protections to meet any regulations and laws, the organization's privacy vision or mission, and the organization's need to perform the intended business transactions.[4]

5.6 Design Effective Employee Policies

An article by Ronald Breaux and Sam Jo reminds us:

> "...that employees and data users are typically the most common cause of data breaches, data loss and data misappropriation if appropriate safeguards are not instituted and enforced. To mitigate these risks, develop comprehensive policies and procedures that dictate which employees have access to particular data by category to ... include instructions on reporting impermissible uses or violations of policies related to confidentiality and security, and contain onboarding and exit procedures to protect against information misappropriation upon termination of employment."[5]

Comprehensive privacy policies must align with supporting documents, including additional policies that respond to the needs and intent of the organization to fix an issue, serve a specific purpose, or meet a specific goal. Higher-level policies and procedures include items such as security configurations and responsibilities, while examples of those that address issues include behavior modification, proper usage of organization property, newer technology threats, social media use, email use and internet use. Documents addressing these issues should be reviewed and updated regularly. Regardless of the intent, supporting policies may contain the following data.

Issue/objective statement. To formulate a policy on an issue, the information owner/steward must first define the issue with any relevant terms, distinctions and conditions included. It is often useful to specify the goal or justification for the policy to facilitate compliance. For example, an organization might want to develop an issue-specific policy on the use of "unofficial software," which might be defined to mean any software not approved, purchased, screened, managed or owned by the organization. The applicable distinctions and conditions might then need to be included for some software, such as software privately owned by employees but approved for use at work or owned and used by other businesses under contract to the organization.

Statements of the organization's position. Once the issue is stated and related terms and conditions are detailed, this section is used to clearly state the organization's position (i.e., management's decision) on the issue. In the previous example, this would mean stating whether the use of unofficial software as defined is prohibited in all or some cases; whether there are further guidelines for approval and use; or whether case-by-case exceptions may be granted, by whom, and on what basis.

Applicability. Issue-specific policies also need to include statements of applicability. This means clarifying where, how, when, to whom and to what a policy applies. For example, it could be that the hypothetical policy on unofficial software is intended to apply only to the organization's own on-site resources and employees and not to contractors with offices at other locations. Additionally, the policy's applicability might need to be clarified as it pertains to employees travelling among different sites, working from home, or needing to transport and use hardware at multiple sites.

Roles and responsibilities. The assignment of roles and responsibilities is also usually included in issue-specific policies. For example, if the policy permits employees to use privately owned, unofficial software at work with the appropriate approvals, then the approval authority granting such permission would need to be stated. (The policy would stipulate, who, by position, has such authority.) Likewise, the policy would need to clarify who would be responsible for ensuring that only approved software is used on organizational system resources and, possibly, for monitoring users regarding unofficial software.

Compliance. Some types of policies may describe unacceptable infractions and the consequences of such behaviors in greater detail. Penalties may be explicitly stated and consistent with organizational personnel policies and practices. When used, they can be coordinated with appropriate officials, offices, and even employee bargaining units. A specific office in the organization may be tasked with monitoring compliance.

Points of contact and supplementary information. For any issue-specific policy, indicate the appropriate individuals to contact in the organization for further information, guidance and compliance. Since positions tend to change less often than the individuals occupying them, specific positions may be preferable as the point of contact. For example, for some issues, the point of contact might be a line manager; for others, it might be a facility manager, technical support person, system administrator or security program representative. Using the above example once more, employees would need to know whether the point of contact for questions and procedural information would be their immediate superior, a system administrator or an information security official.

Many offices in the organization may be responsible for selecting, developing, updating and finalizing policies and all supporting documents, including the privacy office, legal, HR and information security. This distribution of responsibility helps ensure a clear and accurate policy that meets the needs of the organization and any regulatory or external standards.

The following section presents several high-level examples of supporting documents that affect data protection and the privacy vision or mission of the organization, including materials on acceptable use, information security, procurement, and data retention and destruction. These represent only a small subset of topics that can be considered as privacy-supporting policies.

5.6.1 Acceptable Use Policies: Guest Wireless Access

An acceptable use policy (AUP) stipulates rules and constraints for people within and outside the organization who access the organization's network or internet connection. It outlines acceptable and unacceptable use of the network or internet connections to which the user agrees either in written or electronic form. Violation typically leads to loss of use and/or punitive action either by the organization or by law enforcement if necessary. People affected include employees, students, guests, contractors and vendors.

The information security function usually plays a major role in developing acceptable use policies. This type of policy considers the following:

- Others' privacy
- Legal protections (e.g., copyright)
- Integrity of computer systems (e.g., anti-hacking rules)
- Ethics
- Laws and regulations
- Others' network access
- Routing patterns
- Unsolicited advertising and intrusive communications
- User responsibilities for damages
- Security and proprietary information
- Virus, malware protection and malicious programs

- Safeguards (e.g., scanning, port scanning, monitoring) against security breaches or disruptions of network communication

5.6.2 Information Security Policies: Access and Data Classification

Internal information security policies serve several purposes:

- To protect against unauthorized access to data and information systems
- To provide stakeholders with information efficiently, while simultaneously maintaining confidentiality, integrity and availability (CIA)
- To promote compliance with laws, regulations, standards and other organizational policies
- To promote data quality

An information security policy establishes what is done to protect the data and information stored on organization systems, including the following:

- Risk assessments
- User and password policies
- Administrative responsibilities
- Email policies
- Internet policies
- Intrusion detection
- Antivirus and malware policies
- Firewall rules and use
- Wireless management

5.7 Procurement: Engaging Vendors

Vendors should be held to the same privacy standards as the organization. When engaging vendors, an organization may:

- Identify vendors and their legal obligations
- Evaluate risk, policies and server locations

- Develop a thorough contract
- Monitor vendors' practices and performance
- Use a vendor policy

An organization must exercise similar due diligence for mergers, acquisitions and divestitures. More information on these can be found in Chapter 4.

5.7.1 Create a Vendor Policy

Vendor policies should guide an organization in working with third parties from procurement through termination. Policy components may include requirements for vendors, logistics (e.g., where work should be conducted), and onboarding and employee training. A vendor policy may require identification and inventories of all vendors and entry points, such as free survey tools, personal information the vendor can access, and legal obligations on the organization and vendor. The vendor policy may stipulate that the procuring organization evaluate its processes for risk assessment, its risk profile, and categories of vendors based on risk. This may include evaluating the vendor's internal policies; affiliations and memberships with other organizations; mandatory and nonmandatory certifications; location of data servers; and data storage, use, and transport.

5.7.2 Develop a Vendor Contract

It's important to work with the organization's legal and HR departments on any contract, including the following:

- Standard contract language
- Requirement to inform the organization when any privacy/security policies change
- Prohibition against making policy changes that weaken privacy/security protections
- Data migration/deletion upon termination
- Vendor security incident response procedures
- Vendor liability
- Right to audit

5.7.3 Monitor Vendors

After the basic vendor policy and contract are complete, the procuring organization should consider the vendor in its monitoring plan to ensure crossover with its audit and compliance functions. This may include recurring on-site visits, attestations, and/or periodic reassessments.

5.7.4 Implement Procurement/Information Security Policies: Cloud Computing Acceptable Use

Cloud computing technologies can be implemented in a wide variety of architectures, models, technologies and software design approaches. The privacy challenges of cloud computing present difficult decisions when choosing to store data in a cloud. Public, private and hybrid clouds offer distinct advantages and disadvantages.

The privacy aspects of any potential cloud choices should be considered before engaging vendors or external parties. Working from requirements, an organization should determine the purpose and fit of a cloud solution, obtain advice from experts, then contact external cloud vendors. Furthermore, understanding the policies, procedures and technical controls used by a cloud provider is a prerequisite to assessing the security and privacy risks involved.

With the increased use of cloud computing and other offsite storage, vendors that provide cloud computing services may pose distinct privacy challenges, especially because of compliance requirements and security risks. An organization should ensure its acceptable use policy for cloud computing requires the privacy and security of its data as well as compliance with policies, laws, regulations and standards. Risks of processing data using cloud-based applications and tools should be mitigated. The policy should stipulate approval of all cloud computing agreements by appropriate leadership, such as the chief information officer (CIO).

Both information security and privacy teams should agree on the policy and vendor of choice before final decisions are made. This ensures alignment of the stakeholders and the policy that will be used to protect the organization. It may also outline specific cloud services that may be used, restrictions for processing sensitive information in the cloud, restrictions for personal use, and data classification and rules for handling.

5.7.5 Implement HR Policies

HR handles diverse employee personal information and typically will have policies to guide processing. HR policies often provide rules regarding who may access employee data and under what circumstances. Employee data includes any data the employee has created in the process of performing normal business efforts for the organization, including emails, phone calls, voice mail, internet browsing, and use of systems.

When creating or updating any HR policy that concerns privacy, HR should consult with legal and information security to ensure all laws, regulations, and other possible organization policies are met. Especially regarding updates to laws and regulations such as the EU General Data Protection Regulation (GDPR), the privacy professional should consult with all stakeholders prior to creating or updating any HR policy.

HR privacy concerns can be addressed through several types of HR policies. These policies may address the following privacy concerns:

- Employee communications, including employee browser histories, contact lists, phone recordings and geolocations

- Employee hiring and review, including performance evaluations, background checks, and the handling of resumes

- Employee financial information, such as bank account information, benefits information and salary

5.7.5.1 Types of HR Policies

Typical HR privacy policies to consider include the following:

- Handling of applicant information

- Employee background checks

- Access to employee data

- Termination of access

- Bring your own device (BYOD)

- Social media

- Employee/workplace monitoring

- Employee health programs

5.8 Data Retention and Destruction Policies

Data retention and destruction policies should support the idea that personal information should be retained only for as long as necessary to perform its stated purpose. Data destruction triggers and methods should be documented and followed consistently by all employees. These should align with laws, regulations and standards, such as time limits for which records must be saved. Ownership of a data retention/destruction policy may vary and intersect with privacy, legal, IT, operations, finance and the business function.

Actions an organization can take to develop a data retention policy include:

- Determine what data is currently being retained, how and where

- Work with legal to determine applicable legal data retention requirements

- Brainstorm scenarios that would require data retention

- Estimate business impacts of retaining versus destroying the data

- Work with IT to develop and implement a policy

Data management requires answers to questions such as why we have the data, why we are keeping it, and how long we need to keep it. The process begins with identifying all the data contained in the organization and determining how it is used. Next, the organization should match the data to the legal obligations around retention. Data retention and data deletion should be executed with caution. Keeping the data for as long as the organization has a legitimate business purpose is a common best practice. To comply with legal requirements and organization governance standards, the organization should review all associated policies, standards, guidelines and handbooks. This includes every relevant country's required minimum retention time. Legal requirements could change if the company is involved in litigation and discovery actions. Thus, the policy and all supporting standards and technical controls should be flexible.

5.8.1 Implementing Policies

Privacy-related policies will not be effective if individuals do not care about or follow them. An organization should seek ways to enable employees to integrate the policies into their daily tasks. The privacy team can achieve this objective by aligning policies with existing business procedures, training employees and raising awareness.

5.8.2 Aligning with Procedures

Multinational and multisector organizations have additional challenges to ensure policies are consistent and uniform across all locations while satisfying local laws, regulations and industry guidance. Different business functions may have diverse policy needs. The organization should document and review policies of the following functions and others to ensure alignment:

- HR
- Business development (when assessing proposed projects)
- Project management
- Procurement and contract management
- Risk management
- Incident management
- Performance management

Inconsistencies between policies should be explained fully to ensure there are no gaps or misunderstandings.

5.9 Implementing and Closing the Loop

Once policies have been created, approved and put in place, they must be communicated to the organization. Raising awareness and properly training employees and data users is key to knowledge transfer and retention.

Awareness means to be vigilant or watchful. From a privacy perspective, achieving awareness requires communicating the various components of an organization's privacy program, thus creating a vigilant or watchful attitude toward the protection of privacy data. Everyone who handles privacy information must be alert to the constant need to protect data. Yet no one is immune to the daily pressures and deadlines that can distract attention from the big picture. This reality underscores the need for organizations to put reminders in front of their workforces to keep attention focused on the proper handling and safeguarding of personal information. These reminders may take the form of awareness tools such Data Privacy Day on January 28, infographics, tip sheets, comics, posters, postcards, stickers, blogs, wikis, simulations, email campaigns, announcements on the intranet, web sessions, drop-in sessions, and lunch-and-learns. Raising workforce awareness on a consistent basis should be one of the top activities considered by any privacy management team.

Formal training practices are also part of closing the communication loop. Training may be delivered through dedicated classroom, instructor-led courses or online platforms. Employees and data users may be required to train regularly. This is where the privacy vision for the organization and policy enforcement is communicated clearly and consistently. Training and awareness reinforce policies by educating personnel with constant and consistent reminders about why they are important, who they affect, and how they are accomplished. Training is covered in greater detail in Chapter 7.

Finally, policies apply to everyone in the organization. One loophole or one break in the organization's protection can lead to a hack on the entire organization. Leadership, management, the privacy office, and the information security office do not have a waiver to break any policy they believe does not address them. Individual choices that breach policy can place the entire workforce at risk for significant legal consequences and loss of credibility. If a policy is disconnected from reality, it needs to be corrected—and all risk factors mitigated—as soon as possible to protect the data owners' privacy rights and to protect the organization from crippling loss and impacts.

5.10 Summary

A privacy policy should be considered a living document that adapts over time based on the needs of the organization, the evolving business environment, regulatory updates, changing industry standards and many other factors. This could be considered the lifecycle of the policy that continues to be reviewed and updated on a regular basis. Part of this lifecycle should be the communication of the policy through effective training and awareness practices that should also be recurring and mandatory for every employee, vendor, contractor or other data user within the organization.

The privacy policy should contain at a minimum the purpose, scope, responsibilities and compliance reasons to allow the reader a full understanding of how privacy will be managed. In some cases, the privacy policy may also address risks, other organizational responsibilities, data subject rights, data use rules and other privacy-related information and practices. The composition of the policy should align with the needs of the organization in meeting national, state and local laws or other standards for data privacy protection.

Beyond the privacy policy are other supporting policies that provide practical guidance on potential issues or specific intent. These include information security policies that also protect data, but for a different purpose and with potentially different tools, people, and processes to support common goals between privacy and security.

It is important to understand that information security is a complex topic that will span the organization and overlap privacy management. By becoming familiar with information security practices and stakeholders, the privacy professional will open channels of communication with those key players throughout the organization and during any incident response.

Managing privacy within an organization requires the contribution and participation of many members of that organization. Because privacy should continue to develop and mature over time within an organization, functional groups must understand just how they contribute and support the overall privacy program, as well as the privacy principles themselves. Importantly, individual groups must have a fundamental understanding of data privacy because, in addition to supporting the vision and plan of the privacy officer and the privacy organization, these groups may need to support independent initiatives and projects from other stakeholders.

The privacy professional should have awareness of other policies and standards that support privacy or offer other data protections. An example is the data retention/records management strategies that reinforce the basic concept that data should only be retained for the length of time the business needs to use the data. Records management and data retention should meet legal and business needs for privacy, security and data archiving.

Creating privacy policies does not mean employees or other internal data users will know and follow them or understand their purpose and intent. The same is true for any organization policy, standard, guideline or handbook. The privacy policy, like many other business-related policies, has a specific intent to protect data privacy during and after business use. To meet the privacy intent, users of the data will need to be educated and reminded on a regular basis of the organization's vision and mission. Because data users focus on their primary objectives and jobs rather than on privacy, education and reminders about what privacy is and how and why of privacy management is important for the continued success of the organization.

Endnotes

1 Bob Siegal, "Kick-Starting a Privacy Program," *The Privacy Advisor*, IAPP, February 2013, https://iapp.org/news/a/2013-01-22-kick-starting-a-privacy-program/ (accessed February 2019).

2 "An Introduction to Computer Security," NIST Special Publication 800-12 Revision 1, National Institute of Standards and Technology, U.S. Department of Commerce, https://doi.org/10.6028/NIST.SP.800-12r1 (accessed November 2018).

3 *Id.*

4 *Id.*

5 Ronald Breaux and Sam Jo, "Designing and Implementing an Effective Privacy and Security Plan," *The Privacy Advisor*, IAPP, March 2014, IAPP, https://iapp.org/news/a/designing-and-implementing-an-effective-privacy-and-security-plan/ (accessed November 2018).

CHAPTER 6

Data Subject Rights

Amanda Witt, CIPP/E, CIPP/US;
Jon Neiditz, CIPP/E, CIPP/US, CIPM; Tajma Rahimic

Across the globe, privacy and data protection laws are being enacted with a primary goal of strengthening both the rights of data subjects and their control over the processing of their personal information. Data subjects are identified or identifiable individuals whose personal information is being processed by an organization, such as a patient at a medical facility, an employee of a company, a customer of a retail store, or a visitor to a website. Data subject rights vary across jurisdictions and include the right to know how personal information will be used and the right to opt out of certain processing activities. Data subject requests may come directly from the data subject or, under some privacy laws and based on required contractual arrangements, organizations may need to assist business customers with fulfilling data subject requests.

Preparing to respond and efficiently responding to data subject requests is a critical component of any privacy program. Some laws require a response without undue delay or within a certain set period. Organizations also run the risk that a poorly handled response to a data subject request could result in a data subject making a complaint to a regulator or supervisory authority or going public with a complaint against the organization. Thus, a timely and effective response to data subject requests is of paramount importance to excellent customer service and brand protection. The practices outlined in this chapter can help your organization ensure effective communications with data subjects and develop an effective subject request process.

6.1 Privacy Notices and Policies

Transparency is critically important under most privacy laws, so it is crucial to provide data subjects with information about privacy practices at the time personal information is collected. A privacy notice is an external statement directed to current or potential customers or users. Provided when an organization collects information from a data subject, it is a tool used to describe the organization's privacy practices. On the other hand, privacy policies are typically internal documents directed to employees or contractors that describe how the organization will process personal information. Both privacy notices and policies describe how personal information will be collected, used and stored.

A privacy notice can help an organization comply with applicable laws, but it does not provide blanket protection from privacy-related litigation. A privacy notice should be considered a promise the organization makes to data subjects. If the organization breaks those promises, it may face regulatory action or litigation.

Section 5(a) of the Federal Trade Commission Act prohibits unfair and deceptive trade practices and allows the U.S. Federal Trade Commission (FTC) to investigate and bring enforcement actions against companies engaging in unfair and deceptive trade practices.[1] Similarly, most states have consumer protection laws that provide state attorneys general (AGs) with the authority to address unfair and deceptive business practices. In the United States, the FTC and AGs have routinely used this power to investigate whether companies act contrary to the statements made in their privacy notices. Citing breaches of company privacy notices, the FTC has initiated enforcement actions alleging deceptive acts and practices against companies such as Google, Snapchat and MySpace.[2] In connection with the Snapchat settlement in 2014, Edith Ramirez, then chairwoman of the FTC, noted the following: "If a company markets privacy and security as key selling points in pitching its service to consumers, it is critical that it keep those promises. Any company that makes misrepresentations to consumers about its privacy and security practices risks FTC action."[3]

6.1.1 Privacy Notice: Common Elements

Your organization's privacy notice will typically provide the following information:

- Who your organization is and your organization's contact information

- What information is collected, directly or indirectly

- How your organization will use the information

- With whom your organization will share the information

- How the behavior of website users is monitored

- How data subjects may exercise their rights

6.1.2 Privacy Notice: Design Challenges and Solutions

Privacy notices should be living documents, maintained in a lifecycle that includes designing and developing, testing, releasing, and reviewing and updating where necessary. When designing a privacy notice, consider the intended audience and how the users will view it (e.g., on a computer screen, mobile device, home appliance). It is important to not only consider the primary users (e.g., the car owner, homeowner), but also any other individuals whose information could be collected (e.g., car passengers, other home residents, visitors).[4] The goal of the privacy notice should be to "help the recipient make informed privacy decisions."[5]

Several design strategies can help keep privacy notices accessible to your customers or external stakeholders. There are several approaches to providing privacy notices. A layered approach to privacy notices has been endorsed both by the FTC and the EU's Article 29 Working Party (WP29), now the European Data Protection Board (EDPS).[6] A layered approach provides a high-level summary of the various sections of the privacy notice and allows the users to read more about that section by clicking a link to that section or scrolling below. As described by the WP29 in its guidance on transparency, "design and layout of the first layer of the privacy statement/notice should be such that the data subject has a clear overview of the information available to them on the processing of their personal data and where/how they can find that detailed information within the layers of the privacy statement/notice."[7]

Another way to provide data subjects with notices about the information you plan to collect from them is with the just-in-time notice. It is a type of layered approach provided immediately before the data is collected—for instance, when a mobile application asks to track your location. More information is typically available by clicking a link or hovering over the notice. The WP29 recommends using this type of notice when "providing information at various points throughout the process of data collection; it helps to spread the provision of information into easily digestible chunks and reduces the reliance on a single privacy statement/notice containing information that is difficult to understand out of context."[8]

Icons or symbols can also be used to communicate privacy practices to data subjects. As an example, the Digital Advertising Alliance (DAA) regulates the use of its icon on websites and mobile screens by requiring compliance with the DAA principles relating to "notice, opt out and limitations on data collection and use."[9] The DAA icon is intended to represent transparency to consumers and to inform them of their rights under the DAA principles. The use of icons or symbols is another type of layered approach to presenting privacy notice. Hyperlinks connected to the icon or hovering over the icon should lead the data subject to additional information on the meaning of the icon. This approach is especially useful in scenarios where there is limited space to provide a longer privacy notice, such as in internet-of-things (IoT) devices or mobile screens. User testing is recommended so that you confirm that the symbol is meaningful and adequately conveys the required information.

Lastly, another tool for providing transparent privacy notices and user control is a privacy dashboard, which offers a summary of privacy-related information and metrics and is easy to access and navigate. As described by the WP29, a privacy dashboard, which is built into the existing platform, can be a tool for providing more personalized privacy notices and choices to data subjects in that "it will ensure that access and use of it will be intuitive and may help to encourage users to engage with this information, in the same way that they would with other aspects of the service."[10]

6.1.3 Privacy Notice: Communication Considerations and Re-Evaluation of the Fair Information Practice Principles

Privacy notices inform individuals of an organization's privacy practices, but do not solicit or imply consent. If an individual has a choice about the use or disclosure of their information, consent is that person's way of giving permission for the use or disclosure. In the United States, consent may be affirmative (i.e., opt-in or implied), but express (i.e., not implied) is now required in the EU. If relying on consent, it is important to keep a legally admissible record that establishes what the individual consented to and establishes that such individual agreed to the notice.

While consent may be required by law in many instances, it is not always required and may not be the only reliable basis for processing personal information. For example, under the EU General Data Protection Regulation (GDPR), in addition to consent, lawful bases for processing personal data include contract, legal obligation, vital interests, public interest and legitimate interests.

Increasingly, privacy scholars and practitioners question the effectiveness of privacy notices and the illusion of control they create. Lawmakers in the 1990s determined that using "notice and choice" was the best way to protect consumer privacy.[11] Presumably consumers could maintain control of their information and their privacy would be respected if they received notice of a company's data practices and decided to continue using that company's website or services.[12] Over time, the length and complexity of privacy notices have increased, and few consumers actually read them. In a well-known study at Carnegie Mellon, researchers Lorrie Faith Cranor and Aleecia McDonald determined that if every internet user were to spend eight hours per day reading every privacy policy they encountered while using the internet, it would take 76 days to complete the task.[13] The privacy notice is generally a way for organizations to limit their liability by disclosing their practices and providing themselves with maximum flexibility for use of consumer data. Knowing these limitations and the GDPR requirements for increased transparency, organizations should explore ways to provide more meaningful, digestible notices and develop new ways to protect consumer privacy instead of relying on notice and illusory control. Organizations should consider providing more innovative and user-friendly tools to consumers such as the privacy dashboards and other tools discussed above.

6.2 Choice, Consent and Opt-Outs

6.2.1 Choice and Consent

If consent is required by law or regulation, there must be a method for obtaining and recording it. Under the GDPR, electronic consent requires an affirmative act from the individual establishing a freely given, specific, informed and unambiguous indication of the individual's agreement to the processing.[14] A pre-ticked box is not sufficient to imply consent; according to the WP29, a clear action, such as swiping a bar on a screen, waving in front of a smart camera or turning a smartphone around may be sufficient. Individuals who do not have a choice about the processing of their personal information should not be led to believe that they do. Individuals who do have a choice must be given the ability to exercise that choice. Further, organizations should not process personal information in a manner incompatible with the consent. For example, an app on a social media site that collects personal information based on consent for one purpose, such as a personality quiz, may not also use that personal information for a different purpose such as targeted advertising. Individuals who provide consent must be able to revoke that decision. For example, an individual may decide that they no longer want the app to continue processing their personal information, so there should be a mechanism for them to withdraw consent.

In addition to a record of consent, organizations should keep documentation of the privacy notice provided at the time of consent. Consents should be regularly reviewed to determine if a refresh is necessary (if, for example, the organization has made changes to the processing operations or if laws, regulations or standards have changed).

6.2.2 Opt-In versus Opt-Out

There are two central concepts of choice: Data subjects can either give their consent to processing by opting in, or withhold or revoke such consent by opting out.

When individuals opt in, they make an active, affirmative indication of choice; for instance, an individual might check a box to signal their desire to share their information with third parties. Ideally, this choice should be clear and easy to execute.

When individuals opt out, they may do so by performing an affirmative action by hitting an "unsubscribe" link, for example. Alternatively, opting out could be inferred by their lack of action. For example, unless an individual checks or unchecks a box, their information will be shared with third parties.

If an organization will perform different types of processing, as required by the GDPR, an individual should consent to each activity separately. For example, an individual might be asked to check yes or no beside various methods for direct marketing—for instance, email or phone.

6.3 Obtaining Consents from Children

6.3.1 Compliance

The U.S. Children's Online Privacy Protection Act (COPPA) and the GDPR set out specific rules regarding providing privacy notices to children and obtaining parental consent for processing their personal information.[15] Children's information may be considered sensitive information, which warrants heightened protections. COPPA and its implementing rule are designed to provide parents with control over the personal information collected online from children under 13 years of age.[16] Prior to collecting personal information online (including via mobile applications) from a child under 13, organizations must obtain verifiable parental consent from a parent or legal guardian of the child.[17] The law provides parents with the right of access, modification and deletion of their child's personal information.[18] COPPA also provides parents with an opportunity to prevent and limit further collection and use of their child's personal information.[19]

6.3.2 Language and Delivery

Generally, privacy notices directed toward children should be presented in ways children can understand. For example, the Office of the Privacy Commissioner of Canada states, "Organizations should implement innovative ways of presenting privacy information to children and youth that take into account their cognitive and emotional development and life experience."[20] The WP29 suggests "vocabulary, tone and style of the language used is appropriate to and resonates with children [...]"[21] Furthermore, it recommends reviewing the "UN Convention on the Rights of the Child in Child Friendly Language," which provides useful examples of child-centric language.[22]

6.3.3 Age

Laws and regulations may establish an age threshold for consent. In practice, a website may ask users to enter their age before accessing content, or a web application for children may require consent via a parent's or legal guardian's email account before collecting and processing the personal information of a child under 13 years old in the United States. The age threshold may vary depending on jurisdiction. For example, the GDPR sets 16 as the age threshold but allows individual countries to set the age threshold between 13 and 16 years old. The recently enacted California Consumer Privacy Act (as described in Section 6.4.2.4) requires organizations to obtain parental or legal guardian consent for children under the age of 13 years old and the affirmative consent of children between 13 and 16 years of age prior to engaging in data selling.[23]

6.3.4 Purpose of Processing

The purpose of processing may trigger certain rules. For example, organizations may be required to refrain from tracking children for online behavioral advertising purposes or selling their personal information.

6.4 Data Subject Rights in the United States

Many federal and state laws provide data subjects with rights of control over their personal information. Although these rights are not encompassed in one comprehensive federal law, federal laws across different sectors as well as individual state laws grant data subjects rights over how their personal information is processed.

6.4.1 Federal Laws

6.4.1.1 Federal Credit Reporting Act

The Federal Credit Reporting Act (FCRA) grants several important rights to consumers with respect to how their data is used.[24] Under FCRA, customers can obtain access to all the information a consumer reporting agency has on file about them.[25] Such information is usually compiled into a credit report and must be provided to consumers free of charge once a year.[26] FCRA also allows consumers to correct or delete any incorrect information that may be contained in their files by notifying the credit reporting agency.[27] If inaccurate information is discovered in the consumer file, the credit reporting agency must examine the disputed information, usually within 30 days of notification.[28] Consumers also have the right to request removal of outdated negative information such as civil suits, judgments and liens from their consumer reports 7 years after the statute of limitations has expired, while bankruptcies may be removed from credit reports after 10 years.[29] Consumers have several notification rights under the FCRA. For example, consumers have the right to be notified of adverse actions taken against them based on information contained in their credit reports. If a financial institution submits or plans to submit negative information to a credit reporting agency, the financial institution must provide a notice to the consumer prior to furnishing such negative information.[30]

FCRA places obligations upon employers to obtain an applicant or employee's written consent prior to conducting a background check.[31] Additionally, FCRA requires employers to inform the applicant or employee that the information obtained in the background check may be used to make the decision about their employment.[32] This information must be provided in a standalone written notice separate from an employment application.[33]

6.4.1.2 Health Insurance Portability and Accountability Act of 1996

The Health Insurance Portability and Accountability Act (HIPAA), along with its implementing regulations including the Privacy Rule, regulates the use and disclosure of protected health information (PHI) and provides individuals with rights relating to their PHI.[34] Under HIPAA, individuals have the right to obtain a copy of their medical record and other health information.[35] Usually, a copy of this information must be provided within 30 days.[36] An individual has the right to change any incorrect information and add any information that may be missing or incomplete. In most cases, these changes must be implemented within 60 days.[37] Similarly, an individual has the right to know how their information has been shared with others and to limit information that an individual may not want to be shared.[38] For example, when filling out paperwork at a doctor's office, an individual has the right to limit disclosure of health information to other clinics, doctors and insurance companies.

6.4.1.3 Do Not Call Registry

The FTC created the National Do Not Call (DNC) Registry as a part of revisions to its Telemarketing Sales Rule (TSR).[39] The Federal Communications Commission (FCC) also enforces the DNC Registry and adopted its own do-not-call rule, effectively plugging gaps in the FTC's jurisdiction and applying the registry to all telemarketing of goods or services. Consumers may also file a complaint with the FCC if they believe they have received an illegal call or text.[40]

Consumers can sign up without charge for the DNC Registry in order to stop unwanted commercial solicitation calls.[41] The FTC enforces the DNC Registry by taking legal action against companies and telemarketers who violate the applicable law and rules.[42]

6.4.1.4 Controlling the Assault of Non-Solicited Pornography and Marketing Act of 2003

The FTC allows individuals to forward unwanted or deceptive messages to the FTC in order to report and in effect reduce the number of spam emails.[43] The Controlling the Assault of Non-Solicited Pornography and Marketing Act (CAN-SPAM)[44] prohibits business from sending many types of commercial messages.[45] An individual may also file a complaint with the FTC regarding a company's unsolicited emails and/or its refusal to honor a request to unsubscribe from the mailing list.[46]

6.4.1.5 Privacy Act of 1974

The Privacy Act of 1974 provides individuals with a right of access to their own records from each federal agency that maintains a system of records, upon receipt of a written request from an individual.[47] The law also permits an individual to request an amendment of his or her records and to challenge the accuracy of information that an agency has on file. Information collected for one purpose may not be used for a different purpose.[48] Lastly, individuals may bring civil actions against agencies for violations of the act.[49]

6.4.1.6 Freedom of Information Act

Under the Freedom of Information Act (FOIA), federal agencies are required to disclose any federal agency records or information upon request by the public, unless the request falls under one of the nine exemptions and three exclusions that protect national security interests, personal privacy and law enforcement interests, for example.[50] The nine exemptions to information that may be requested under FOIA are:

1. Information that is classified to protect national security

2. Information related solely to the internal personnel rules and practices of an agency

3. Information that is prohibited from disclosure by another federal law

4. Trade secrets or commercial or financial information that is confidential or privileged

5. Privileged communications within or between agencies

6. Information that, if disclosed, would invade another individual's personal privacy

7. Information compiled for various law enforcement purposes

8. Information that concerns the supervision of financial institutions

9. Geological information on wells

Congress has provided special protection for information requests for three categories of law enforcement and national security records, and these records are not subject to the requirements of the FOIA. The first exclusion protects the existence of an ongoing criminal law enforcement investigation when the subject of the investigation is unaware that it is pending and disclosure could reasonably be expected to interfere with enforcement proceedings. The second exclusion is limited to criminal law enforcement agencies and protects the existence of informant records when the informant's status has not been officially confirmed. The third exclusion is limited to the FBI and protects the existence of foreign intelligence or counterintelligence, or international terrorism records when the existence of such records is classified.[51]

6.4.2 State Laws

Increasingly, states have begun enacting laws that grant data subjects rights over their information. California has served as the national trendsetter in its enactment of various laws aimed at providing individuals with rights over how their information is processed.

6.4.2.1 California Online Privacy Protection Act and Delaware Online Privacy Protection Act

California was the first state in the nation to require commercial website or online service operators to conspicuously post a privacy notice on their websites or online services.[52] The impact of the California Online Privacy Protection Act (CalOPPA) is wide-reaching, as the law applies to any website or online service operator in the United States and possibly the world whose website collects personally identifiable information (PII) from California consumers.[53] The law requires the disclosure of specific information in the privacy notice such as categories of PII collected, description of a process by which a website operator notifies consumers of material changes to the privacy notice, and disclosure of how an operator honors Do Not Track requests, among others.[54]

The Delaware Online Privacy Protection Act (DOPPA) is materially similar to CalOPPA; however, there are a few notable differences.[55] CalOPPA applies to "consumers" while DOPPA applies to "users" and therefore has a broader application. Under CalOPPA, a consumer is defined as "any individual who seeks or acquires, by purchase or lease, any goods, services, money, or credit for personal, family, or household purposes."[56] DOPPA defines a user as an "individual that uses an internet website, online or cloud computing service, online application or mobile application [...]"[57] DOPPA covers a broader range of entities that could be handling PII, including websites, cloud computing services, online apps and mobile apps, while CalOPPA is limited to commercial websites and apps.[58] Both CalOPPA and DOPPA require that operators disclose in their privacy notices how they respond to Do Not Track requests regarding the collection of consumers' and users' PII.[59]

6.4.2.2 California "Shine the Light" Law

Separate but related to CalOPPA is California's "Shine the Light" law, which is already in effect and gives California residents the right to request and be notified about how businesses use and share their personal information with other businesses for direct marketing purposes.[60] The law also gives consumers a private right of action in the event a business fails to respond to a consumer's request.

6.4.2.3 California "Online Eraser" Law

California's "Online Eraser" law, which is designed to protect individuals under the age of 18, requires operators of websites, online services, online applications and mobile applications to permit minors who are registered users of services to request and remove content a minor may have posted on the operator's website or application.[61] However, there are exceptions to the law that limit its effectiveness in application. A service operator is not required to comply with the request for removal and deletion if the content about the minor was posted by a third party other than the minor, who is a registered user of a website. This exception may make it less effective in combating online bullying, for example. Further, if a minor does not follow instructions provided to the minor on how to request removal of content, or if a minor received compensation or other consideration for the content, the service operator is not legally obligated to comply with this law.[62]

6.4.2.4 California Consumer Privacy Act of 2018

On June 28, 2018, the governor of California signed into law a landmark privacy bill. While lawmakers are discussing amending the law prior to its January 1, 2020, effective date, as the bill is currently written, the California Consumer Privacy Act of 2018 (CCPA) impacts businesses around the world, including, according to IAPP estimates, more than 500,000 U.S. companies, most of which are small- to medium-sized enterprises.[63] Given the haste with which it was adopted and the need for the attorney general to issue interpretative regulations, there will likely be additional changes to the CCPA prior to its effective date.

The CCPA, as initially adopted, extends existing privacy rights of California residents in the California constitution, including:

- The ability to request a record of:
  - ° What types of personal information an organization holds about the requestor, its sources and the specific personal information that has been collected
  - ° Information about the use of the individual's personal information in terms of both business use and third-party sharing

- A right to erasure—that is, deletion of the personal information (with exceptions for completion of a transaction, research, free speech, and some internal analytical use), as well as disclosure of this right to consumers

- In relation to businesses that sell personal information, the option for consumers to opt out of having their data sold to third parties.

6.4.2.5 Biometric Privacy Laws

Illinois, Washington and Texas have enacted biometric privacy laws that govern how biometric identifiers, or unique identifying characteristics, may be used.[64] The Illinois Biometric Information Privacy Act (BIPA) provides the most robust consumer rights of the biometric laws adopted thus far. BIPA requires that a private entity notify an individual in writing of its intent to collect biometric information, inform the individual of the purpose and length of term for which biometric information is being collected and used, and receive a written release authorizing the use.[65] A private entity must also obtain consent for further disclosure of biometric identifiers.[66] BIPA grants individuals a private right of action for violations of the act.[67] Statutory damages against an entity that negligently violates a provision of BIPA are $1,000 of liquidated damages or actual damages, whichever amount is greater, and $5,000 of liquidated damages or actual damages, whichever is greater, for intentional or reckless violation of BIPA.[68] Successful plaintiffs may also recover reasonable attorneys' fees and costs.[69]

> *Sections 6.5 through 6.5.11 on data subject rights in Europe is excerpted from Chapter 9 of* European Data Protection: Law and Practice: Data Subjects' Rights, *by Jyn Schultze-Melling.*[70]

6.5 Data Subject Rights in Europe

European data protection law has always provided individuals with a range of rights enforceable against organizations processing their data.

Compared to the Data Protection Directive ("Directive"), the General Data Protection Regulation (GDPR, or "Regulation") is considerably more complex and far-reaching in this respect, as it includes an extensive set of rights. This is in part because bolstering individuals' rights was one of the main ambitions of the European Commission ('Commission') in proposing the new data protection framework. Data subjects' rights, set forth in Articles 12 to 23 of the Regulation, may not only limit an organization's ability to lawfully process personal data, but they can also have a significant impact upon an organization's core business processes and even its business model.

These rights encompass the following:

- *Articles 12–14:* **Right of transparent communication and information.**

- *Article 15:* **Right of access.** The data subject is entitled to have information concerning his or her personal data that is undergoing processing as well as a copy of such data.

- *Article 16:* **Right to rectification.** The data subject has the right to have inaccuracies related to his or her personal data corrected.

- *Article 17:* **Right to erasure (or the "right-to-be-forgotten").** The data subject has the right to require the data controller to delete his or her personal data if the continued processing of those data is not justified.

- *Recitals 42 and 65 and Article 7(3):* **Right to withdraw consent** (when processing is based on consent). In order for a consent to be valid, the data subject must have the right to withdraw such consent, and the data subject has the right to withdraw such consent at any time.

- *Article 18:* **Right to restrict processing.** The data subject has, in some situations, the right to limit the processing of his or her personal data to some purposes. This means that the data controller must refrain from using such personal data during the period for which the right applies. This right may be used for example, when the data subject contests the lawfulness of the processing or the accuracy of the data, and data controller is in the process of verifying the accuracy of the data.

- *Article 19*: **Obligation to notify recipients.** A controller has an obligation to communicate any rectification or erasure of personal data or restriction of processing carried out in accordance with Articles 16, 17(1) and 18 to each recipient to whom the personal data have been disclosed, unless this proves impossible or involves disproportionate effort. The controller shall inform the data subject about the recipients of such personal data if the data subject requests such information.

- *Article 20*: **Right to data portability.** Under certain conditions, the data subject may require his or her data to be provided to himself or herself or to another company in a commonly used machine-readable format.

- *Article 21*: **Right to object.** The data subject has the right to object to certain processing, upon which the processing shall cease. The data subject also has the right, on grounds relating to his or her particular situation, to object to processing if the processing is based on legitimate interest or public interest. When personal data is processed for the purposes of direct marketing, the data subject always has the right to object to such processing, including profiling. The data subject must be informed of this right clearly and separately from other information.

- *Article 22*: **Right to not be subject to automated decision-making (to profiling).** The data subject's right to not be subject to a decision based solely on automated processing, including profiling, which produces legal effects concerning him or her or similarly significantly affects him or her.

6.5.1 The Modalities—to Whom, How and When

Article 12(2) of the Regulation requires organizations to facilitate the exercise of data subject rights. Whereas the Directive did not explicitly require organizations to confirm data subjects' identities, the Regulation now requires the controller to use all reasonable efforts to verify the identity of data subjects. Consequently, where the controller has reasonable doubts as to a data subject's identity, the controller may request the provision of additional information necessary to confirm it. The controller, however, is not obliged to collect any additional personal data just to link certain pieces of data it holds to a specific data subject.

Under the Regulation, companies must protect the confidentiality, integrity and availability of personal data. On the other hand, the method of confirming identity should be reasonable (not unduly burdensome) and companies should avoid collecting excessive amounts of personal data for the authentication itself.[71]

Another operational aspect refers to the time frame to honor data subjects' requests. Preliminarily, the controller should acknowledge receiving the request and confirm or clarify what is requested. Article 12(3) sets out the relevant time windows for responding: one month, starting with receipt of the request, should be the normal time frame, which can be extended by two further months for cases of specific situations and/ or especially complex requests. During the first month, however, the organization has to decide whether it can act on the users' request at all—if the organization decides not to proceed, it must inform the data subjects about this and inform them of their right to lodge complaints with regulators. In situations where there are multiple controllers or processors who have some or all of the relevant information, it is important to have processes in place to ensure that the requested information can be provided within the applicable deadlines under the Regulation.

In terms of form, the Regulation aims to establish and rely on technology-based processes—electronically received requests should be answered electronically, unless the data subject requests something else. While this seems like a straight-forward requirement, companies should not underestimate the potential security implications of honoring rights through technological means alone. As email encryption is still not a thoroughly widespread mean of providing secure communication for sensitive information, companies will be challenged to adopt ways to deliver this information electronically in a safe and accountable way.

6.5.2 The General Necessity of Transparent Communication

As mentioned earlier in this chapter, transparency is fundamental to any data protection system, as individuals' right to privacy cannot be assured if they are not properly informed about the data controllers' activities. In essence, the rights established by the Regulation require that data subjects have all the information they need in order to understand the nature of the processing and to exercise their further statutory rights. Consequently, Article 12(1) requires that any information communicated by the organization be provided in a "concise, transparent, intelligible and easily accessible form, using clear and plain language."

6.5.3 Right to Information (About Personal Data Collection and Processing)

Under Article 13 of the Regulation, data subjects have the right to be provided with certain pieces of information that describe their relationship with the controller. This includes the controller's identity and contact details, the reasons or purposes for processing their personal data, the legal basis for doing so, recipients of that data (especially if those reside in third countries), and other relevant information necessary to ensure the fair and transparent processing of the data. Additionally, the controller must identify the source of data if collected or obtained from a third party, in order to effectively enable the data subject to pursue their rights.[72]

6.5.4 Right of Access

The Regulation's right of access set out in Article 15 is in some ways a counterpart to the more passive right of information in Articles 13 and 14. Any data subject who exercises his or right to know must be told about the personal data the organization holds about him or her and, more specifically, why and how it does so. In comparison to the Directive, the Regulation expands considerably the mandatory categories of information that a company must provide.

The Regulation prescribes that the data subject has the right to obtain from the controller confirmation as to whether or not personal data that concerns him or her is being processed. Where that is the case, in addition to providing access to the personal data, the data subject is entitled to receive the following information:

- the purposes of the processing;
- the categories of personal data concerned;
- the recipients or categories of recipients to whom the personal data have been or will be disclosed, in particular, recipients in third countries or international organizations;
- where possible, the envisaged period for which the personal data will be stored or, if not possible, the criteria used to determine that period;
- the existence of the right to request from the controller rectification or erasure of personal data or restriction of processing of personal data concerning the data subject or to object to such processing;
- the right to lodge a complaint with a supervisory authority;
- where the personal data are not collected from the data subject, any available information as to their source; and
- the existence of automated decision-making, including profiling, referred to in Article 22(1) and (4) and, at least in those cases, meaningful information about the logic involved, as well as the significance and the envisaged consequences of such processing for the data subject.

In practice, these types of requests are likely to pose a substantial administrative burden on organizations, so they should consider upfront what types of processes need to be in place to assist with this task. Some of the most burdensome requests likely to be received will be from employees who are hoping to use their new rights under the Regulation in the context of litigation.[73]

6.5.5 Right to Rectification

The scope of this right under the Regulation is largely unchanged from the Directive. In a nutshell, data subjects have the right to rectification of inaccurate personal data, and controllers must ensure that inaccurate or incomplete data is erased, amended or rectified. This right can generate a considerable amount of effort operationally.

Rectifying wrong entries in databases is typically not an isolated issue for most organizations. Because data is often interconnected and together and in duplicate, any changes to any piece of data may have wider, unforeseen consequences.

6.5.6 Right to Erasure ("Right to be Forgotten")

The so-called right to be forgotten (RTBF) is probably one of the most actively scrutinized aspects of the original proposal by the Commission.[74]

Article 17(1) establishes that data subjects obtain the right to have their personal data erased if:

- the data is no longer needed for its original purpose and no new lawful purpose exists;

- the lawful basis for the processing is the data subject's consent, the data subject withdraws that consent, and no other lawful ground exists;

- the data subject exercises the right to object, and the controller has no overriding grounds for continuing the processing;

- the data has been processed unlawfully; or

- erasure is necessary for compliance with EU law or the national law of the relevant member state.

In addition, Article 17(2) of the Regulation requires that, where the controller has made any personal data public (e.g., in a telephone directory or in a social network) and the data subject exercises the right to erasure, the controller must take reasonable steps (including applying technological solutions, but taking costs into account) to inform third parties which are processing this published personal data as controllers that the data subject has exercised this right. Given how prominent the right to be forgotten was during the legislative process, it seems reasonable to assume that regulators will emphasize the importance of honoring this right in full.

Exemptions to the right of erasure are listed in Article 17(3), which allows organizations to decline data subjects' requests to the extent that processing is necessary:

- for exercising the right of freedom of expression and information;

- for compliance with a legal obligation which requires processing by Union or member state law to which the controller is subject or for the performance of a task carried out in the public interest, like public health, archiving and scientific, historical research or statistical purposes; or

- for the establishment of, exercise of or defense against legal claims.

The Regulation also entitles data subjects to request information about the identities of recipients to whom the personal data has been disclosed. Consequently, Article 19 requires that where a controller has disclosed personal data to particular third parties, and the data subject has subsequently exercised his or her right of rectification, erasure or blocking, the controller must notify those third parties of the data subject's exercise of those rights. The controller is exempt from this obligation only if it is impossible to comply with it or would require disproportionate effort, which must be proven by the controller. As Recital 66 mentions, this extension of the right of erasure is meant to strengthen the right to be forgotten specifically in the online environment, where personal data is notoriously difficult to control once it has been shared and distributed—so online service providers will probably find dealing with this obligation especially difficult.

In terms of operational impact, this means that organizations, in addition to implementing systems and procedures for giving effect to the new rights that the Regulation grants to data subjects, are also required to implement systems and procedures for reliably notifying affected third parties about the exercise of those rights. For organizations that disclose personal data to a large number of third parties, these provisions may be particularly burdensome.

6.5.7 Right to Restriction of Processing

Article 18 of the Regulation establishes something similar to a prior right under the Directive that allowed the "blocking" of data. Data subjects have the right to restrict the processing of their personal data if:

- the accuracy of the data is contested (and only for as long as it takes to verify that accuracy);

- the processing is unlawful, and the data subject requests restriction (as opposed to exercising the right to erasure);

- the controller no longer needs the data for their original purpose, but the data is still required by the data subject to establish, exercise or defend legal rights; or

- verification of overriding grounds is pending in the context of an erasure request.

From an operational point of view, organizations face a broad range of circumstances under which data subjects can require that the processing of their personal data is restricted under the Regulation. How this will be done technologically remains to be seen. Recital 67 at least provides some guidance by suggesting that compliance with this right could be achieved by 'temporarily moving the selected data to another processing system, making the selected personal data unavailable to users, or temporarily removing it from a website.

6.5.8 Right to Data Portability

Data portability is an entirely new term in European data protection law.[75] Article 20 of the Regulation states that data subjects have the right to receive their own personal data, which they have provided to a controller, in a structured, commonly used and machine-readable format. They also have the right to transmit the data to another controller without hindrance from the controller. Technically, the controller must either hand the data over to the data subject in a usable fashion, or—at their request (Article 20(2))—transfer the data directly to the recipient of the data subject's choice, where technically feasible.

For some organizations, this new right to transfer personal data between controllers creates a significant additional burden, requiring substantial investment in new systems and processes. On top of that, many issues with this particular provision still need further guidance by the regulatory community in order to allow companies to set up their processes. In particular, it remains to be seen what is meant by a "structured, commonly used and machine-readable" format for modern information services or how the threshold of "hindrance" and "technical feasibility" is determined in the context of direct controller-to-controller transfers.

6.5.9 Right to Object

In accordance with Article 21(1), whenever a controller justifies the data processing on the basis of its legitimate interests, data subjects can object to such processing. As a consequence, the controller is no longer allowed to process the data subject's personal data unless it can demonstrate compelling, legitimate grounds for the processing. These grounds must be sufficiently compelling to override the interests, rights and freedoms of the data subject, such as to establish, exercise or defend against legal claims.

Under Article 14 of the Directive, data subjects already had the right to object to the processing of personal data for the purpose of direct marketing. Under the Regulation, this now explicitly includes profiling. In addition, the data subject must be explicitly, clearly and separately notified of the right to object—at the latest, at the time of the first communication.

Under Article 21(6), which states that personal data is processed for scientific and historical research purposes or statistical purposes, the right to object exists only as far as the processing is not considered necessary for the performance of a task carried out for reasons of public interest.

6.5.10 Right to Not be Subject to Automated Decision-Making

The right not to be evaluated on the basis of automated processing is closely connected with the aforementioned right to object. It is important to take into consideration, though, that Article 22 has a narrow application. The right not to be subject to automated decision-making applies only if such a decision is based solely on automated processing and produces legal effects concerning the data subject or similarly significantly affects them. Because of their ambiguity, however, these terms will need further explanation and probably additional guidance from the regulators. There is no common understanding of what "solely automated process" means, and there are no commonly accepted rules as to what kind of decisions have significant effects on individuals.

Yet, if a decision-making process falls within these parameters, the underlying processing of personal data is allowed if it is authorized by law, necessary for the preparation and execution of a contract, or done with the data subject's explicit consent, provided that the controller has put sufficient safeguards in place. Such safeguards might include the right to obtain human intervention on the part of the controller or another equally effective opportunity to express the data subject's point of view to contest the decision.

6.5.11 Restrictions of Data Subjects' Rights

In spite of the Regulation's prescriptive nature, controllers must also be prepared to comply with additional EU and member state law that could further impose obligations and provide rights in addition to those provided for in Articles 12 to 22. Individual EU countries have the right to provide additional guidelines on the principles of Article 5, insofar as its provisions correspond to the rights and obligations provided for in Articles 12 to 22. In particular, while they must still respect data subjects' fundamental rights and freedoms, member states may enact additional restrictions on data subject rights under the GDPR that are deemed necessary to safeguard interests of national security, defense or public security.

In order to comply with the Regulation's requirements relating to data subject rights, controllers should revise their privacy notices and internal privacy policies. If the controller does not already have such policies, the controller will also need to prepare a data subject access request policy and privacy by design policy. These policies will need to be implemented at every business level and training will need to be provided to the employees in such business units—from entry-level employees through leadership of an organization.

6.6 Responding to Data Subject Requests

6.6.1 Responding to Withdrawals of Consent and Data Access Requests

For consent to be freely given, it must also be freely revocable. Therefore, it is important to have a process and policy in place for enabling data subjects to withdraw their consents.

6.6.1.1 Responding to Withdrawals of Consent

Choice and control should be offered to individuals even after the opt-in stage. If an organization relies on consent to process personal data, it may want to—or be required to—state in the privacy notice that the individual can withdraw consent.

An organization's procedures around withdrawal of consent may address:

- When and how consent may be withdrawn

- Rules for communicating with individuals

- Methods for withdrawing consent

- Documentation of requests and actions taken

The process for withdrawing consent should be publicized—via privacy notices, consent requests, and so on—to inform individuals about the steps they should take.

6.6.1.2 Responding to Data Subject Access and Rectification Requests

Under certain circumstances, laws and regulations may require an organization to provide individuals, upon request, with access to their personal information—and information about the processing performed on it—and allow them to correct their information. The information must be provided:

- Completely

- In a timely manner

- Without charge to the individual

- In the same form that the request was made

There may be limits to this right, such as protections for the rights and freedoms of others.

A privacy team should work with the legal team to establish policies and procedures that align with legal requirements.

It is important for an organization to have a documented process and follow it. The process may be the first thing a regulator asks about in the event of an issue. The regulator will also likely want to know if the employees charged with implementing such policies understand them and have received training on them.

6.7 Handling Complaints: Procedural Considerations

Complaints about how the organization manages data subject rights may come from both internal sources, such as employees, and from external sources, such as customers, consumers, competitors, patients, the public, regulators and vendors. Individuals handling complaints or requests for an organization must be trained to identify these requests, because they may be submitted in a variety of ways such as by email, phone or social media.[76] If an individual makes any request relating to his or her personal data, it is safe to assume that such a request that may be subject to the GDPR.[77] Therefore, all employees who may come across such requests should be trained on how to recognize them and instructed on how to quickly send them to the person or team within the organization who has the responsibility of handling them.

Internal procedures should define and enable mechanisms for:

- Differentiating between sources and types of complaints

- Designating proper recipients

- Implementing a centralized intake process

- Tracking the process

- Reporting and documenting resolutions

- Redressing

Departments and roles designated for receiving complaints should be easy to reach, whether through dedicated phone numbers, email addresses or physical addresses.

Complaints from data subjects should go through some centralized process. There needs to be a central point of control that deals with data subject complaints. Because you have a limited time to respond and may need cooperation from other parties (e.g., other controllers, processors), it is critical to have an efficient and consistent process. If you have a centralized process, you have trained people who know the organization and can quickly determine how to resolve most complaints. The individuals who will respond to these complaints need to understand how to properly authenticate the individuals making the complaints or requests. They also need to be trained to identify fraud and phishing. It has become somewhat common for terminated or disciplined employees to use subject access requests in litigation or threatened litigation, so it is important to make sure the organization's subject access request policies contemplate all likely scenarios. Individuals handling these requests for an organization must be trained on the types of requests the organization may receive, how to respond to such requests and when such requests can be declined or limited in accordance with applicable law. Such individuals must also be able to consult with the legal team when any uncertainty arises in responding to such requests.

To better operationalize a response to a large volume of access requests and complaints, some organizations are exploring the use of technology in order to increase their efficiency in responding to such requests and complaints. This technology includes complaint forms and software that can be used to automate responses.[78] When designing processes to respond to data subject requests and complaints, it is also important to consider special situations, including responses to visually impaired individuals, handling of multiple languages across multiple jurisdictions, and tracking of metrics related to such requests both for resolution and for efficiency.

Companies that handle a large volume of requests have realized the value in having a strong records retention program that facilitates finding the requested information, ensures that years of information have not been unnecessarily retained, and provides a defensible rationale for deleting data on a regular basis (subject to applicable legal holds).

Data subject access requests can be time-consuming and labor-intensive, especially when a large volume of documents must be provided.[79] When providing such documents, which may include the personal data of third-party data subjects, it is critical to redact or remove such data if the third parties have not consented to disclosure or, as permitted in the UK, it is otherwise reasonable to comply with the request without the third party's consent.[80] In many ways, responding to data subject access requests may remind American organizations of complex e-discovery production exercises. Given the timing requirements in responding to such subject access requests, a sound process and solid record retention program become even more important.

6.8 Data Subject Rights Outside the United States and Europe

Clearly there is a trend toward strengthening privacy and cybersecurity-related laws globally. Many countries in Latin America, for example, have either adopted or are in the process of adopting GDPR-like laws. Canada has also recently strengthened its privacy laws with recent changes in its Personal Information Protection and Electronic Documents Act (PIPEDA) relating to breach notification.[81] Canada is also exploring additional changes to its Anti-Spam Legislation (CASL).[82] In Canada, PIPEDA generally provides data subjects with a general right to access their personal information (defined as "information about an identifiable individual") held by businesses subject to the law.[83]

Latin American privacy laws are composed both of constitutional protections and, where adopted in certain countries, comprehensive privacy legislation. As of February 2018, 11 Latin American countries had comprehensive privacy or data protection laws.[84] In the laws that have been adopted thus far, there are some common elements such as requiring notice and giving access and correction rights to data subjects.[85] In Mexico, these rights are referred to as "ARCO" rights and specifically grant Mexican citizens the right of access, rectification, cancellation and opposition to processing of their personal data.[86]

In China, Article 40 of the Constitution of the People's Republic of China (PRC) and several sets of laws and regulations expressly protect privacy. For example, the PRC Criminal Law prohibits selling or providing Chinese citizens' personal information in breach of relevant state requirements.[87] The PRC General Provisions of the Civil Law prohibits the unlawful collection, use, processing, transfer, sale, provision or disclosure of another person's information.[88] Also, the National People's Congress Standing Committee Decision regarding the Strengthening of Network Information Protection

("NPCSC Decision") stipulates that no organization or individual can steal or obtain citizens' personal digital information by other unlawful means, or sell or provide citizens' personal digital information to others unlawfully.[89]

The Chinese National Information Security Standardization Technical Committee, or TC260, circulated a draft *Information Security Technology - Personal Information Security Specification* (draft "PI Security Specification") and *Information Security Technology - Guide for De-Identifying Personal Information* on May 29, 2017 and August 15, 2017, respectively. Under the draft PI Security Specification, the handling of "personal information" and "personal sensitive information" must follow the seven principles of (1) consistent rights and responsibilities, (2) clear purpose, (3) choice and consent, (4) minimal and necessary uses, (5) openness and transparency, (6) security assurance, and (7) data subject participation.[90]

South Korea's privacy regime is one of the strictest in the world and requires the personal information processor to provide detailed notices to data subjects and obtain explicit consent in a manner that is similar to the requirements of the GDPR in that matters requiring consent should be segregated from the personal information not requiring consent.[91] The Korean Personal Information Protection Act, which was enacted on September 30, 2011, prohibits denying goods and services to a data subject on the basis that such individual denied consent to certain processing (e.g., receiving marketing messages).[92] Furthermore, the Korean law gives data subjects the right to access, correction, deletion and destruction of their personal information.

Given the requirements of various global privacy laws, it is critical for global organizations to have robust data subject access request policies in place and the ability to respond in a timely manner to these requests.

6.9 Summary

The trend in global privacy is to endow data subjects with greater control over their personal data and require increased transparency regarding how organizations communicate to data subjects about the ways they process the data subjects' personal data. It will be critical for your organization's brand to handle data subject access requests in a way that engenders trust in your organization and does not instead lead the dissatisfied data subject to complain to the regulator or on social media. Organizations that are responsive and have sound processes will come to view each interaction with a data subject as a trust-building exercise and an opportunity to improve how their organization is viewed internally and externally.

Endnotes

1 15 USC § 45(a)(1); "IAPP Guide to FTC Privacy Enforcement," IAPP, https://iapp.org/media/pdf/resource_center/Scully-FTC-Remedies2017.pdf (accessed November 2018).

2 "FTC Charges Deceptive Privacy Practices in Google's Rollout of its Buzz Social Network," FTC, March 30, 2011, https://www.ftc.gov/news-events/press-releases/2011/03/ftc-charges-deceptive-privacy-practices-googles-rollout-its-buzz (accessed November 2018); "Snapchat Settles FTC Charges That Promises of Disappearing Messages Were False," FTC, May 8, 2014, https://www.ftc.gov/news-events/press-releases/2014/05/snapchat-settles-ftc-charges-promises-disappearing-messages-were (accessed August 2018); and "Myspace Settles FTC Charges That It Misled Millions of Users About Sharing Personal Information with Advertisers," FTC, May 8, 2012, https://www.ftc.gov/news-events/press-releases/2012/05/myspace-settles-ftc-charges-it-misled-millions-users-about (accessed August 2018).

3 "Snapchat Settles FTC Charges That Promises of Disappearing Messages Were False."

4 "A Design Space for Effective Privacy Notices," 2015 Symposium on Usable Privacy and Security, (2015), https://www.ftc.gov/system/files/documents/public_comments/2015/10/00038-97832.pdf (accessed November 2018).

5 Id.

6 "Mobile Privacy Disclosures: Building Trust Through Transparency," FTC staff report, February 2013, (noting that the "Commission staff supports this type of innovation as a way to provide a starting point for improved disclosures"), https://www.ftc.gov/sites/default/files/documents/reports/mobile-privacy-disclosures-building-trust-through-transparency-federal-trade-commission-staff-report/130201mobileprivacyreport.pdf (accessed November 2018); Müge Fazlioglu, "What's new in WP29's final guidelines on transparency," IAPP, April 18, 2018, https://iapp.org/news/a/whats-new-in-wp29s-final-guidelines-on-transparency/ (accessed November 2018).

7 Article 29 Working Party Guidance on Transparency Under Regulation 2016/679, Section 30, p. 17, http://ec.europa.eu/newsroom/article29/item-detail.cfm?item_id=622227 (accessed November 2018).

8 Article 29 Working Party Guidance on Transparency Under Regulation 2016/679, Section 32, p. 18, http://ec.europa.eu/newsroom/article29/item-detail.cfm?item_id=622227 (accessed November 2018).

9 "New Creative Guidelines for DAA Icon Placement on Mobile Devices," Digital Advertising Alliance, April 7, 2014, https://digitaladvertisingalliance.org/press-release/new-creative-guidelines-daa-icon-placement-mobile-devices (accessed November 2018).

10 Article 29 Working Party Guidance on Transparency Under Regulation 2016/679, Section 32, p. 18.

11 Woodrow Hartzog, "User Agreements are Betraying You," Medium, June 5, 2018, https://medium.com/s/trustissues/user-agreements-are-betraying-you-19db7135441f (accessed November 2018).

12 Id.

13 Alexis Madrigal, "Reading the Privacy Policies You Encounter in a Year Would Take 76 Work Days," The Atlantic, March 1, 2012, https://www.theatlantic.com/technology/archive/2012/03/reading-the-privacy-policies-you-encounter-in-a-year-would-take-76-work-days/253851/ (accessed November 2018).

14 GDPR, Recital 32.

15 15 U.S.C.A. § 6501 et. Seq; GDPR, Article 8, www.privacy-regulation.eu/en/article-8-conditions-applicable-to-child's-consent-in-relation-to-information-society-services-GDPR.htm (accessed November 2018).

16 16 C.F.R. § 312.1 et. seq.

17 16 C.F.R. § 312.4(a).

18 16 C.F.R. § 312.6.

19 16 C.F.R. § 312.4(a)(iii).

20 Guidelines for Online Consent, Office of the Privacy Commissioner of Canada, April 2013, https://www.oipc.ab.ca/media/383662/guidelines_for_online_consent_may2014.pdf (accessed November 2018).

21 Page 10, Section 14 of Article 29 Working Party Guidance on Transparency Under Regulation 2016/679, http://ec.europa.eu/newsroom/article29/item-detail.cfm?item_id=622227 (accessed November 2018).

22 *Id.*

23 "Analysis: The California Consumer Privacy Act of 2018," IAPP, July 2, 2019, https://iapp.org/news/a/analysis-the-california-consumer-privacy-act-of-2018/ (accessed August 2018).

24 15 U.S.C.A. § 1681.

25 15 U.S.C.A. § 1681(g).

26 15 U.S.C.A. § 1681(a)(1)(A).

27 15 U.S.C.A. § 1681(i).

28 15 U.S.C.A. § 1681(i)(a)(1)(A).

29 15 U.S.C.A. § 1681(c)(a).

30 15 U.S.C.A. § 1681s-2(a)(7)(A)(i).

31 *Background Checks: What Employers Need to Know,* U.S. Equal Employment Opportunity Commission, https://www.eeoc.gov/eeoc/publications/background_checks_employers.cfm (accessed November 2018).

32 *Id.*

33 *Id.*

34 Pub. L. 104-191; 45 C.F.R. § 160.103 et.seq; 45 C.F.R. § 162.100 et. seq; 45 C.F.R. § 164.102 et. seq.

35 45 C.F.R. § 164.524.

36 45 C.F.R. § 164.524(b)(1)(2)(i).

37 45 C.F.R. § 164.526.

38 45 C.F.R. § 164.510.

39 National Do Not Call Registry, https://www.donotcall.gov/ (accessed November 2018); Telemarketing Sales Rule, FTC, https://www.ftc.gov/enforcement/rules/rulemaking-regulatory-reform-proceedings/telemarketing-sales-rule (accessed November 2018).

40 Stop Unwanted Robocalls and Texts, Consumer Guides, FCC, https://www.fcc.gov/consumers/guides/stop-unwanted-robocalls-and-texts (accessed November 2018).

41 National Do Not Call Registry, https://www.donotcall.gov/ (accessed November 2018).

42 Enforcement of the Do Not Call Registry, FTC, https://www.ftc.gov/news-events/media-resources/do-not-call-registry/enforcement (accessed November 2018). In 2017, for example, a federal court ordered Dish Network to pay penalties totaling $280 million and injunctive relief for Dish's failure to

comply with the FTC's Telemarketing Sales Rule, the Telephone Consumer Protection Act, and state law.

43 *CAN-SPAM Act: A Compliance Guide for Business,* FTC, https://www.ftc.gov/tips-advice/business-center/guidance/can-spam-act-compliance-guide-business (accessed November 2018).

44 15 U.S.C.A. § 7701 et. seq.

45 *CAN-SPAM Act: A Compliance Guide for Business,* FTC, https://www.ftc.gov/tips-advice/business-center/guidance/can-spam-act-compliance-guide-business (accessed November 2018).

46 "Spam," Consumer Information, FTC, https://www.consumer.ftc.gov/articles/0038-spam (accessed February 2019).

47 5 U.S.C.A. § 552a; 5 U.S.C.A. § 552a(d)(1).

48 5 U.S.C.A. § 552a(d)(3).

49 5 U.S.C.A. § 552a(g)(1).

50 5 U.S.C.A. § 552.

51 Frequently Asked Questions, FOIA.gov, https://www.foia.gov/faq.html (accessed November 2018).

52 Cal. Bus. & Prof. Code § 22575(a).

53 Cal. Bus. & Prof. Code § 22575 et. seq; COPPA, Consumer Federation of California Education Foundation, https://consumercal.org/about-cfc/cfc-education-foundation/california-online-privacy-protection-act-caloppa-3/ (accessed November 2018).

54 Cal. Bus. & Prof. Code § 22575(b).

55 Del. Code Ann. tit. 6, § 1201C et seq.

56 Cal. Bus. & Prof. Code § 22577(d).

57 Del. Code Ann. tit. 6, § 1201C(17).

58 Del. Code Ann. tit. 6, § 1201C(14); Cal. Bus. & Prof. Code § 22575(a).

59 Del. Code Ann. tit. 6, § 1201C(b)(5); Cal. Bus. & Prof. Code § 22575(b)(5).

60 Cal. Civ. Code § 1798.83 et. seq.

61 Cal. Bus. & Prof. Code § 22580 et seq.; Cal. Bus. & Prof. Code § 22581.

62 *Id.*

63 California Consumer Privacy Act of 2018 (CCPA), CAL. CIV. CODE § 1798.100(a) et. seq. (2018); Sam Pfeifle, "California passes landmark privacy legislation," IAPP, June 28, 2018, https://iapp.org/news/a/california-passes-landmark-privacy-legislation/ (accessed November 2018).

64 740 Ill. Comp. Stat. Ann. 14/1 et. seq.; Wash. Rev. Code Ann. § 19.375.010 et seq.; Tex. Bus. & Com. Code Ann. § 503.001.

65 740 Ill. Comp. Stat. Ann. 14/15.

66 *Id.*

67 740 Ill. Comp. Stat. Ann. 14/20.

68 *Id.*

69 *Id.*

70 Jyn Shultze-Melling, *Data Subjects' Rights, European Data Protection Law and Practice* (Portsmouth, NH: IAPP, 2018), 159.

71 Piotr Foitzik, "How to verify identity of data subjects for DSARs under the GDPR," IAPP, June 26, 2018, https://iapp.org/news/a/how-to-verify-identity-of-data-subjects-for-dsars-under-the-gdpr/ (accessed November 2018).

72 GDPR: Regulation (EU) 2016/679 of the European Parliament and of the Council of 27 April 2016 on the protection of natural persons with regard to the processing of personal data and on the free movement of such data, and repealing Directive 95/46/EC ("General Data Protection Regulation"), Art. 14, OJ 2016 L 119/1.

73 "New Europe law makes it easy to find out what your boss has said about you," *The Guardian*, April 24, 2018, https://www.theguardian.com/technology/2018/apr/23/europe-gdpr-data-law-employer-employee (accessed November 2018).

74 "Factsheet on the 'Right to be Forgotten' ruling"(C-131/12), European Commission, https://www.inforights.im/media/1186/cl_eu_commission_factsheet_right_to_be-forgotten.pdf (accessed February 2019).

75 'Guidelines on the right to data portability' (16/EN: WP 242), 13 December 2016, http://ec.europa.eu/newsroom/document.cfm?doc_id=43822.

76 Sophie Lalor-Harbord and Ian Gatt, "Dealing with subject access requests under the GDPR," Stewarts, September 11, 2018, https://www.lexology.com/library/detail.aspx?g=c2ea32d0-c695-4d60-93dc-8702aa5d8b6f (accessed November 2018).

77 *Id.*

78 Ryan Chiavetta, "DSAR tool seeks to help large companies locate user data." IAPP, March 5, 2018, https://iapp.org/news/a/dsar-tool-seeks-to-help-large-companies-located-their-data/ (accessed February 2019).

79 Sophie Lalor-Harbord and Ian Gatt, "Dealing with subject access requests under the GDPR."

80 *Id.*

81 The Personal Information Protection and Electronic Documents Act, Office of the Privacy Commissioner of Canada, https://www.priv.gc.ca/en/privacy-topics/privacy-laws-in-canada/the-personal-information-protection-and-electronic-documents-act-pipeda/ (accessed November 2018).

82 S.C. 2010, c. 23, Government of Canada, Justice Laws website, https://laws-lois.justice.gc.ca/eng/acts/E-1.6/index.html (accessed November 2018).

83 "Accessing your personal information," Office of the Privacy Commissioner of Canada, https://www.priv.gc.ca/en/privacy-topics/access-to-personal-information/accessing-your-personal-information/ (accessed August 2018).

84 "Latin American Privacy with GDPR as Model," Baker McKenzie, February 26, 2018, https://www.intlprivacysecurityforum.com/wp-content/uploads/2018/02/LatAm_Privacy_with_GDPR_as_Model-v2.pdf (accessed November 2018).

85 "Privacy in Latin America and the Caribbean," Bloomberg BNA, (2015), https://www.bna.com/uploadedFiles/BNA_V2/Legal/Pages/Custom_Trials/PVRC/Privacy_Laws_Latin_America.pdf (accessed November 2018).

86 "Personal Data Held by Government Agencies Now Heavily Protected in Mexico," Jones Day, May 2017, http://www.jonesday.com/personal-data-held-by-government-agencies-now-heavily-protected-in-mexico-05-15-2017/# (accessed November 2018).

87 Article 253-1 of the PRC Criminal Law.

88 Article 111 of the PRC Civil Law.

89 Article 1 of the NPCSC Decision.

90 Article 4 of the draft PI Security Specification.

91 Alex Wall, "GDPR matchup: South Korea's Personal Information Protection Act," IAPP, January 8, 2018, https://iapp.org/news/a/gdpr-matchup-south-koreas-personal-information-protection-act/ (accessed November 2018).

92 *Id.*

CHAPTER 7

Training and Awareness

Chris Pahl, CIPP/C, CIPP/E, CIPP/G, CIPP/US, CIPM, CIPT, FIP

Employees have many issues to consider as they perform their daily duties. While privacy offices believe appropriate collection and use of personal information is the most important priority for employees, to the employee, the focus is on task completion. This disconnect between expected and actual behavior can frustrate the privacy office, but closing the gap requires ongoing and innovative efforts to keep privacy integrated with everyday responsibilities. Management needs to approve funding to support privacy initiatives such as training and awareness and hold employees accountable for following privacy policies and procedures. Building a privacy strategy may mean changing the mindset and perspective of an entire organization through training and awareness. Effectively protecting personal information within an organization means all members of the organization must do their share.

Ponemon's *2018 Cost of a Data Breach Study* estimates the average cost of a data breach is USD $148 per record, or $3.86 million, which is a 4.8 percent increase over 2017. The United States, Canada and Germany have the highest per capita costs at $233, $202 and $188 respectively, with Turkey, India and Brazil at $105, $68 and $67. The study finds the likelihood of a recurring material breach in the next two years is 27.9 percent. These figures do not include the impact on productivity, resource reassignment, delays in executing the strategic plan, and civil or regulatory lawsuits. However, deployment of an incident response team reduces costs by $14 per record.[1]

Verizon's *2018 Data Breach Investigations Report* cites 53,308 security incidents and 2,216 data breaches in 65 countries, with criminals continuing to exploit the same weakness—the human. In 76 percent of the cases, cybercriminals were financially motivated, and 28 percent of the attacks were committed by insiders. Verizon's report states that 17 percent are due to employee errors such as "failing to shred confidential information, sending an email to the wrong person or misconfiguring web servers."[2] Most shocking is that 4 percent of employees will click on *any* given phishing campaign.

The frequency with which large-scale issues are triggered by clicking on suspicious links should come as no surprise to privacy professionals. In early 2014, a Yahoo! employee allegedly opened a "spear fishing email that created a massive vulnerability for the company."[3] Half a billion Yahoo! accounts were exposed to Russian hackers, who allegedly forged cookies to directly access more than 6,500 Yahoo! accounts. The hackers sought access to the accounts of Russian and U.S. government officials as well as high-ranking international executives. For two years, Yahoo! was pillaged of user data and its own technology. A simple click has turned into an ongoing nightmare for the company. It is estimated that three billion Yahoo! accounts have been affected, and courts are allowing data breach victims and Yahoo! investors to sue the company.[4]

Failures to protect personal information can become expensive. On September 26, 2018, the New York attorney general reached the largest data breach settlement to date with Uber Technologies. Uber agreed to pay $148 million to settle a 2016 data breach in which hackers stole data on 57 million Uber customers, including 25.6 million riders and drivers in the United States. Although the company was aware of the breach, it chose to conceal it from regulators and paid the hackers $100,000 to delete the stolen data and keep the incident quiet. This decision later resulted in the firing of Uber's chief security officer.[5]

Corporate culture has a profound impact on the effectiveness of a compliance program; however, making employees aware of their obligations to observe data minimization principles and safeguard personal information begins with training and awareness.

7.1 Education and Awareness

Education and awareness reinforce the organization's privacy policy and practices. Education allows for communication and social acceptance of the privacy policy and supporting processes. It is critical to the successful delivery of the privacy message and sets the stage for reception and acceptance throughout the organization. Education efforts may be recorded in employee records and include formal and informal methods such as:

- Classroom training
- Online learning through streaming, videos and websites
- Poster campaigns
- Booklets
- Workshops

The education strategy and budget typically determine the best or approved methods for education within the organization. The privacy professional should first understand these areas to ensure they align with and meet corporate standards before offering any solutions.

> *Tip: Have a regular coffee and catch-up on one privacy topic via a 15-minute web conference or a face-to-face meeting.*

Training is a key control, and under some regulations—such as the U.S. Health Insurance Portability and Accountability Act (HIPAA) of 1996—it is required. However, training must go beyond checking a box. It must address applicable laws and policies, identify potential violations, address privacy complaints and misconduct, and include proper reporting procedures and consequences for violating privacy laws and policies. Where appropriate, the training delivered internally must extend to business partners and vendors. Companies should require trainees to acknowledge in writing that they have received training and agree to abide by company policies and applicable law, which should also be overseen by the privacy team.[6] This step can easily be accomplished by concluding a course with a simple signoff, requiring the employees to check multiple boxes regarding three to five principles they must follow at all times.

If people are not aware of what they are processing, they are also unaware of the consequences and liabilities that may result from mishandling data. The privacy office cannot assume understanding without ensuring there are sufficient learning opportunities. The words *training* and *awareness* are used interchangeably, but they serve different functions. Training communicates the organization's privacy message, policies and processes, including those for data usage and retention, access control and incident reporting. Training must be engaging—for example, using gamification or creating friendly competitive contests—to motivate individuals to protect information. In some cases, training should be personal, teaching employees how to implement appropriate privacy controls at their homes, which will make them more aware in the office. Its impact must be measured using attendance and other metrics. Metrics give leaders a powerful picture of what is occurring in the company.

An organization's privacy awareness program reinforces the privacy message through reminders; continued advertisement; and mechanisms such as quizzes, posters, flyers, and lobby video screens. Reinforcement of this message ensures greater privacy awareness, which can effectively reduce the risk of privacy data breach or accidental disclosure. If implemented effectively, training and awareness programs can communicate beyond what is written in privacy policies and procedures to shape expected behaviors and best practices. Where possible, integration with other training and awareness programs reinforces the messaging.

Some mistakes typically associated with education and awareness include:

- Equating education with awareness

- Using only one communication channel

- Lacking effectiveness measurements

- Eliminating either education or awareness due to budget concerns

> *Awareness-raising is one of the key aspects of the privacy framework and should be prioritized for all organizations. It can come in different forms, none of which require huge budgets. If people are not aware of what they are processing, they are also unaware of the consequences and liabilities that result from not knowing.*

7.2 Leveraging Privacy Incidents

Most privacy compliance programs have mechanisms for gathering information regarding privacy incidents. While these incidents result in investigative work by the privacy office, they also provide training opportunities. Where possible, the privacy office should provide targeted training to the affected department. When privacy incidents occur, it is important to consider the following:

- **Where possible, leverage lessons learned from events that make the headlines.** Use the events as learning opportunities, including discussions of how the incidents described suggest ways to improve your company's processes.

- Doing business means mistakes will happen. **Use mistakes as learning opportunities to improve processes rather than as cause for complaint.** Mistakes are best handled when they are approached constructively.

- **Use stories.** It is human nature to want to hear other people's stories. Share a privacy incident with others, or ask a victim of identity theft to speak about their experience.

- **Hold "lunch and learn" sessions.** Lunch and learn is a perfect way to educate employees during their lunch hour. Allow them to bring their lunch and listen to an expert speaker on a topic of personal interest, such as how to protect families from identity theft. These sessions could be held on one of the dedicated privacy and cybersecurity days sponsored by the cybersecurity industry. For example, ask a law enforcement expert to speak during lunch on worldwide Data Privacy Day, January 28, about data breaches or identity theft and make free resources, such as information available through the Federal Trade Commission (FTC) or StaySafe Online, available to attendees. At the end of the lunch, connect personal privacy with the responsibilities each employee has to protect the organization's data.

- **Make it fun.** Admit it: Privacy training is not fun, and those around you have no idea why you are passionate about your job. However, take that passion and share it through games, stickers, competitions and giveaways. The IAPP can assist by sending you a six-foot foam superhero cutout of Prudence the Privacy Pro, with her sidekick, Opt-Out, for a nominal charge.[7]

- **Develop slogans that can be used in presentations to capture the essence of the message.** For example, the word *security* is frequently used. However, privacy professionals know the human element is the concern. Consider playing off the word like this: "there can be all the security in the world, but at the end SECU-R-ITY." The letters SECTY fade away, and employees are told U-R-IT.

7.3 Communication

Communication is one of the most effective tools an organization has for strengthening and sustaining the operational lifecycle of its privacy program. Privacy information is dynamic and constantly changing, so for privacy policies and procedures to remain effective, organizations must continually communicate expectations and policy requirements to their representatives—including contractors and vendors—through training and awareness campaigns.

Improvements to the privacy program will also depend on the organization providing ongoing communication, guidance and awareness to its representatives regarding proper handling and safeguarding of all privacy data. All available means should be used to take the message to everyone who handles personal information on behalf of the organization. A good question to ask regularly is: How effectively are we communicating the expectations of our privacy program to the workforce—everyone who is using the data? Measure understanding through metrics or other objective means. This requires use of multiple metrics to assess an overall trend, which will demonstrate to the privacy office where additional, or refined, training is required.

Each organization needs a communications strategy to create awareness of its privacy program and a specific, targeted training program for all employees. A goal of this communications strategy is to educate and develop privacy program advocates for each affected business unit within the organization. One of the best ways to accomplish this goal is by employing a variety of methods to communicate the message.

The privacy office is responsible for updating employees' knowledge when changes occur. However, employees cannot be expected to be trained on every aspect of a privacy regulation—just on the guiding principles of compliance and expected behavioral outcomes. Additionally, training to the details of a regulation will require more frequent retraining when changes are made. Taking a big-picture approach for protecting personal data is easier to manage than addressing the details of what constitutes personally identifiable information (PII).

Creating a strategic activities plan for the year is a good way to provide for regular updates. Some groups specifically build into their plans a calendar of workforce communications to ensure ongoing reinforcement throughout the year. For example, the plan might specify that "every quarter we will produce a targeted email campaign that will instruct employees on how to do x, y, z. We will conduct knowledge tests (contests) to assess learning."

7.4 Creating Awareness of the Organization's Privacy Program

As discussed in Chapter 5, *awareness* means to be vigilant or watchful. From a privacy perspective, achieving awareness requires communicating the various components of an organization's privacy program, thus creating a vigilant or watchful attitude toward the protection of personal data. The need for the privacy office to constantly put reminders in front of their workforce requires innovative thinking to identify different reminder techniques. Trying new approaches should not be impeded by the fear of failure— sometimes the best planned reminders fail, but the failures spark new, more effective ideas.

7.4.1 Internally

How does an organization build an awareness program internally? A good place to start is through interdepartmental cooperation working toward the shared goal of privacy protection. For example, the marketing department could work with information security and tie in its campaign with the awareness program. You may also look at including your organization's ethics and integrity department, as well as human resources (HR), in planning effective ways for departments to share their awareness programs and experiences. Discuss how different groups can work together to reinforce the privacy message with the workforce, creating an even greater awareness of your privacy program.

You could also take an interdepartmental approach to assessing the various privacy awareness programs throughout the organization. This can reveal both strengths and weaknesses in individual programs, contributing to an overall strengthening of all internal awareness programs.

Conferences and seminars can be rich sources of information and expert suggestions on effective ways to build a privacy program and address privacy governance. An individual may learn about various approaches from privacy professionals by attending presentations or panel discussions on these topics. And often, a person learns about governance structures and approaches to privacy through presentations on other topics.

Managing security incidents, creating a sustainable training and awareness program, and designing and implementing programs or presentations on privacy challenges can educate the workforce on privacy topics and provide insights into how an organization manages these issues and assigns accountability.

Information can also be obtained through informal exchanges of ideas. Most privacy professionals are engaged in some phase of launching a privacy program. The challenge is that technologies are always changing, new laws are always being adopted, and processes can always be improved.

7.4.2 Externally

Creating external awareness of a privacy program requires different resources and methods than building internal awareness. External awareness is more directed toward building confidence through brand marketing. This occurs, for example, when an organization makes statements such as, "We respect your personal information, and we take steps to make sure that your information is secure with us." Increasing external awareness will also require obtaining partner agreements and, in certain cases, providing training or obtaining attestations of compliance. The challenge is to meet the reasonable expectations of consumers and regulators and provide proof of compliance if challenged, otherwise state agencies or the FTC may file civil penalties against your company for misleading its consumers.

External awareness is aimed at building consumer confidence in a brand by creating recognition of a corporation's commitment to security or to fulfilling a legal requirement. Organizations must have integrity when it comes to handling personal information if customers are to remain loyal.

An example of creating external awareness is found in the growing cloud computing industry. Many corporations are now exclusively, or at least heavily, involved in providing infrastructure, platform and software services for individuals and businesses. The marketing of cloud services is built on the consumers' perception of the ability of the host organization to protect their personal information.

Much of this information is personal information that other organizations are transferring to an external site for storage. The most successful cloud-hosting organizations are those that inspire confidence in their ability to provide security for the personal data consumers entrust to them.

7.5 Awareness: Operational Actions

The privacy team, along with all relevant departments, can take the following operational actions to ensure ongoing awareness:

- Develop and use internal and external communication plans to ingrain operational accountability

- Communicate information about the organization's privacy program

- Ensure policy flexibility for incorporating changes to compliance requirements from laws, regulations and standards

- Identify, catalog and maintain all document requirements updates as privacy requirements change

7.6 Identifying Audiences for Training

Staff, managers, contractors and other third parties may need privacy training. The key is to identify who has access to personal information and provide targeted training to those people. Targeted training implies there may be a variety of training programs, depending on the department, the type of information that is being handled, how that information is processed, and who handles it.

7.7 Training and Awareness Strategies

Training and awareness must have the intention of changing bad behaviors and reinforcing good ones that are integral to the success of the privacy program. Many organizations have a learning and development group managing activities related to employee training. This function enables policies and procedures to be translated into teachable content and can help contextualize privacy principles into tangible operations and processes. In smaller companies, these responsibilities may fall on the privacy function. Whatever the size of the organization, the privacy team will always need to approve the training materials that have been produced.

Steps for a successful communication and awareness campaign include:

- Assessing the organization's education and awareness initiatives
- Sustaining communication via awareness and targeted employee, management, and contractor training
- Partnering with HR or training functions, or an organizational change management expert
- Using badges and slogans
- Repeating training over a predetermined period (e.g., annually, biannually)
- Using microlearning or blended learning
- Inserting privacy messaging into other department trainings
- Going to road shows and staff meetings
- Tracking participation and comprehension

The communications group can assist by publishing periodic intranet content, communicating via email, and providing posters and other collateral that reinforce good privacy practices.

7.8 Training and Awareness Methods

Companies must think of innovative ways to communicate training and awareness opportunities to their employees. Methods may differ based on the company's culture and budget. Some methods are low-cost. It is not uncommon for companies to use different ways for delivering messaging. Examples include:

- **Formal education** utilizes a classroom environment to deliver official training that may be recorded and documented. Training may also be delivered just-in-time; for instance, an organization might provide a brief training session when an individual has been authorized to perform a new task. Instructors can use out-of-the-box modules (e.g., IAPP Privacy Core®).

  - Different training methods include instructor/classroom, online, hybrid and gamification

  - Awareness includes email, posters, blogs, internal social media, games and expos

- **E-learning** includes computer-based training (CBT), internet-based training (IBT) or web-based training (WBT). E-learning can be self-paced or live (with the active support of an instructor). Simulations can be used.

- **Road shows and department team meetings** offer opportunities to provide training pamphlets or other material for individuals to pick up at booths or to receive at staff meetings.

- **Newsletters, emails and posters** have been used for many years. Delivery methods include email, websites, print materials, and physical displays among other options. Stickers are also a unique way to deliver messages.

- **Handouts** containing frequently asked questions and tip sheets are helpful for answering common questions or dispelling myths.

- **Slogans and comics** can be used to summarize important aspects of the program and promoted as giveaway items.

- **Video teleconferencing** delivers content via videos that can be recorded live and replayed.

- **Web pages** can be used to communicate data, knowledge bases, and frequently asked questions.

- **Voicemail broadcast** provides an automated means to deliver a broadcast message to all employees without having to contact each one separately.

Communication should be consistent at all levels of the organization and among all stakeholders to ensure they understand the framework and how it affects and improves the organization.

7.9 Using Metrics

Privacy programs are generally not seen as revenue-generating; however, they can reduce risk. For privacy programs to show how they support the company's mission and prove to regulators they are actively addressing compliance risks, they must keep records regarding training and awareness programs, including any remediation taken after an event. Metrics must go beyond the numbers enrolled in a training or communication event and tell a story regarding process improvement. They should be linked to other program metrics, such as reduction in the number of privacy events. It may take time to measure the impact of training and awareness activities.

Sample training and awareness metrics include:

- Number of training or awareness opportunities by topic
- Number of individuals who enrolled or received awareness communication
- Training method (e.g., live, online, poster, road shows)
- Percent of training completed
- Results of quizzes or knowledge tests
- Changes to the number of privacy incident reports or requests for consultation or additional training

Table 7-1: Metric Template Example: Awareness and Training Measure[8]

Field	Data
Measure ID	Security Training Measure 1 (or a unique identifier to be filled out by the organization)
Goal	• Strategic goal: ensure a high-quality workforce supported by modern and secure infrastructure and operational capabilities • Privacy goal: ensure that organization's personnel are adequately trained to carry out their assigned information-security-related duties and responsibilities
Measure	Percentage of information system security personnel who have received security training (see NIST SP 800-53 Controls: AT-3: Security Training for definitions)
Measure Type	Implementation
Formula	Number of personnel who have completed security training within the past year/total number of information system security personnel *100
Target	High percentage defined by the organization
Implementation Evidence	• Training records maintained • Percentage of those with significant privacy responsibilities who have received the required training
Frequency	• Collection frequency: organization-defined (e.g., quarterly) • Reporting frequency: organization-defined (e.g., annually, monthly, weekly)
Responsible Parties	• Information owner: organization-defined (e.g., training manager) • Information collector: organization-defined (e.g., information system security officer (ISSO), training manager, privacy officer) • Information customer: chief information officer (CIO), ISSO, chief information security officer (CISO)

Field	Data
Data Source	Training and awareness-tracking records
Reporting Format	Pie chart illustrating the percentage of personnel who have received training versus those who have not received training; if performance is below target, pie chart illustrating causes of performance falling short of targets

Training programs dealing with privacy policies should be based on clear policies and standards and have ongoing mechanisms and processes to educate and guide employees in implementation. Everyone who handles personal information needs to be trained in privacy policies and how to deploy them within their area to ensure compliance with all policy requirements. This applies to employees, management, contractors, and other entities with which the organization might share personal information.

7.10 Summary

As companies continue to closely monitor training seat time, the privacy compliance program should seek out innovative ways to ensure its message continues to be heard. This means the program must build alliances with other similar organizations, such as cybersecurity and physical security, to ensure a consistent message is carried through all applicable training. Where possible, the topic of privacy should become a core topic within the company, ensuring its importance is emphasized in the code of conduct. Awareness is an ongoing journey, during which the privacy program can leverage company technology to build a privacy coalition and facilitate friendly competitions but, more importantly, make protecting information personal through practical application. An effective training and awareness program makes a complex topic comprehensible and enables people to integrate key aspects of it effortlessly into their daily routines.

Endnotes

1 Ponemon Institute, *2018 Cost of a Data Breach Study: Global Overview*, IBM, July 2018, https://www.ibm.com/security/data-breach (accessed November 2018).

2 *2018 Data Breach Investigations Report*, Verizon, https://enterprise.verizon.com/resources/reports/DBIR_2018_Report_execsummary.pdf (accessed February 2019).

3 James Tennent, "Users Affected by Yahoo's Massive Data Breach Will be Able to Sue, A Judge Has Ruled," *Newsweek*, March 12, 2018, https://www.newsweek.com/users-affected-yahoos-massive-data-breach-will-be-able-sue-judge-has-ruled-841799 (accessed November 2018).

4 *Id.*

5 Austin Carr, "Uber to Pay $148 Million in Settlement Over 2016 Data Breach," *Bloomberg Law News*, September 26, 2018, https://www.bloomberg.com/news/articles/2018-09-26/uber-to-pay-148-million-in-settlement-over-2016-data-breach (accessed November 2018).

6 "Developing a Privacy Compliance Program," Practical Law, n.d. https://content.next.westlaw.com/5-617-5067?transitionType=Default&contextData=(sc.Default)&__lrTS=20180705135935578&firstPage=true&bhcp=1 (accessed November 2018).

7 "Prudence the Privacy Pro," IAPP, https://iapp.org/resources/article/prudence-the-privacy-pro/ (accessed November 2018).

8 "National Institute of Standards and Technology, Special Publication 800-55, revision 1, Performance Measurement Guide for Information Security," 32–33, http://csrc.nist.gov/publications/nistpubs/800-55-Rev1/SP800-55-rev1.pdf (accessed November 2018).

CHAPTER 8

Protecting Personal Information

Jonathan Fox, CIPP/US, CIPM

For information privacy, protecting personal information (which is sometimes referred to as personal data or personally identifiable information) starts with privacy by design; includes determining which information security privacy controls are needed; and continues through ensuring those controls are successfully designed, engineered, deployed and monitored in whatever it is (e.g., product, service, IT system, business process) that is processing personal information.

8.1 Privacy by Design

Originating in the mid-1990s and developed by Ann Cavoukian, former information and privacy commissioner of Ontario, the Privacy by Design (PbD) framework dictates that privacy and data protection are embedded throughout the entire lifecycle of technologies, from the early design stage through deployment, use and ultimate disposal or disposition. The foundational concept—that organizations need to build privacy directly into technology, systems and practices—has gained recognition around the globe, including from the U.S. Federal Trade Commission (FTC) and the European Commission.

PbD consists of seven foundational principles:[1]

1. **Proactive, not reactive; Preventative, not remedial.** PbD anticipates and prevents privacy invasive events before they happen, rather than waiting for privacy risks to materialize.

2. **Privacy as the default.** No action is required by individuals to maintain their privacy; it is built into the system by default. This concept has been introduced in the EU General Data Protection Regulation (GDPR).

3. **Privacy embedded into design.** Privacy is an essential component of the core functionality being designed and delivered. The FTC has adopted this principle in its consumer privacy framework, calling for companies to promote consumer privacy throughout the organization and at every stage of product development.

4. **Full functionality—positive-sum, not zero-sum.** PbD seeks to accommodate all legitimate interests and objectives, rather than making unnecessary trade-offs.

5. **End-to-end security—full lifecycle protection**. Strong security measures are essential to privacy, from start to finish of the lifecycle of data.

6. **Visibility and transparency.** Component parts and operations remain visible and transparent to users and providers alike. Visibility and transparency are essential to establishing accountability and trust.

7. **Respect for user privacy**. Above all, PbD requires keeping the interests of the individual uppermost by offering such measures as strong privacy defaults, appropriate notice, and empowering user-friendly options.

When followed, the principles of PbD (see Figure 8-1) ensure that an organization establishes a culture of privacy as realized through the privacy framework, mission statement, training and awareness. The organization, having implemented a tactical strategy to reduce privacy-associated risks, may then be viewed favorably by its peer industry partners and consumers.

Figure 8-1: The Foundational Principles of Privacy by Design (after Cavoukian)

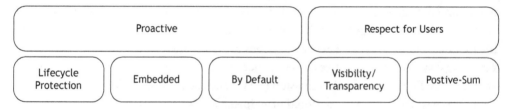

8.1.1 Paradigm of Privacy by Design

The PbD paradigm ensures that privacy and security controls are aligned with an organization's tolerance for risk, its compliance with regulations, and its commitment to building a sustainable privacy-minded culture. Notably, though, the paradigm is not a formal security/privacy engineering process [i.e., a system development lifecycle (SDLC)].

The qualities of the paradigm include:

- **Being proactive.** By default, privacy controls are part of the system engineering requirements. They are tested for effectiveness and monitored continuously.

- **Embedded privacy controls.** This involves putting them into systems and applications, auditing them for regulatory compliance, and evaluating them when new threats to information systems are discovered.

- **Demonstrating respect for users**. Privacy and security controls coexist transparently to a user. They do not diminish the necessary authorizations to access data. The protection of organizational information assets is enabled without unnecessary trade-offs.

> *Privacy has historically been viewed as an impediment to innovation and progress, but that's so yesterday and so ineffective as a business model. Without user trust, technologies can't move forward.*[2]
> —Ann Cavoukian, PhD, former Ontario information and privacy commissioner, who has been encouraging organizations since the 1990s to embrace the concept of Privacy by Design.

8.2 Data Protection by Design and by Default

Following are Article 25 from Chapter IV of the EU GDPR and Recital 78, which articulate what is meant by data protection by design and default from an EU perspective. While different in language and principles, they are highly similar in concept and in goal: that information privacy should be built in to the design process and not added on as an afterthought.

Article 25—Data protection by design and by default

1. *Taking into account the state of the art, the cost of implementation and the nature, scope, context and purposes of processing as well as the risks of varying likelihood and severity for rights and freedoms of natural persons posed by the processing, the controller shall, both at the time of the determination of the means for processing and at the time of the processing itself, implement appropriate technical and organizational measures, such as pseudonymisation, which are designed to implement data-protection principles, such as data minimization, in an effective manner and to integrate the necessary safeguards into the processing in order to meet the requirements of this Regulation and protect the rights of data subjects.*

2. *The controller shall implement appropriate technical and organizational measures for ensuring that, by default, only personal data which are necessary for each specific purpose of the processing are processed. That obligation applies to the amount of personal data collected, the extent of their processing, the period of their storage and their accessibility. In particular, such measures shall ensure that by default personal data are not made accessible without the individual's intervention to an indefinite number of natural persons.*

3. *An approved certification mechanism pursuant to Article 42 may be used as an element to demonstrate compliance with the requirements set out in paragraphs 1 and 2 of this Article.*[3]

Recital 78—Appropriate technical and organizational measures

The protection of the rights and freedoms of natural persons with regard to the processing of personal data require that appropriate technical and organisational measures be taken to ensure that the requirements of this Regulation are met.

In order to be able to demonstrate compliance with this Regulation, the controller should adopt internal policies and implement measures which meet in particular the principles of data protection by design and data protection by default.

Such measures could consist, inter alia, of minimising the processing of personal data, pseudonymising personal data as soon as possible, transparency with regard to the functions and processing of personal data, enabling the data subject to monitor the data processing, enabling the controller to create and improve security features.

When developing, designing, selecting and using applications, services and products that are based on the processing of personal data or process personal data to fulfil their task, producers of the products, services and applications should be encouraged to take into account the right to data protection when developing and designing such products, services and applications and, with due regard to the state of the art, to make sure that controllers and processors are able to fulfil their data protection obligations.

The principles of data protection by design and by default should also be taken into consideration in the context of public tenders.[4]

Like PbD, it sets an expectation for privacy to be designed to whatever is being developed and outlines what this means. With this, privacy by design, as a concept, has moved from something recognized as good practice to compliance requirement—at least for systems, applications and products that will process data in the EU or data collected in the EU.

Although PbD and the GDPR's notion of data protection by design and by default both have similar goals. The GDPR's principles are tethered to the requirements of the Regulation:[5]

- Lawfulness, fairness and transparency of processing in relation to the data subject

- Purpose limitation: collecting and processing for the specified purpose only

  ° Compatibility test for further processing: link between purposes, nature of the data, method of collection, consequences of secondary uses and safeguards

- Data minimization: relevance and limit to what is necessary

- Accuracy: complete and up-to-date data

- Storage limitation: kept only as long as needed to conduct the specified processing

- Integrity and confidentiality: security

- Accountability: responsibility and demonstration of compliance

Privacy by Design and Privacy Engineering
Privacy engineering (see Figure 8-2) is an emerging discipline within, at least, the software or information systems domain, that aims to provide methodologies, tools and techniques such that the engineered systems ensure acceptable levels of privacy.

Figure 8-2: Relationship between PbD and Privacy Engineering[6]

Privacy engineering is a concept for which PbD is a facilitator. It provides valuable design guidelines that privacy engineers should follow. In turn, privacy engineering adds to and extends PbD. It provides a methodology and technical tools based on industry guidelines and best practices, including the Unified Modeling Language.[7]

8.3 Diagramming Privacy by Design

One way to approach PbD is to visually lay out, at a high level, data flow diagrams, include administrative and end users, first-party and third-party processors, and geographic locations (see Figure 8-3), then add the data flow (see Figure 8-4).

Figure 8-3: Data Flow Diagram 1: Actors

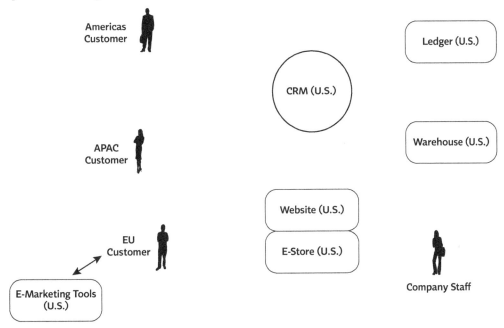

Figure 8-4: Data Flow Diagram 2: Data Flow

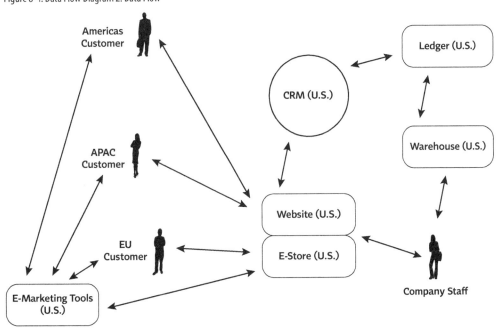

Next, begin to work through likely, less likely, and edge-case risks (harms, threats, vulnerabilities) and, with each, identify what privacy and information security controls are warranted or what must change about the design (see Figure 8-5).

Figure 8-5: Data Flow Diagram 2: Risks

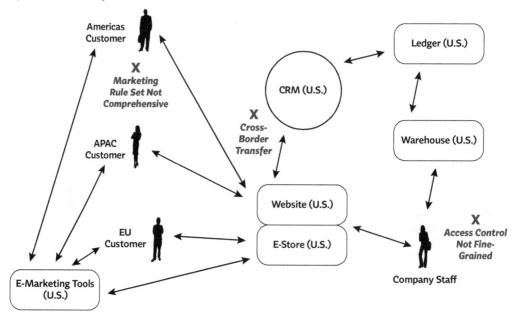

8.4 Information Security

Whether you use PbD, the GDPR's Article 25 data protection by design and default, or privacy engineering as the means to design, develop, deploy, manage and retire things that process personal information, throughout the things lifecycle, there will be a dependency on information security in the protection of the data that is being processed.

Therefore, as a privacy program manager, it is important to understand the connections and disconnects information security has with information privacy.

Just as information privacy has a set of objectives that need to be achieved to assert that privacy is maintained, so does information security. Also, just as information privacy has terms and concepts with specific definitions, so does information security.

8.4.1 Confidentiality, Integrity, Availability

Information security aims to ensure the confidentiality, integrity and availability of information throughout the data lifecycle. Confidentiality, integrity and availability are often referred to as CIA. *Confidentiality* means prevention of unauthorized disclosure of information. *Integrity* ensures information is protected from unauthorized or unintentional alteration, modification or deletion. *Availability* means information is readily accessible to authorized users

Additionally, information security includes the concepts of *accountability* and *assurance*. For information security, accountability means entity ownership is traceable, while assurance means all other four objectives are met.[8]

8.4.2 Information Security Practices

Like information privacy, information security involves a continual, ongoing set of practices that are applied throughout the data lifecycle—from creating/collection of data to its destruction. Information security defines *risk* as the combination of the probability of an event and its consequence (ISO/IEC 73).[9]

Information security builds upon risk management practices to provide:

- Identification of risk

- Selection and implementation of controls and measures to mitigate risk

- Tracking and evaluation of risk to validate the first two parts

Examples of information security risks include:[10]

- Technology with weak security

- Social media attacks

- Mobile malware

- Third-party entry

- Neglect of proper configurations

- Outdated security software

- Social engineering

- Lack of encryption

- Corporate data on personal devices

- Inadequate security technology

8.4.3 Controls

Information security uses controls to manage risk. ISACA defines controls as "The means of managing risk, including policies, procedures, guidelines, practices or organizational structures, which can be of an administrative, technical, management, or legal nature."[11]

Controls are divided into the following categories:

- **Preventive controls** are intended to prevent an incident from occurring. They are used to avoid undesirable events, errors and other occurrences that an enterprise has determined could have a negative impact on a process or end product (e.g., by locking out unauthorized intruders).[12]

- **Detective controls** are intended to identify and characterize an incident in progress. They detect and report when errors, omissions and unauthorized uses of entries occur (e.g., by sounding an alarm and alerting the appropriate person).[13]

- **Corrective controls** are intended to limit the extent of any damage caused by the incident. They are designed to correct errors, omissions and unauthorized uses and intrusions once they are detected (e.g., by recovering the organization to normal working status as efficiently as possible).[14]

According to their nature, for example:

- **Physical controls** govern physical access to hard copies of data and the systems that process and store electronic copies (e.g., fences, doors, locks and fire extinguishers).[15]

- **Administrative or policy controls** govern an organization's business practices (e.g., incident response processes, management oversight, security awareness and training, policies regarding how the organization handles data).[16]

- **Technical controls** govern software processes and data [e.g., user authentication (login) and logical access controls, antivirus software, firewalls].[17]

Here are some information security controls:[18]

- Information security policies

- Organization of information security

- Human resource (HR) controls

- Asset management

- Access control

- Cryptography

- Physical and environmental security

- Operational security

- Communications security

- Systems acquisition, development and maintenance

- Supplier relationships

- Information security incident management

- Information security aspects of business continuity management

- Compliance

8.4.4 Information Security Standards

Information security practices use standards and guidelines for consistent application of management, technical, and operational controls to reduce the risks to confidentiality, availability, and integrity of information.

The best known and most prominent are the International Organization for Standardization (ISO) Standards. ISO/IEC 27001 Annex A contains a summary of security controls, while ISO/IEC 27002 examines controls and control objectives in more depth. These include:

- **ISO/IEC 27000. Information security management systems—Overview and vocabulary.** ISO/IEC 27000:2018 provides the overview of information security management systems (ISMS). It also provides terms and definitions commonly used in the ISMS family of standards.[19]

- **ISO/IEC 27001. Information security management systems—Requirements.** ISO/IEC 27001 is the best-known standard in the family providing requirements for an ISMS.[20]

- **What is an ISMS?** An ISMS is a systematic approach to managing sensitive company information so that it remains secure. It includes people, processes and IT systems by applying a risk management process.

- **ISO/IEC 27002. Code of practice for information security management.** ISO/IEC 27002:2013 gives guidelines for organizational information security standards and information security management practices, including the selection, implementation and management of controls taking into consideration the organization's information security risk environment(s).[21]

- **ISO/IEC 27003. Information security management system implementation guidance.** ISO/IEC 27003:2017 describes the process of ISMS specification and design from inception to the production of implementation plans. It describes the process of obtaining management approval to implement an ISMS, defines a project to implement an ISMS, and provides guidance on how to plan the ISMS project, resulting in a final ISMS project implementation plan.[22]

- **ISO/IEC 27004. Information security management—Measurement.** ISO/IEC 27004:2016 provides guidelines intended to assist organizations in evaluating the information security performance and the effectiveness of an information security management system.[23]

- **ISO/IEC 27005. Information security risk management.** ISO/IEC 27005:2018 provides guidelines for information security risk management and is designed to assist the satisfactory implementation of information security based on a risk management approach.[24]

- **ISO/IEC 27006. Requirements for bodies providing audit and certification information security management systems.** ISO/IEC 27006:2015 specifies requirements and provides guidance for bodies providing audit and certification of an ISMS. It is primarily intended to support the accreditation of certification bodies providing ISMS certification.[25]

- **ISO/IEC 27010. Information technology, security techniques, information security management for inter-sector and inter-organizational communications.** ISO/IEC 27010:2015 provides guidelines in addition to the guidance given in the ISO/IEC 27000 family of standards for implementing information security management within information-sharing communities.[26]

- **ISO/IEC 27011. Information security management guidelines for telecommunications organizations based on ISO/IEC 27002.** The scope of Recommendation | ISO/IEC 27011:2016 is to define guidelines supporting the implementation of information security controls in telecommunications organizations.[27]

- **ISO/IEC 27031. Guidelines for information and communications technology readiness for business continuity.** ISO/IEC 27031:2011 describes the concepts and principles of information and communication technology (ICT) readiness for business continuity and provides a framework of methods and processes to identify and specify all aspects (such as performance criteria, design, and implementation) for improving an organization's ICT readiness to ensure business continuity.[28]

- **ISO/IEC 27033-1. Network security overview and concepts.** ISO/IEC 27033-1:2015 provides an overview of network security and related definitions. It defines and describes the concepts associated with, and provides management guidance on, network security.[29]

- **ISO/IEC 27035. Information security incident management.** ISO/IEC 27035-1:2016 is the foundation of this multipart international standard. It presents basic concepts and phases of information security incident management and combines these concepts with principles in a structured approach to detecting, reporting, assessing, and responding to incidents, and applying lessons learnt.[30]

  ISO 27799. Information security management in health using ISO/IEC 27002. ISO 27799:2016 gives guidelines for organizational information security standards and information security management practices including the selection, implementation and management of controls taking into consideration the organization's information security risk environment(s).[31]

8.5 Information Privacy and Information Security

Privacy addresses the rights of individuals to control how and to what extent information about them—their personal information—is collected and further processed. Information security is about assuring the confidentiality, integrity and availability of information assets. While privacy and information security overlap, they are also different in certain respects (see Figure 8-6).

Figure 8-6: Privacy versus Information Security

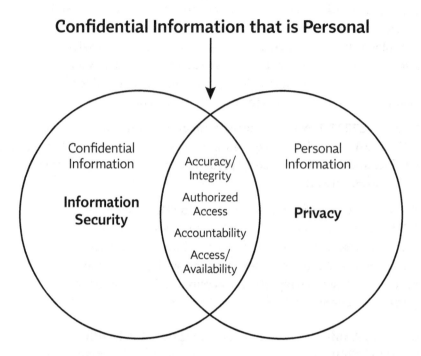

Confidential Information that is Personal

Confidential Information

Information Security

Accuracy/ Integrity

Authorized Access

Accountability

Access/ Availability

Personal Information

Privacy

The safeguards enable the "authorized" in the "authorized access and use" element that is a cornerstone of the operational definition of privacy. This is the first overlap between privacy and information security.

In addition to the fact that both information security and privacy are data protection regimens, other areas of overlap are:

- Integrity (information security) and accuracy (privacy)

- Availability (information security) and access (privacy)

- Accountability (both)

- Confidentiality (when the data is both personal information and nonpublic)

Information security's focus on data integrity overlaps with privacy's accuracy requirement in that both target ensuring the data is not altered without authorization.

Information security's availability requirement supports privacy's access requirement because if the data is not available, it cannot be accessed.

Both information security and privacy doctrines require data owners and custodians to be responsible for protecting the data in accordance with the respective protection regimen, which is a form of accountability.

And when the information is both nonpublic and personal information, confidentiality supports privacy because nonpublic data needs to be kept nonpublic.

8.5.1 The Disconnects

The reason there is not a complete overlap between privacy and information security is threefold.

First, privacy has a wider set of obligations and responsibilities than information security does, such as:

- Collection limitation

- Openness

- Relevancy

- Use limitation

This means there are issues privacy addresses that information security does not.

The second disconnect is confidentiality. Because personal information is not always nonpublic (consider the phone book), the notion of confidentiality does not apply.

Also, in a resource-constrained world, if the data is not considered confidential, it is not always valued and the necessary measures to ensure authorized access and use will be overlooked.

Third, and perhaps most important, while information security techniques can be privacy-enabling technologies (PETs) (which means they are tools that enable privacy) and are often necessary, these PETs can also become "feral" if applied incorrectly (i.e., in an invasive manner). This is why you can have security without privacy, but you cannot have privacy without security.[32]

Privacy and information security have orthogonal information classification systems:

- Information privacy classifies personal information into two categories: private information and sensitive private information

- Information security protects information differently, usually along the lines of degree of confidentiality: public, confidential, highly confidential, restricted or top secret

Sometimes, but not always, that which is public, confidential, highly confidential, or restricted/top secret will contain personal information that is public, confidential, highly confidential, or restricted/top secret, depending on the specifics and context.

In addition, confidentiality is state-determined by two parties regarding how to manage access to some kind of information. While personal information is more organic, the degree to which data identifies an individual determines whether it is personal. If it does, it is personal; if it has characteristics of a person, it is de-identified or pseudonymized. If it has no characteristics of an individual, it is anonymized.

8.5.2 Alignment

Information privacy and information security are both data protection regimes and, as noted, while they have different focuses, they do have significant overlaps. Information privacy professionals have a vested interest in ensuring security controls are implemented and are operating effectively. The business partners of both, information privacy and information security, also have a vested interest in privacy and security being effectively and efficiently implemented, so that assets and people are protected but not unnecessarily encumbered from getting work done.

As the information privacy function within organizations has matured and has been translated into controls and embedded into development processes and reviews, this overlap (as well as the distinctions) of information privacy and information security have become increasingly clear. With this clarity, the opportunity for the two domains to align and support each other to the benefit of both has become increasingly clear and achievable.

A survey commissioned by the IAPP and TrustArc (formerly TRUSTe) found the nexus of this alignment and support was driven by the mutual goal of preventing or mitigating data breaches.[33] Thus, both are interested in driving data minimization, having good data maps and inventories, and ensuring the right controls and measures are in place and accessed. As such, often privacy review and assessment processes have been embedded in secure development lifecycle processes.

With this nexus identified, it is not surprising that the same survey found that some of the ways for information privacy and information security programs to align are:

- Increased involvement of privacy personnel on information security teams and vice versa

- Employment of core privacy functions with an IT motivated to get a better handle on their data and the extent of their corporate risk

- Increased investment in privacy technology

- Increased use of privacy impact assessments and data inventory and classification

- Increased use of data retention policies

Another reason for this increased alignment is the recognition that many PETS and standards are, in many cases, information security technologies and standards. The details of use and implementation are crucial, however.

Finally, driving this increased alignment is the limitation of time and money. Rarely are privacy and information security programs awash with cash and so, to maximize efficiency and productivity and to lessen the burden on themselves and the business, information privacy and information security have found ways to improve how they work together. To realize better alignment, consider these four principles:

The first is **teaming**. Information privacy teams should work closely with information security and development teams (e.g., product, IT, web) to evaluate security controls. Be part of the process. Train colleagues in information security and development (including quality assurance) on information privacy.

Second is **don't reinvent**. Leverage existing reviews [e.g., System and Organization Controls for Service Organizations (SOC 1 and SOC 2) audits, internal audits, pen test, ISO certifications] and review processes for security assurances whenever possible. Layer in—don't become a silo or parallel activity.

Third, **stay aware**. Make sure security risks relevant to your organization or enterprise are part of your privacy risk framework. If security risks are not part of your risk framework, it is much harder to evaluate and ensure that controls are in place and correctly implemented.

Fourth, **rank and prioritize**. Not all problems can be solved or mitigated at once, and having an agreed-upon ranking of risk factors is key to prioritizing and allocating resources and evaluating outcomes.

8.5.3 Access Control

Access to an organization's information systems should be tied to an employee's role. No employees should have greater information access than is necessary to perform their job functions.

An access control policy should be established, documented and reviewed based on business and security requirements for access.

The privacy team should work with information security and IT to ensure effective access controls. Basic security principles for role-based access controls (RBAC) include the following:

- **Segregation of duties.** Ensure one person cannot exploit or gain access to information inappropriately.

- **Least privilege.** Grant access at the lowest possible level required to perform the function.

- **Need-to-know access.** Restrict access to only information that is critical to the performance of an authorized, assigned mission.

Guidelines for user access management (also known as identity access management) include the following:

- Unique user IDs

- Credentials for ID (e.g., smart card, password, two-factor authentication, machine certificate)

- Level of access based on business purpose

- Formal logical access process for granting and removing

- Password management

- Review of user access rights (e.g., privileged accounts, job function changes, employment termination)

- User responsibility

- Users required to follow good security practices in selecting and protecting passwords

- Clean desk policy for papers and removable storage media

8.5.4 Data Classification

To properly protect data, it needs to be classified. Most information security classification schemas use the following categories:

- Public

- Confidential

- Highly confidential

- Restricted

They have associated definitions for each category based on the risk to the business in the event of unauthorized access or loss of the data.

Information privacy traditionally classifies personal information based on whether it is sensitive personal information or not, which is defined by both policy and law.

Another axis with which to classify personal information is identifiability and linkability. This becomes useful in calibrating risk—especially when contemplating big data analytics—or finding ways to use data, or articulating how and to what degree personal information has been de-identified. See Table 8-1 for an example of a classification scheme.

Table 8-1: Classification Scheme Example[34]

Identifiability	Linkability	System Characteristics
Identified	Linked	• Unique identifiers across databases • Contact information stored with profile information
Pseudonymous	Linkable with reasonable and automatable effort	• No unique identifiers across databases • Common attributes across databases • Contact information stored separately from profile or transaction information
	Not linkable with reasonable effort	• No unique identifiers across databases • No common attributes across databases • Random identifiers • Contact information stored separately from profile or transaction information • Collection of long-term personal characteristics on a low level of granularity • Technical enforced deletion of profile details at regular intervals
Anonymous	Unlinkable	• No collection of contact information • No collection of long-term personal characteristics • K-anonymity with large value k

8.6 Privacy Policy and Technical Controls

For data protection, controls need to be implemented with privacy in mind.

Required (or suggested) administrative or policy controls for privacy can be found in four areas. See Table 8-2 for examples.

Table 8-2: Policy Control Examples

Type	Source	Control	Implementation
Laws and regulations	GDPR: Right to erasure	Delete data upon request.	Have a delete button that actually deletes data.
Self-regulatory regime	Payment Card Industry Data Security Standard (PCI DSS)	Encrypt cardholder data.	Use AES 256 in transit.
Industry practices	Generally Accepted Privacy Principles (GAPP)	Get explicit consent for sensitive data.	Require opt-in selection for specified uses.
Corporate ethos/policy	Google's former motto: "Don't be evil."	Do not be deceptive in search results.	Always clearly identify advertising as a "sponsored link."

It is the policy that dictates the controls, which in turn establish what mechanism or process must be implemented to ensure the control is enabled.

Technical controls fall into four main areas: [35]

- **Obfuscation:** Personal data is made obscure, unclear or unintelligible (e.g., masking, tokenization, randomization, noise, hashing)

- **Data minimization:** The collection of personal information is limited to that which is directly relevant and necessary to accomplish a specified purpose (e.g., granulation, data segregation, deletion, de-identification, aggregation)

- **Security:** Protective privacy measures are used to prevent unauthorized access (e.g., encryption, access controls for physical and virtual systems, data loss management, destruction, auditing, testing)

- **Privacy engineering technologies:** Technologies ensure engineered systems provide acceptable levels of privacy (e.g., secure multiparty computations, homomorphic encryption, differential privacy, mix networks, anonymous digital credentials)

> ### *Data Destruction*
>
> *One important way to protect personal information and privacy is to destroy personal information when it is no longer needed.*
>
> *Two ways of electronically destroying data are overwriting and degaussing.*
>
> *Three ways of physically destroying data are shredding, melting and burning.*
>
> *Regardless of the methodology selected, privacy professionals should work with their data retention functions so agreed-upon policies, standards and guidelines are in place to ensure personal information is destroyed when it is supposed to be destroyed.*[36]

8.7 Summary

Protecting personal information is an ongoing effort. Many failures are related to inability to imagine the worst or to understand evolving technologies. It is important to stay abreast of new technologies, to ensure that system, product, and application updates are reviewed, and that new or different privacy controls are not needed. As a privacy program manager, you will need not only to help design and engineer privacy, but also to design and engineer processes that will enable easy adoption of change.

Endnotes

1 Ann Cavoukian, "Privacy by Design: The 7 Foundational Principles, Information and Privacy Commissioner," https://iab.org/wp-content/IAB-uploads/2011/03/fred_carter.pdf (accessed November 2018).

2 Kashmir Hill, "Why 'Privacy by Design' Is the New Corporate Hotness," July 28, 2011, *Forbes*, www .forbes.com/sites/kashmirhill/2011/07/28/why-privacy-by-design-is-the-new-corporate-hotness/ (accessed November 2018).

3 GDPR, Article 25, www.privacy-regulation.eu/en/article-25-data-protection-by-design-and-by-default-GDPR.htm (accessed November 2018).

4 GDPR, Recital 78, www.privacy-regulation.eu/en/r78.htm (accessed November 2018).

5   GDPR, Article 5, www.privacy-regulation.eu/en/article-5-principles-relating-to-processing-of-personal-data-GDPR.htm (accessed November 2018).

6   Ian Oliver, *Privacy Engineering: A Dataflow and Ontological Approach* (CreateSpace, 2014)

7   Jonathan Fox, Michelle Dennedy and Tom Finneran, *The Privacy Engineer's Manifesto: Getting from Policy to Code to QA to Value*, p. 71 (Apress Media, 2014).

8   GDPR Article 32 includes the notion of "resiliency" when referencing confidentiality, integrity, and availability. Resiliency is the ability to quickly recover. An example of this would be a failover server, which replaces another server as soon as it goes down.

9   ISACA Cybersecurity Fundamentals Glossary, https://www.isaca.org/Knowledge-Center/Documents/Glossary/Cybersecurity_Fundamentals_glossary.pdf (accessed November 2018)

10 Top 10 Threats to Information Security, Georgetown University, https://scsonline.georgetown.edu/programs/masters-technology-management/resources/top-threats-to-information-technology (accessed November 2018).

11 Definition: Control, ISACA Cybersecurity Fundamentals Glossary, https://www.isaca.org/Knowledge-Center/Documents/Glossary/Cybersecurity_Fundamentals_glossary.pdf (accessed November 2018).

12 Definition: Preventive Control, ISACA Glossary, https://www.isaca.org/Pages/Glossary.aspx?tid=1698&char=P (accessed November 2018).

13 Definition: Detective Control, ISACA Glossary, https://www.isaca.org/Pages/Glossary.aspx?tid=1322&char=D (accessed November 2018).

14 Definition: Corrective Control, ISACA Glossary, https://www.isaca.org/Pages/Glossary.aspx?tid=1265&char=C (accessed November 2018).

15 Travis Breaux, *Introduction to IT Privacy: A Handbook for Technologists* (Portsmouth, NH: IAPP, 2014).

16 *Id.*

17 *Id.*

18 ISO/IEC 2702:2013 Information technology—Security techniques—Code of practice for information security controls, ISO, https://www.iso.org/standard/54533.html (accessed November 2018).

19 ISO/IEC 27000:2018 Information technology—Security Techniques—Information management systems—Overview and vocabulary, ISO, https://www.iso.org/standard/73906.html (accessed November 2018).

20 ISO/IEC 27000-family Information security management systems, ISO, https://www.iso.org/isoiec-27001-information-security.html (accessed November 2018).

21 ISO/IEC 27002:2013 Information technology—Security techniques—Code of practice for security controls, ISO, https://www.iso.org/standard/54533.html (accessed November 2018).

22 ISO/IEC 27003:2017 Information technology—Security techniques—Information security management systems—Guidance, ISO, https://www.iso.org/standard/63417.html (accessed November 2018).

23 ISO/IEC 27004:2016 Information technology—Security techniques—Information management—Monitoring, measurement, analysis and evaluation, ISO, https://www.iso.org/standard/64120.html (accessed November 2018).

24 ISO/IEC27005:2018 Information technology—Security techniques—Information security risk management, ISO , https://www.iso.org/standard/75281.html (accessed November 2018).

25 ISO/IEC 27006:2015 Information technology—Security techniques—Requirements for bodies providing audit and certification of information security management systems, ISO, https://www.iso.org/standard/62313.html (accessed November 2018).

26 ISO/IEC 27010:2015 Information technology—Security techniques—Information security management inter-sector and inter-organizational communications, ISO, https://www.iso.org/standard/68427.html (accessed November 2018).

27 ISO/IEC 27011:2016 Information technology—Security techniques—Code of practice for Information security controls based on ISO/IEC 27002 for telecommunications organizations, ISO, https://www.iso.org/standard/64143.html (accessed November 2018).

28 ISO/IEC 27031:2011 Information technology—Security techniques—Guidelines for information and communication technology readiness for business continuity, ISO, https://www.iso.org/standard/44374.html (accessed November 2018).

29 ISO/IEC 27033-1:2015 Information technology—Security techniques—Network security—Part 1: Overview and concepts, ISO, https://www.iso.org/standard/63461.html (accessed November 2018).

30 ISO/IEC 27035-1:2016 Information technology—Security techniques—Information security incident management—Part 1: Principles of incident management, ISO, https://www.iso.org/standard/60803.html (accessed February 2019).

31 ISO 27799:2016 Health Informatics—Information security management in health using ISO/IEC 27002, ISO, https://www.iso.org/standard/62777.html (accessed November 2018).

32 Jonathan Fox, Michelle Dennedy and Tom Finneran, *The Privacy Engineer's Manifesto: Getting from Policy to Code to QA to Value*, p. 71.

33 IAPP and TRUSTe, "How IT and InfoSec Value Privacy," March 2016, IAPP, https://iapp.org/resources/article/how-it-and-infosec-value-privacy/ (accessed November 2018).

34 R. Jason Cronk, Embedding Privacy by Design, IAPP Recorded Web Conference, December 2, 2016, https://iapp.org/store/webconferences/a0l1a000002m05dAAA/ (accessed November 2018).

35 *Id.*

36 Bob Violina, "The in-depth guide to data destruction," February 6, 2012, *CSO from IDG*, https://www.csoonline.com/article/2130822/it-audit/the-in-depth-guide-to-data-destruction.html (accessed November 2018).

CHAPTER 9

Data Breach Incident Plans

Liisa Thomas

For corporations, having a clear plan to respond to a possible data breach is often a core and critical issue. There are a wide range of laws that apply when a company is responding to a data breach. In the United States, there are laws in every state as well as industry-specific federal laws. In Europe, the General Data Protection Regulation (GDPR) addresses how a company responds to a breach, and other countries have laws as well. After addressing notification requirements, corporations often find themselves exposed to post-notice scrutiny. This can take the form of regulatory inquiries or lawsuits, including lawsuits from class action lawyers.

How, then, can corporations best handle these choppy waters? Every corporation needs to be prepared to respond to a potential data breach. No matter the type of request, they need to be prepared to properly receive, assess and respond to it.

> *Breach notification laws in the United States are numerous, and lawsuits often arise post-notification.*

9.1 Incident Planning

9.1.1 What's at Risk

In the United States, there are laws that require companies to provide notification to affected individuals and/or government authorities in the event of a data breach. When notification must be given depends on the jurisdiction and the law in question. How notification must be given, and the contents of the notification, similarly may vary. Failure to give notice properly can give rise to liability and exposure.

Even a company that notifies properly faces risks. Those risks may be in the form of public relations (PR) scrutiny and bad press. Or they may be in the form of follow-on lawsuits or regulatory action accusing the company of having failed to take proper actions to protect information.

9.1.2 Legal Exposure and Liability

Companies that suffer a data breach may face both litigation exposure, reputational liability, and potential regulatory scrutiny. Reputational liability is difficult to anticipate. Similarly, it is not always clear when a fact pattern will result in a lawsuit or regulatory investigation. Should a company face such scrutiny, factors that will be considered include:

- A purported obligation to prevent unauthorized access to or use of the data

- If the company satisfied an applicable industry standard of care

- Whether there were damages or injury, and if the organization's conduct (or lack thereof) was the proximate cause of the damages

9.1.3 Costs When Addressing an Incident

Another significant exposure to an organization is the underlying cost of a data incident. According to the Ponemon Institute's *2018 Cost of a Data Breach Study,* the average cost of an incident is $3.86 million and the cost per individual record lost or compromised is $148.[1] Translating statistics to monetary values can help senior executives see the value of planning for a data incident or breach.

Other risks include not just the cost of the incident itself, but potential loss of revenue. If a company does face litigation or regulatory scrutiny, it may find itself subject to fines. Harder to quantify, but no less risky, is the possible loss of existing and potential business. There might also be an impact on business relationships and third-party contracts, which can be especially problematic during mergers.

In addition to costs to the company, there are arguably also potential costs to the affected individuals, who might suffer identity theft or personal reputational harm. They might also have financial damage from misuse of financial account information.

9.2 How Breaches Occur

The same Ponemon Institute study revealed that malicious actors or criminal attacks are the most common cause of data breaches.[2] The root causes of breaches cited in the study include malicious or criminal attack (48 percent), human error (27 percent) and systems glitch (25 percent).[3]

Employee error or negligence is reported to be one of the biggest causes of privacy breaches. Even malicious and criminal attacks often take the form of phishing attacks, which rely on unsuspecting employees. Ongoing training and awareness-raising around information security policies and practices is therefore essential in reducing the risk of a privacy breach.

In sum, breaches can occur in many ways, including through hacking or malware, device loss or theft, and unintended disclosure of information. Breaches are more than just a technical or IT issue; everyone in an organization can and should play a role in following responsible data privacy and collection practices.

9.3 Terminology: Security Incident versus Breach

When faced with a potential security incident, there is often a temptation to call the situation a data breach. However, that term is a legal one, defined in different ways under various laws around the globe. Until a lawyer has made a determination that a fact pattern meets the legal definition, corporations should refer to a security incident as just that, an incident or a potential incident.

An incident is a situation in which the confidentiality, integrity or availability of personal information may potentially be compromised. For a data breach to exist, typically there must be some sort of unauthorized access or acquisition of the information, although the definition of *breach* varies. If a breach exists, impacted individuals and, in many cases, regulatory authorities must be notified.

In sum, all breaches are incidents, but not all incidents are breaches. Only the privacy office or legal office can declare a breach, based on certain triggers.

9.4 Getting Prepared

Companies generally recognize they may be subject to a data incident. The common phrase is "not if, but when." With this in mind, what measures can a company take to prepare for an incident? Preparedness does not prevent an incident. Instead, while prevention focuses on tasks and technologies that stop a breach from occurring, preparedness focuses on measures a company can take to respond optimally—in other words, to answer the question, "What will the company do when prevention fails?"

Preparedness falls into five categories: training, getting an incident response plan in place, understanding key stakeholders, getting insurance coverage where appropriate, and managing vendors who might be a part of an incident.

9.4.1 Training

Organizations typically face the following questions when they're making the case for training or planning its execution.

Why train? The answer to this is straightforward. Training exposes gaps in applications, procedures and pre-incident plans. It can also cultivate greater overall security for customers, partners and employees. As a result, training has the potential to reduce financial liability and regulatory exposure while lowering breach-related costs, including legal counsel and consumer notification. If appropriate training has been put in place, it can help a company get through an incident with brand reputation and integrity preserved.

Which function within an organization should fund training? Leaders often disagree, and what is appropriate will vary by company. Considerations to take into account include where most of the data is housed, how other similar projects have been funded, what is driving the compliance efforts, and what functions would be most negatively affected by an incident. Many companies find it helpful to consider a shared-cost arrangement, for example, between information technology (IT), finance, human resources (HR) and legal. Quantify the benefits of training by calculating return on investment (ROI) and savings.

Who should receive training? The entire organization will likely need some form of training. Many may only need to learn how to report a potential incident. Others may require more in-depth training. For example, the incident response team will need thorough training. The IT and security teams will similarly need in-depth training. While there will need to be—and should be—different levels and programs for different employee groups, all employees should have a basic understanding of security procedures and how to report a suspected incident.

What form should training take? Training will take various forms, and content should be customized to the audience. It might be a short video or a structured readiness-testing simulation. A training exercise could also simulate an actual incident, for instance, circulating a fake phishing email. Regardless of form, record results and update the plan accordingly.

9.4.2 Creating an Incident Response Plan

A key step in incident preparation is the formal creation of an incident response plan. To create the plan, the drafting team will need to gather a vast amount of information and then use the information they have gathered to develop processes and procedures. This team should be led by the privacy office and the legal department and include help from IT, communications, HR and senior management. The exact stakeholders will vary by organization.

When you put together the plan, you should be thinking about some key factors. These include what types of personal information your organization collects, and in what format you collect that information, as well as the method of collection. You will, of course, also want to consider the applicable laws, which is one of the many reasons working with legal is so important. Third-party relationships are also critical. What vendors are most likely to have a breach that would affect you? Another key factor is internal administration: What works for another company may not work for you. Have there been prior incidents? If so, there may be learnings you can take away from them as you put together your plan.

The plan should touch on some key areas, including how to protect privilege, the roles and responsibilities of team members, how to escalate possible issues and report suspicious activities, severity rankings (i.e., what triggers escalation and what type of escalation), and interactions with external parties (e.g., regulators, vendors, investigators for impacted individuals, insurance providers). A good plan will also consider integration with business continuity plans (BCPs) and provide a mechanism for engaging in learnings post-incident.

The purpose of a good plan is to map out for people in an organization what to do. The lawyers within your organization will also want to ensure the plan appropriately includes any regulatory requirements. This is not the place to list every law that applies, but to help the team understand what they may be facing if an incident occurs.

There are several schools of thought about listing specific team members and contact information. Many plans include these, but keep in mind that the information changes. Do you want to be updating your plan constantly depending on new contact details or new job roles? That may make sense for many organizations. For others, having the key starting point may be enough. As always, your plan will be customized to the realities of your organization.

9.4.3 Know Your Roster of Stakeholders

Effective incident response requires systematic, well-conceived planning before a breach occurs. The success of an incident-response plan ultimately depends on how efficiently stakeholders and constituent teams execute assigned tasks as a crisis unfolds.

The potential size and scope of breach-related consequences can't be understated. At issue are current and future revenue streams, brand equity and marketplace reputation. Other risks resulting from bad publicity include opportunity costs, such as high churn and diminished rates of new customer acquisitions.

These high stakes demand the inclusion and expertise of stakeholders from a wide range of job functions and disciplines. The most common locations of personal or sensitive information within an organization are:

- IT or information security
- HR

- Marketing

- Customer relationship management (CRM) systems of customer care and sales departments

- Audit and compliance

- Shareholder management

Reasons for including stakeholders from these functions in incident response planning are obvious. However, it's also essential to involve other senior leaders in formulating and executing a plan that minimizes a breach's financial and operational impact. Their involvement will ultimately result in a stronger, more richly multidisciplinary plan that enables breached companies to effectively restore security, preserve the evidence, and protect the brand. Examples of departments that should be involved include:

- Business development (BD)

- Communications and PR

- Union leadership

- Finance

- President, chief executive officer (CEO)

- Board of directors

9.4.4 Insurance Coverage

Insurance may be a viable source of funding to offset breach-response and recovery costs. While traditional policies may provide a certain level of protection, they do not normally cover expenses resulting from a data compromise. To reduce exposure, risk managers must work closely with insurance carriers and finance stakeholders to select the right type and level of coverage prior to an incident. A relatively new type of coverage, called cyber-liability insurance, may cover many breach-related expenses, including:

- Forensic investigations

- Outside counsel fees

- Crisis management services

- PR experts

- Breach notification
- Call center costs
- Credit monitoring
- Fraud resolution services

Any preparedness process should take insurance coverage into account. When looking at coverage, keep in mind that you will be asked to fill out questionnaires that speak to your level of preparedness. Before completing them, coordinate with the legal department, as you will be making disclosures about internal operations to external third parties.

9.4.5 Management of Vendors Who May Be the Source of an Incident

Often, vendors are the ones that suffer a data breach. But because of the way data breach notification laws are drafted, the obligation to notify may fall on your company, not the vendor. For this reason, it's important to have a good understanding of what information your vendors have, how they use it, and what they will do if they suffer. This exercise goes beyond merely reviewing contracts and updating language. For vendors with key information, it may be necessary to do on-the-ground diligence to understand their preparedness level and to ensure their coordination in the event of an incident.

9.5 Roles in Incident Response Planning, by Function

This section covers the core elements of incident response planning, incident detection, incident handling, and consumer notification. The focus is on the U.S. approach to responding to data breaches, since the United States has some of the world's strictest and financially consequential breach notification requirements. The section begins by identifying the roles and responsibilities previously identified stakeholders may play during a breach.

Different stakeholder teams have different responsibilities in planning for a possible breach. Table 9-1 details sample departmental responsibilities for the planning period. In reviewing these responsibilities, remember that your organization is unique; just because a plan worked in one corporate structure does not guarantee that it will work in yours. Nevertheless, Table 9-1 provides guidelines for common planning expectations by function.

Table 9-1: Sample Departmental Responsibilities

Function	Planning Role
Information security	Provide guidance regarding how the organization address detection, isolation, removal and preservation of affected systems
Legal	Ensure the response program is designed to protect privilege and think about and design the program with an eye toward limiting legal liability
HR	Provide an employee prospective
Marketing	Advise about customer relationship management
BD	Represent knowledge in handling and keeping the account
PR	Plan strategic and tactical communication to inform and influence
Union leadership	Represent union interests
Finance	Calculate and manage the bottom-line impact of containment and correction
President/CEO	Demonstrate value of preventing breaches through actions
Customer care	Offer insight on customer/caller behavior

9.5.1 Information Security and/or Information Technology

Knowledge of enterprise-wide configurations, networking and protocols, and security measures gives information security a broad enough perspective on the organization's electronic assets to help it identify vulnerabilities before criminals exploit them. As part of the incident response planning process, the information security group will provide guidance regarding the detection, isolation, removal and preservation of affected systems.

9.5.2 Legal

When developing an incident response plan, companies should always seek the advice of competent counsel experienced in the field of data breach response. If it's uncertain whether your legal department possesses the requisite knowledge, an assessment, overseen by the senior legal stakeholder, should be undertaken.

Legal stakeholders are central to incident response planning because they, more than any other executives, understand the legal precedents and requirements for handling data and reporting a breach. Their guidance helps companies limit the liability and economic consequences of a breach, including avoidance of litigation and fines. In addition, most data breach legislation requires intensive legal knowledge to implement a proper procedure. During incident response planning, organization attorneys may negotiate any requirements the organization wishes to impose upon its business partners. Conversely, the organization may also use attorneys to help determine what it is willing to do in the event data belonging to a client is compromised.

Finally, legal involvement in planning for an incident is critical given the need to protect privilege during an incident investigation process, as well as the level of legal exposure and risk that can arise depending on how a company handles an incident. After notification, companies may often find themselves subject to regulatory scrutiny or class action lawsuits. The involvement of a lawyer who understands these risks is a key part of successfully handling an incident.

9.5.3 Human Resources

Given the extensive amount of personal information that typical HR departments have on hand, it is highly advisable to include HR team members when discussing incident response planning. HR staff may also be included because of their unique perspective regarding employees or for notification of current or past employees.

During incident response planning, the HR stakeholders will normally address topics such as employee data handling, security awareness training, and/or incident recognition and response.

9.5.4 Marketing

The typical marketing department has spent years, even decades, gathering, slicing, dicing and warehousing vast amounts of customer data, much of it personal information, individually or in the aggregate (e.g., name, address, date of birth, Social Security number, driver's license number). Through segmentation and analysis of such data, they gain the necessary insight to be both the voice of the brand to external audiences and the voice of the customer to engineering, research and development, and other internal teams.

However, being stewards of such a rich data storehouse also increases marketing's vulnerability to hacking and unintentional breaches. This exposure, combined with the team's access to campaign and CRM databases, more than qualifies marketing decision makers for a role in incident response planning.

9.5.5 Business Development

The BD stakeholder, often aided by a dedicated account support team, monitors and manages vital business relationships. Companies with a certain level of value or prestige receive regular, personalized attention aimed at building trust, nurturing loyalty, and sustaining the bond over time.

Stakeholders in this position gain firsthand knowledge into handling and keeping key accounts, developing an understanding of their corporate culture, organizational strengths and weaknesses, decision-makers' personalities, and management styles of potential customers. These insights can prove invaluable in incident response planning, which is why BD stakeholders should have a seat at the table when the planning process begins.

9.5.6 Communications and Public Relations

PR and communications stakeholders are usually senior, media-savvy professionals who are highly adept at media relations and crisis management. They serve as stewards of public image and reputation, overseeing the development of strategic and tactical programs aimed at informing and influencing audiences.

9.5.7 Union Leadership

Though their numbers have declined since the 1980s, unionized workers still comprise a sizable percentage of the American workforce. According to the Bureau of Labor Statistics, the number of wage and salary workers belonging to unions stood at 14.8 million, or 10.7 percent, in 2017.[4] The AFL-CIO, the U.S.'s most prominent and well-known union, is a labor federation consisting of more than 12.5 million members of 55 different unionized entities.[5]

Data belonging to union workers, like that of all employees, is stored on an organization's servers and is vulnerable to breach by accidental or unauthorized access. If their employer reports a data breach, union members will naturally look to stewards or other union leaders for information and guidance.

These individuals represent union interests and are authorized to act and speak on members' behalf—both to internal groups and to the media at large. For these reasons, any organization whose workers are unionized should consider including a senior union stakeholder in data breach planning and response.

9.5.8 Finance

In their response-planning capacity, the main role of finance stakeholders is to calculate and manage the bottom-line impact of breach containment and correction. Once the potential costs of responding to a breach are computed, it is up to finance to allocate the necessary resources to fund resolution and recovery. The chief financial officer (CFO) should also champion more cost-effective measures that might help mitigate the risk of having a breach in the first place. To further aid in containing costs, finance executives or procurement leaders can help negotiate agreements with new or returning data-breach-resolution providers.

9.5.9 President, Chief Executive Officer

Executives lead; employees and stakeholders follow. In central business functions, the president/CEO's attitude and behavior set the tone for the entire organization. This is especially true with policies and practices surrounding data security. Through actions taken or not taken, and training funded or not, employees can easily discern the value their leaders truly place on preventing breaches. Once data is compromised and the shortcomings of an organization's security practices become public, it is the top executive who will ultimately bear the blame.

9.5.10 Board of Directors

Boards of directors are becoming more aware of—and concerned about—companies' level of preparedness for an incident. Many board members have received training about data incidents, and all are concerned about fulfilling their fiduciary obligations to their organizations. While boards are not tasked with running the day-to-day operations of a company, many members will want to make sure their business is ready in the event of an incident.

Boards often have a wealth of knowledge about handling a data incident, sometimes from their direct experiences with other incidents.

9.5.11 Customer Care

The head of the customer care operation must contend with issues such as high employee turnover and access to large amounts of potentially sensitive CRM data. These factors make customer care teams susceptible to various forms of attacks by intruders looking to access personal information.

Social engineering is an increasingly prevalent threat that can surface in a call center, as criminals call repeatedly to probe and test how security procedures are applied and how often they are enforced. According to Wombat Security, a subsidiary of Proofpoint, 76 percent of organizations experienced a phishing attack in 2017.[6] Respondents to Wombat's survey reported various impacts stemming from the phishing attacks, including malware infections, compromised accounts and a loss of data.[7]

Aside from deployment of the necessary technology as a first line of defense, employee training and awareness of phishing attacks can help to reduce the potential instances of an attack. Companies are increasingly training their employees and, according to the survey, 54 percent say training has led to a quantified reduction in phishing susceptibility.[8]

When trained to recognize unusual employee or caller behaviors or to notice trends in certain types of calls, customer care teams can help deter criminal activity and prevent potential breaches.

9.6 Integrating Incident Response into the Business Continuity Plan

To help operations run smoothly in a time of crisis, many companies depend on a BCP. The plan is typically drafted and maintained by key stakeholders and spells out departmental responsibilities and actions teams must take before, during and after an event. Situations covered in a BCP often include fires, natural disasters (e.g., tornadoes, hurricanes, floods), and terrorist attacks.

To ensure proper execution of the BCP, all planning and response teams should know which stakeholder is responsible for overseeing the plan and who, within a specific job function, will lead them during an event. Knowledge of the plan and preparation for executing it can mean the difference between a successful response and a failed one, especially during the first 24 hours.

In terms of overall organizational impact, a serious or protracted data breach can rival big disasters. Like a fire, tornado or terrorist attack, a breach can strike unexpectedly at any time and leave in its wake damages of immeasurable cost and consequence. As with other calamitous events, cleaning up a digital disaster can take weeks, months or longer; in the aftermath, victims' lives may be changed forever.

In a 2016 study of more than 350 executives, 63 percent said their companies had a BCP in place.[9] An additional 17 percent of respondents said they were in the process of developing a plan.[10] The remaining 20 percent either did not have a business continuity management program or were just beginning to develop such a program and had not yet reached a point where they could write a plan.[11] Two-thirds of respondents reported having to invoke the plan within the previous two years.[12]

Considering a breach's potential repercussions and the benefits than can result from informed and thoughtful preparation, it's imperative that companies integrate breach response planning into their broader BCP.

9.6.1 Tabletop Exercises

Once breach preparedness is integrated into the BCP, or if the company decides to have a standalone incident response plan, incident response training will likely be required.

This training may take many forms, including workshops, seminars and online videos, but often includes tabletop exercises, a strategic mainstay of corporate trainers and business continuity planners.

A tabletop exercise is a structured readiness-testing activity that simulates an emergency situation (such as a data breach) in an informal, stress-free setting. Participants, usually key stakeholders, decision makers and their alternates gather around a table to discuss roles, responsibilities and procedures in the context of an emergency scenario.

The focus is on training and familiarization with established policies and plans. Most exercises last between two and four hours and should be conducted at least semiannually—more often if resources and personnel are available.

9.6.2 Updating the Plan

Soon after concluding the exercise, results should be summarized, recorded and distributed to all participants. Perhaps most importantly, fresh or actionable insights gained from the exercise should be added to the BCP.

It's imperative to keep the incident response plan (or the BCP) current. There is little strategic, practical or economic value to a plan that is painstakingly developed but seldom tested or improved. Those responsible should always ensure the plan includes the most up-to-date timeline, action steps, policies and procedures, and current emergency contact information (vital, but often overlooked) for all plan participants. All those involved should be notified of any changes or updates to the plan.

9.6.3 Budgeting for Training and Response

Breach preparedness training, especially in a large organization, represents a significant investment. Creating an environment that ingrains data security into the corporate culture and prepares teams to respond effectively requires an organization-wide commitment backed by the resources to see it through.

In most cases, the long-term financial and operational benefits of teaching employees to prevent, detect, report and resolve data breaches far outweigh the costs. The strategic upside of investing in breach preparedness includes:

- Exposure of critical gaps in applications, procedures and plans in a pre-incident phase

- Greater overall security for customers, partners and employees

- Reduced financial liability and regulatory exposure

- Lower breach-related costs, including legal counsel and consumer notification

- Preservation of brand reputation and integrity in the marketplace

Though organization leaders often agree about the value of breach awareness and training, there is rarely consensus about who should foot the bill. Many businesses utilize a shared-cost arrangement that equitably splits training costs among participating stakeholder groups, such as IT, finance and HR. Negotiations between them can include everything from funding levels and oversight to allocation of unused funds.

However costs are divided, companies should ensure that adequate funding is available to support business continuity and breach preparedness training. To facilitate the negotiation, parties should focus on quantifying benefits, ROI and savings, rather than the bottom-line expense to any individual group.

9.6.4 Breach Response Best Practices

Allocating funds for breach response is just as important as training, perhaps even more so. Typical costs incurred in responding to a breach include threat isolation, forensic investigation, engaging of legal counsel, PR communications and media outreach, and reporting and notification (including printing, postage and call center).

Without a breach response budget in place, companies may be forced to redistribute funds from other critical projects or initiatives. Having to openly debate the merits and value of one department's initiatives over another's may lead to tension between groups and ultimately delay or detract from optimal breach response.

9.7 Incident Handling

The process of responding to a breach involves tasks that are not necessarily linear. Companies facing a potential incident will deal with incident detection, ensure that stakeholders collaborate and know their roles, investigate, ask their legal teams to conduct a legal analysis, address reporting obligations, and recover from the situation. While these steps are all part of a well-run response, many of them must happen in parallel. It can be helpful to think about breach response tasks in broad categories: secure operations, notify appropriate parties, and fix vulnerabilities.

While these groupings help keep you organized, they are not necessarily meant to be used as a checklist, as many steps will happen concurrently. For example, a company's CEO needs to know about a breach as soon as possible—even if the breach has not yet been contained. In this case, notifying appropriate parties would happen simultaneously with containment efforts.

9.7.1 Incident Detection

Unfortunately, there's not one definitive way to detect a breach. Customer calls or news reports may alert an organization to trouble before internal sources even recognize a problem. Consider, for your organization, how you will determine whether to classify an event as an incident or a breach. Remember also that privacy is a business function— not a technical function—and relies on other organizations and departments to execute breach detection and response.

Generally, a privacy incident may be described as any potential or actual compromise of personal information in a form that facilitates intentional or unintentional access by unauthorized third parties.

9.7.2 Employee Training

From their first day at an organization, new employees should be taught and encouraged to assume a privacy-first mindset. When they observe that leaders and fellow associates are genuinely committed to data security and privacy protection, new hires are more likely to respect and comply with established reporting and data-handling policies.

Initial security indoctrination and training should also teach employees to recognize vulnerabilities and to capture and report basic information when encountering a potential or actual breach. Employees must understand when and how to report suspicious incidents to their supervisors, who, in turn, should know how to properly escalate the incident to internal authorities, such as the privacy office.

9.7.3 Reporting Worksheets

To emphasize employees' personal responsibilities when encountering a breach, policies and procedures should be a regular component of security training and refreshers. The following worksheet provides a foundation for developing your own incident-reporting or privacy-training worksheets. These are merely suggestions and not intended to be a comprehensive list. Keep in mind as well how these materials are distributed. Does the incident involve a bad actor who has possibly accessed your email system? If so, then reporting should not be occurring through that potentially compromised system!

All breach planning and preparedness resources should be reviewed and approved by internal or external legal counsel or by an expert privacy team. Part of the analysis by the legal team will be to think about the issues of privilege and determine what content should be documented and how it should be documented. In many circumstances, materials will need to be prepared at the direction of counsel.

Sample Worksheet—Prepared at the Direction of Counsel

Facts as they are known:

- *Name and contact information of person discovering the incident*

- *Date and time the incident was discovered or brought to your attention*

- *Incident date, time and location*

- *Type of data suspected to be involved*

  - *Internal organization or employee data*

  - *Client or customer data*

  - *Third-party partner or vendor data*

Employee's description of what occurred:

- *Brief description of how the incident or breach was discovered.*

- *Does the incident involve paper records, electronic information or both?*

- *What type of records or media do you believe were involved?*

  - *Paper: letter, office correspondence, corporate document, fax or copies thereof?*

  - *Electronic: data file or record, email, device such as laptop, desktop, or pad-style computer, hard drives in other electronic equipment (e.g., copy machines)*

  - *Media: external hard drive, flash/thumb drive, USB key*

- *Do you know if the device or information was password-protected?*

- *Do you know if the device or information was encrypted?*

- *Do you believe personally identifiable information (PII) such as Social Security numbers, account information, user names or passwords were exposed?*

- *Can you estimate how many records were involved?*

- *To the best of your knowledge, has the incident been contained? (That is, has the data leak or loss stopped or is there still potential for additional data to be lost?)*

9.7.4 Collaboration Among Stakeholders

Within any organization, data is viewed and handled by any number of individuals and groups and is often stored in several disparate locations—even across multiple states or continents. The potential for compromising sensitive data exists throughout every business of every size in every industry.

Regardless of organization size, however, all employees have a vested interest in being vigilant about safeguarding data. The cost of recovering from a single breach could potentially cripple an organization or business unit and render it unable to operate or fully employ its workforce.

For example, whenever IT conducts security training, instructors may keep logs to record who has attended and who has not. IT may then share this information with HR to help ensure every employee receives the instruction required by organization policies.

> *The potential for compromising sensitive data exists throughout every business of every size in every industry.*

Another example of cooperation between departments is how IT and HR might work together following detection of a virus or other cybersecurity threat. Typically, IT would detect the intrusion and prepare very specific containment instructions for all employees. They could autonomously issue these instructions or work with HR or communications to assure distribution to the complete employee base via all available channels.

9.7.5 Physical Security

In many organizations, the level of technical integration between IT and facilities is so deep and so extensive that regular contact through established lines of communication is essential to maintaining security.

As technology advances, the lines of responsibility can begin to blur. Computers and systems managed by IT, for example, directly control doors, electromechanical locks, remote cameras and other access-limiting security measures maintained by facilities staff. This close association demonstrates the need for ongoing collaboration if the safety and integrity of physical and digital assets are to be maintained.

9.7.6 Human Resources

Hiring, transfers, promotions or other changes in employment status may require revisions to an individual's data access privileges. When such changes are needed, HR, IT and facilities should follow established policies for monitoring and managing data access.

Other occasions requiring group coordination are employee layoffs or terminations. These unfortunate but not uncommon events can affect thousands of individuals or just a handful. In either case, the resulting threat to data security can take many forms, for which HR and other teams must prepare.

Disgruntled or resentful employees, for example, may try to exact revenge for the dismissal by stealing or destroying sensitive information. Others may attempt to obtain organization secrets or intellectual property to sell to or gain favor with key competitors. Before employees are terminated, HR must inform IT and facilities so that physical and electronic access for those departing may be turned off immediately after, or in some cases even simultaneously with, the announcement. Phones, equipment and other employee devices must also be wiped of login and password credentials.

> *Every organization must ensure that it has a procedure for retrieving portable storage devices or media from departing employees.*

9.7.7 Third Parties

Sensitive data is seldom handled or processed in a single location. In today's global economy, huge volumes of personal information for which companies are directly responsible reside in systems and facilities managed by outside vendors, partners and contractors. These groups should always be accounted for in incident detection and planning.

For example, companies should make standard a clause requiring third parties to notify them within a certain time frame when servers, websites or other business-critical systems are taken offline. It goes without saying that companies should always require third parties to promptly communicate any breach of data so that contingencies can be made to mitigate resulting threats.

Conversely, it's vital for companies that work with third parties to remember that such communication flows both ways. If the organization's network is hit with a virus or comes under a cyber attack, or if there are changes to call center procedures or employee data-handling policies, the organization has an obligation to notify its partners immediately.

9.7.8 Tools of Prevention

To those on the front lines, prevention and detection bear many similarities to defending an occupied fortress. They must protect sensitive information against treachery and attacks that could come at any time. Regardless of how they originate, if the fortress is to remain secure, threats must be detected and eliminated before it's too late.

Today, there are numerous weapons in a security team's arsenal of prevention. Some techniques are familiar but still quite effective, while others are emerging and showing tremendous promise. The successful privacy professional will be mindful of the need to understand various prevention techniques and their intended applications and to be purposeful about keeping up with new ones as security technology advances.

Once breach investigators conclude that an actual compromise of sensitive information has occurred, the prenotification process is triggered. Steps taken may vary depending on several factors, but the purpose is to confirm that the event does indeed constitute a reportable breach.

9.8 Team Roles During an Incident

Immediately following the decision to notify affected parties, tactical portions of the incident response plan begin to unfold. Companies dealing with an incident may find themselves balancing two possibly conflicting issues: containment and legal exposures. Companies want to contain and remediate the problem. At the same time, should the situation be viewed as a data breach, impacted individuals and, potentially, government agencies must be notified. These notices often result in lawsuits or regulatory scrutiny.

An incident response process will need to balance these objectives. A successfully handled plan will be directed by legal (to address the legal exposures and privilege concerns), who will work hand in hand with an IT leader who is focused on containment and remediation. Other key stakeholders will also need direct involvement.

Depending on your organization's structure, your incident program will need a clearly delineated leader to rally the troops and keep the process on track. When thinking about incident response leadership, it is important to keep legal risks in mind. While an organization may have many lawyers on staff, not all are engaged in the practice of law. The chief privacy officer (CPO) or chief compliance officer (CCO), for example, may have legal degrees but not be functioning as lawyers (i.e., providing legal advice to the organization). General counsels may at times also be concerned about whether their roles will be questioned during litigation. For this reason, many turn to outside counsel, who are often best positioned to advise on breach-related matters. The distinction of individuals with law degrees who are not serving in the role of lawyers is important, because in order to protect attorney-client privilege, the investigation will need to be done at the direction of counsel. Thus, in many organizations, the leader is, of necessity, legal counsel.

Organizations often have many individuals with extensive knowledge about data breach matters. In addition to legal counsel, who are concerned with privilege, the CPO or CCO wants to ensure that a breach is handled correctly from a compliance standpoint, and the chief information security officer (CISO) will be focused on the nuts and bolts of investigation and containment. The CISO's role may include recommending outside forensic experts to help ascertain the incident's cause, size and scope. The CISO, in connection with the rest of the IT department, may also oversee evidence preservation, taking affected systems offline and correcting vulnerabilities that facilitated the incident.

Team leadership, keeping containment and privilege in mind, will include contacting and activating appropriate response team members or their alternates. Meetings during the investigation may be necessary, and the team leadership should think about how best to schedule these to gather and analyze status reports and provide guidance as needed. Convening with individual stakeholders to discuss lawsuits, media inquiries, regulatory concerns and other pressing developments is another of the team leader's tasks.

During the breach, team leaders will also:

- Keep individual response-team members on track to meet their performance objectives and timelines

- Track budget adherence for all response activities

- Contact outside incident response resources to confirm engagement and monitor performance

- Prepare a final analysis of the response effort and lead the post-event evaluation process

The team leader may also choose to provide senior executives with an overview of the event and of the team's expected course of action. The breach response team leader must manage expectations around communications, so executives know they are always as informed as possible and do not need to continually check in during the response process, which would hinder the team leader's work.

Below is a list of tips to help manage expectations and communicate with executives:

- Manage executive leaders' expectations by establishing the frequency of updates/communications

- Determine what is appropriate for the situation and communicate when/if the frequency needs to change

- Hold a kickoff meeting to present the team with the known facts and circumstances

- Provide senior executives with an overview of the event and of the team's expected course of action

- Engage remediation providers to reduce consumers' risk of fraud or identity theft

- Convene with individual stakeholders to discuss lawsuits, media inquiries, regulatory concerns and other pressing developments

- Keep individual response-team members on track to meet their performance objectives and timelines

- Track budget adherence for all response activities

- Contact outside incident response resources to confirm engagement and monitor performance

- Prepare a final analysis of the response effort and lead the post-event evaluation

There is sometimes confusion about who—between legal, CPO/CCO and CISO—should be directing and leading an incident response. The best incident response teams are those in which the three work together, ensuring maintenance of privilege, containment and swift investigations.

9.8.1 Legal

In addition to ensuring the protection of privilege during the investigation, legal will be focused on determining whether there is a duty to notify under breach notification laws, and if so, what form that notice should take. The entities to notify vary by breach.

Legal stakeholders may also recommend forensically sound evidence collection and preservation practices and engage or prepare statements for state attorneys general, the Federal Trade Commission (FTC) and other regulators. Stakeholders' knowledge of laws and legal precedents helps teams more effectively direct and manage the numerous related elements of incident investigation and response.

Drafting and reviewing contracts is another vital area in which legal stakeholders should be involved. If data belongs to a client, it can interpret contractual notification requirements and reporting and remediation obligations. Should the organization become the target of post-breach litigation, the legal stakeholder may also guide or prepare the defense.

9.8.2 Information Security

While some data incident matters do involve paper records, given the cyber nature of most incidents, it is almost certain that the information security group will be engaged to address data compromises. The CISO or the chief technology officer (CTO) or their designated person on the incident team will focus the group's expertise on facilitating and supporting forensic investigations, including evidence preservation. Information security will also likely be tasked with overseeing the deletion of embedded malware and hacker tools and correcting vulnerabilities that may have precipitated the breach. Larger companies may establish a computer emergency response team (CERT) to promptly address security issues.

While internal IT resources may have the experience and equipment to investigate incidents, it is often more advantageous to bring in outside experts to identify the cause and scope of the breach and the type and location of compromised data.

To support other groups with their breach response efforts, the technology team may also:

- Provide a secure transmission method for data files intended for the print vendor or incident call center

- Identify the location of potentially compromised data (e.g., test development and production environments)

- Determine the number of records potentially affected and the types of personal information they contain

- Clean up mailing lists to help facilitate the printing process

- Sort through data to identify populations requiring special handling (e.g., minors, expatriates, deceased)

- Monitor systems for additional attacks

- Fix the gaps in the IT systems, if applicable

9.8.3 Other Response Team Members

There are typically two levels to a response team. First are the leaders who will make the key decisions about how an incident is handled. Second are the individuals who will be providing input and support to the core team. Those in the second group will vary depending on the type of incident. A balance should be struck between ensuring that the appropriate stakeholders are included but that communications are controlled to avoid legal exposure. Legal counsel can be very helpful in this regard.

Core team members will be the legal lead as well as the IT or security head investigating and handling containment. Additional support may be needed from other areas as described in Table 9-2.

Table 9-2: Incident Response Support Roles by Function

Function	Potential Role
HR	Serve as information conduit to employees
Finance	Secure resources to fund resolution
Marketing	Establish and maintain a positive and consistent message
PR	Assume positions on the front line
Customer care	Handle breach-related call traffic
BD	Notify key accounts
Union leadership	Communicate and coordinate with union
President/CEO	Promptly allocate funds and personnel and publicly comment on breach

The following describes the typical roles these functions fulfill in most organizations. Every company is unique, however, and care should be taken to ensure you are following the protocols of your own organization when thinking about the roles of team members.

9.8.3.1 Human Resources

Whether breaches affect employees' data or not, the chief human resources officer (CHRO) or vice president of HR must guide the HR team's response activities. Concerns over the organization's solvency or stock value can make it necessary to inform employees of the incident. Moreover, employees might be contacted regarding the incident by affected persons, the media or other parties and need to be directed on how to respond.

If employee data is compromised, the CHRO's role will become more prominent, including directing the HR team in identifying the cause and scope and overseeing communications between management and staff. If the breach is attributed to an employee, the HR group will take one or more of the following actions: provide training, make procedural changes, administer the appropriate corrective action, or terminate the individual. If criminal behavior is discovered, the legal department and/or law enforcement officials may become involved.

During and after a breach, the HR team may be called upon to perform a variety of other corrective or educational tasks, such as:

- Facilitating employee interviews with internal and external investigators

- Identifying individuals who need training

- Holding daily meetings to summarize breach updates and create appropriate communications for employees

- Escalating concerns to the appropriate department heads

In the aftermath of a breach, the HR stakeholder may serve as the organization's informational conduit, working closely with PR or corporate communications to inform and update employees about the incident. During the breach, employees may become concerned about the effects an event might have on their employment, organization, stock or strategic business relationships. Therefore, HR might work with internal or external resources to address and allay such concerns.

If an incident affects employee records, the HR team might also help investigators determine the location, type and amount of compromised data. If the breach is traced to an organization employee, HR would be expected to collaborate with the individual's manager to document the individual's actions and determine the appropriate consequences.

9.8.3.2 Finance

The CFO or the chief financial and operating officer (CFOO) will be responsible for guiding the organization's post-breach financial decisions. Since breaches tend to be unplanned, unbudgeted events, the CFO should work closely with senior management to allocate and acquire the funds necessary to fully recover from the event.

The CFO may help negotiate with outside providers to obtain favorable pricing and terms of service. The finance team may also collaborate with the legal group to create cost/benefit models that identify the most practical or economical approaches.

Tasks commonly undertaken by the finance team during a breach include:

- Setting aside and managing appropriate reserves to pay for rapidly mounting expenses

- Working with vendors to extend payment terms and secure potential discounts

- Promptly paying invoices for breach-related activities

- Meeting daily with the response team leader to track incident expenses

- Requesting ongoing reports from breach providers to manage and track call center, printing and credit-monitoring costs

During a data breach, finance stakeholders apply their knowledge of the organization's financial commitments, obligations and cash position to recommend budget parameters for responding to the event.

In companies where incident response is an unbudgeted expense, the finance team is often tasked with being both proactive and creative in securing the resources necessary to fund resolution and notification. This sum can range from several thousand to several million dollars.

Before or after a breach, finance executives may work with insurance carriers to negotiate insurance policy updates, including improvements to the general commercial liability (GCL) policy and the addition of cyber insurance coverage.

Cyber insurance is a relatively new form of protection that fills gaps typically not covered by the GCL plan. Organizations seeking first-party cyber insurance coverage have a surprisingly diverse range of choices, including protection against losses stemming from data destruction and theft, extortion and hacking, and revenue lost from network intrusion or interruption.

Notification expenses such as printing, mailing, credit monitoring, and call center support may be included in a policy, along with third-party cyber liability coverage for vendors and partners. The CFO or other finance stakeholder can offer invaluable assistance in assessing the necessity and cost of updating insurance coverage.

9.8.3.3 Marketing and Public Relations

The chief marketing officer (CMO) is the person best qualified to help mitigate brand and reputational damage that can follow a data breach. By collaborating with the PR team or crisis management firm, the CMO can oversee content development for press releases, blog and website updates, and victim notification letters. Monitoring and responding to media coverage and arranging spokesperson interviews will also fall to members of the CMO's team.

Since the marketing department may already have the expertise and infrastructure in place to support large-scale mailings, the CMO could divert resources necessary to facilitate the notification process. In support of the effort, the team may also:

- Suggest direct marketing best practices to maximize notification letter open rates

- Perform address/database hygiene to improve breach notification delivery and response rates

- Analyze media coverage and report relevant developments to the response team

- Draft scripts for the incident response call center

- Develop customer retention and win-back campaigns to minimize churn and encourage loyalty

Marketers are expert communicators, especially skilled at researching and crafting highly targeted, consumer-driven messaging. Marketing can work with management and PR teams to establish and maintain a positive, consistent message during both the crisis and the post-breach notification.

Direct mail expertise may also prove beneficial in supporting the data-breach response. Depending on organization size, marketing may control the physical infrastructure to help launch and manage a high-volume email or letter notification outreach. Gaining internal agreement on the post-breach allocation of marketing resources is an essential element of breach response planning.

When a data breach occurs, and response teams are thrust into the fray regardless of the severity, PR and communications stakeholders quickly assume positions on the front lines, preparing for the response to potential media inquiries and coordinating internal and external status updates.

Among their chief roles is to oversee the preparation and dissemination of breach-related press releases, interviews, videos and social media content. As the crisis develops, they also work to ensure message accuracy and consistency and to minimize leaks of false or inaccurate information.

During and after a breach, PR and communications teams closely monitor online and offline coverage, analyzing what's being said and to what degree negative publicity is shaping public opinion. Resulting analysis and recommendations are shared among key stakeholders and used to adapt or refine PR messaging.

9.8.3.4 Customer Care

In the aftermath of a breach, customer service can recommend ways of using internal sources to serve the needs of breach victims and identify an appropriate outsourced partner. This stakeholder is also likely to work with others to coordinate the release of breach-related communications with call center readiness and activities.

Given the customer service training and experience of most call center teams, using existing staffing and assets to address breach-related inquiries may be a viable time- and cost-saving option for some companies. If an outsourced provider is retained to answer incoming calls, the customer service executive can play a crucial role in determining acceptable service levels, reporting duties and necessary service-representative training.

As part of their normal duties, customer care reps are trained to remain calm when confronted and to defuse potentially volatile encounters before they escalate. Such training, along with experience working and delivering scripted messages in a pressure-filled environment, can enable deployment of these team members to effectively handle breach-related call traffic.

Using internal resources in this manner, however, could potentially degrade service quality for other incoming service calls, so the prospect of leveraging existing resources to minimize breach response expenditures may only be attractive for certain organizations.

In companies where using in-house employees to answer breach-related calls is not an option, the executive of customer service should consider hiring experienced outsourcers to handle call overflow or perhaps manage the entire initiative.

9.8.3.5 Business Development

In the hands of a skilled sales or BD executive, high-value relationships can flourish for many years. Because of their unique association with customers and the bond of trust built carefully over time, BD decision makers are often asked to notify key accounts when their data has been breached. Receiving unfavorable news from a trusted friend and partner may lessen the impact and mitigate any potential backlash, such as a loss of confidence or flight to a competitor.

After obtaining the facts from IT, legal, PR or other internal teams, the BD stakeholder should contact the account and carefully explain what happened. Accuracy and transparency are essential. The stakeholder should stick to the known facts and under no circumstances speculate about or downplay any aspect of the breach.

Whenever possible, updates or special instructions regarding the breach should be promptly delivered by the stakeholder in charge of the account. This will provide reassurances that someone with executive authority is proactively engaged in safeguarding the account's interests and security.

9.8.3.6 Outside Resources

In addition to the support of internal functional leaders, a successful response may depend heavily on the aid of outside specialists retained to manage notification, call center and breach remediation activities. It is a best practice to negotiate agreements with experienced breach response providers prior to having to respond to an incident.

Professional forensic firms prepare themselves to deploy at a moment's notice. Once on the scene, investigators work closely with the organization's IT group to isolate compromised systems, contain the damage, preserve electronic evidence, establish a chain of custody, and document any actions taken.

Depending on the type of evidence uncovered, the affected organization may need to confer with outside counsel regarding its legal obligations. Breach definition and applicable reporting requirements usually depend on a variety of state and federal laws and international regulations, as well as the compromised organization's industry. Healthcare, for example, is subject to a different set of regulations than non-healthcare businesses. With so many variables influencing the notify/don't notify decision, advice from an experienced breach or privacy attorney can prove invaluable in meeting legal obligations and mitigating unnecessary costs.

As the forensic and legal analysis concludes, the decision whether to notify affected parties must be made. If notification is indicated, the incident response plan must be activated and "go-live" preparations quickly initiated. While the organization's focus shifts to executing the incident response plan, it is also important to continue addressing the cause of the breach.

Whether through training employees, replacing equipment, installing new software, adding staff, creating a new oversight position, or replacing the responsible vendor, some action must be taken, and quickly. The situation that led to the breach should not be allowed to continue unchecked, or the entire costly exercise may be repeated unnecessarily.

9.8.3.6.1 Print Vendors

A reputable print provider, for example, can be invaluable in leveraging its equipment and assets to produce, stuff, mail and track large volumes of letters. The print vendor may also guide the breach response team leader and appropriate support staff through the notification effort's many technical details. Important but less obvious support activities such as gathering logos, sample signatures, letter copy, and address files must also be completed as production and delivery deadlines approach.

9.8.3.6.2 Call Center

Once notification letters are delivered, recipients will begin calling and emailing the organization to inquire about the event and its impact on their lives. In situations where projected call volume is large enough for call center outsourcing, it is crucial that the team leader fully understand the vendor's overall capabilities. As soon as possible, agreements should be reached and the timeline set for training and assignment of agents, call-routing programming, message recording, preparation of service level agreements (SLAs) and call center reporting.

9.8.3.6.3 Remediation Providers

Depending on the nature of the information compromised, breached organizations may choose to engage remediation providers to reduce consumers' risk of fraud or identity theft. This may include a third-party service to monitor credit activity. The service should be offered free to the consumer and include, at minimum: daily monitoring and alerts of activity from all three national credit bureaus, identity theft insurance, and fraud resolution services. In some cases, supplemental services, such as internet scanning (for compromised information), may also be deployed to help protect consumers.

9.8.3.7 Union Leadership Role During an Incident

In preparation for a breach, union stakeholders should identify appropriate contacts within the organization and become familiar with its overall breach response plan. Specifically, they should know the roles, responsibilities and sequence of events to be taken by other nonunion stakeholders and response teams.

After a breach occurs, the primary roles for the union stakeholder are communication and coordination. Working with IT, HR or PR executives, the union steward may oversee the use of electronic communication channels, such as social media or union intranet or website, to provide members with timely updates and instructions. If member directories and databases are supplied ahead of time, marketing and call center teams can notify or update members directly through mail, email or phone calls.

9.8.3.8 President, Chief Executive Officer

One of the first and arguably most critical steps taken by the top executive is to promptly allocate the funds and manpower needed to resolve the breach. Having resources readily available helps teams quickly contain and manage the threat and lessen its overall impact.

In the period immediately after a breach, PR or communications teams will handle most of the media interaction. At some point, however, top executives could be called upon to publicly comment on the breach's cause or status. As with any organization attempting to manage a crisis, accuracy, authenticity and transparency are essential. Regular status updates from IT and legal, as well as coaching support from PR/ communications can prepare the president/CEO for scrutiny from a potentially hostile media corps.

When addressing the public, executives would do well to follow messaging recommendations set forth by the communications team. This helps ensure message consistency and reduces the risks of speaking in error or going off topic. The CEO, supported by the privacy team, might also be well-advised to get in contact with the responsible data protection authorities or regulators to discuss the incident and assure them that the breach is being handled from the top down. With personal information exposed, peoples' lives and even livelihoods are at risk. Therefore, language and tone used to address the public should always be chosen with great care. The sensitivity with which an organization responds to a breach and executives' actions during the event will affect how quickly the organization's brand trust and customer relations are restored afterward.

9.8.3.9 Board of Directors

The board is responsible for ensuring that a company is well run and focuses on ensuring that the company properly handles risk exposure. During an incident, company personnel and management will find themselves in frequent communication with the board. The board will ask questions about how an incident is being handled and whether the company is properly mitigating its risks.

9.9 Investigating an Incident

Breach investigation is a subset of breach response and occurs once breach investigators have concluded that sensitive information has been compromised. Professional forensic investigators can capture forensic images of affected systems, collect and analyze evidence, and outline remediation steps. During an investigation, on the containment side, the focus is on isolating compromised systems, containing the damage, and documenting any actions taken. On the legal side, the focus is on determining whether the event constitutes a "breach" as defined by the relevant laws, preserving electronic evidence, and establishing a chain of custody.

9.9.1 Containment

During the investigation phase of an incident, containment will be top of mind for the IT/information security team. The need to prevent further loss by taking appropriate steps is critical. These include securing physical areas and blocking bad actors' access to impacted data. The approach to these issues, however, needs to be balanced with the legal steps discussed in the next section.

Another part of containment is fixing the vulnerabilities that allowed the bad actor to access the systems in the first place. After ensuring any breach is contained, begin analyzing vulnerabilities and addressing third parties that might have been involved. Where appropriate, it may be necessary to share learnings, but this should be done in conjunction with the legal steps discussed in the next section. Factors to consider include:

- **Service providers**. Were they involved? Is there a need to change access privileges? What steps do they need to take to prevent future breaches? How can you verify they have taken these steps?

- **Network segmentation**. Ensure your segmentation plan was effective in containing the breach.

9.9.2 The Importance of Privilege

When investigating an incident, a company will want to make sure that its investigation and related communications and work product are protected by attorney-client privilege. Attorney-client privilege protects any communication between a lawyer and their client made for the purpose of giving or obtaining legal advice. The attorney work product doctrine protects documents or analyses made by a lawyer or at the direction of a lawyer in anticipation of litigation. A company should involve its attorneys as soon as it discovers a breach has occurred and ensure that the attorneys are directing the investigation for the purpose of legal advice or in anticipation of litigation. (CC'ing an attorney on an email is not enough to create privilege.) It is better to have the process directed by outside counsel than by inside counsel, because courts have in some instances ruled that there was no privilege where inside counsel appeared to be acting in a business rather than a legal capacity. A proper investigation may generate communications and documents containing facts and opinions that reflect badly on the company, or sensitive materials such as trade secrets. An investigation directed by counsel will maintain privilege so the company has the freedom to perform a thorough and effective investigation into the incident without fearing that the communications and documents created during that process will be used against it in later litigation.

9.9.3 Notification and Cooperation with Insurer

After a cyber incident, a company should notify all its insurance providers, because there may be coverage under more than just a standalone cyber policy. After notification, the company should receive a coverage letter from the insurer outlining the scope of coverage. Depending upon the policy, the insurer may require the company to use the insurer's preferred service providers during the investigation. The costs of breach response including notification, credit monitoring, PR and data recovery can add up quickly. Accordingly, it is important for companies to seek ongoing updates on the status of their coverage levels.

9.9.4 Credit Card Incidents and Card Schemes

Companies that have contracted with credit card companies to accept credit card payments must notify those credit companies in case of a breach. The contract should be consulted because it is likely to contain specific requirements not only about notification but also about post-breach procedures and cooperation with the credit company.

9.9.5 Third-Party Forensics

It may be necessary to engage outside forensics vendors in a complex breach. To ensure the investigation is privileged, those vendors should be engaged by the attorneys (preferably by outside counsel) rather than the company. Furthermore, to the extent the company is insured, it should check with the insurer in case the insurer requires the company to use particular vendors. The engagement letter with the vendors should specify that their work is undertaken at the direction of counsel as "work for hire" for the purpose of providing legal advice, and all documents and communications with the vendor should be labeled confidential and proprietary.

9.9.6 Involve Key Stakeholders During Investigations

Think carefully about how it is most appropriate to involve key stakeholders. What is the culture of your company? What are the legal and practical risks in your situation of involving large groups in potentially sensitive matters? In some cases, daily meetings with your core response team will be needed. There may also need to be some reporting out to other stakeholders, especially company leadership.

9.10 Reporting Obligations and Execution Timeline

Not all breaches require notification. There are various types of notification requirements to regulators and affected individuals. If data was encrypted, or if an unauthorized individual accidentally accessed but didn't misuse the data, potential harm and risk can be minimal and companies may not need to notify (based on applicable laws). Notification may be required even without harm to an individual. Coordinating with legal counsel to understand notification obligations is critical.

Breach-reporting obligations for legal compliance vary by jurisdiction, but tend to adhere to certain principles, including harm prevention, collection limitation, accountability, and monitoring and enforcement. The legal team will determine, based on the facts, whether the situation constitutes a breach as defined by relevant laws such that notification is necessary.

If notification is needed, it must occur in a timely manner. (The specific time frame is often dictated under the relevant statutes.) To best accomplish notification, a timeline to guide the execution and administration of breach resolution activities is critically helpful. Close coordination among internal and external stakeholders will also help ensure that all plan elements are executed in the proper sequence.

No strategy is bulletproof, and no timeline perfect. But the crucial execution phase of the incident response plan is particularly susceptible to setbacks if realistic, properly sequenced timelines are not observed.

Because of organizations' vastly differing cultural, political and regulatory considerations, it is usually not practical to prescribe a rigid, one-size-fits-all breach event timeline. There is value, however, in including some or all the following communication tactics when formulating a breach response.

9.10.1 Notification Requirements and Guidelines

Escalation refers to the internal process whereby employees alert supervisors about a security-related incident, who in turn report the details to a predefined list of experts—typically the privacy office—which will then engage IT, information security, facilities or HR. Notification is the process of informing affected individuals that their personal data has been breached.

> *During the management of a privacy incident, it is imperative that all internal communications are locked down so that inaccurate or incomplete details regarding the incident are not sent around the organization. The incident response team should be responsible for all internal communications regarding the incident; these communications should only be forwarded to staff on a need-to-know basis.*

Many statutes prescribe specific time frames for providing notification—either to impacted individuals and/or relevant regulators. The legal requirements change regularly. For planning purposes, however, it is enough to know that when investigating an incident, time is of the essence. Timing is even more critical once the incident has been confirmed to be a breach. Organization privacy professionals and those charged with incident response planning and notification should be intimately familiar with the prevailing notification requirements and guidelines and should work with qualified legal counsel to assist in making the legal determination about the need to give notice.

> *Incident response teams should always confirm requirements with legal counsel experienced in data privacy litigation prior to initiating or forgoing any notification campaign.*

Because of the potential consequences to the organization and to those whose data has been exposed, organizations must quickly initiate the notification process. This includes verifying addresses; writing, printing and mailing notification letters; setting up a call center; and arranging support services such as identity theft protection for affected individuals.

In the United States, some states mandate that notification letters contain specific verbiage or content, such as toll-free numbers and addresses for the three major credit bureaus, the FTC and a state's attorney general. Multiple state laws may apply to one breach, and notification may be delayed if law enforcement believes it would interfere with an ongoing investigation.

The notification deadline weighs heavily, in addition to the public scrutiny and already stressful ordeal of a data breach. Mishandling notifications can lead to severe consequences, including fines and other unbudgeted expenses. For extra support, some companies enlist the services of a third-party breach resolution provider to assist with notification, call-handling and credit-monitoring offers. Lining up providers in advance can sometimes reduce response times and related costs. Coordinating with your legal counsel—who will be familiar with a wide range of providers—as well as your insurance carrier (if you have insurance) is important in making these assessments.

9.10.2 Internal Announcements

Attempting to keep employees from learning of a data loss is neither prudent nor possible. On the contrary, transparency is typically paramount to maintaining integrity and credibility. When a breach occurs, in most situations all employees should receive properly worded communications about the event, along with specific guidelines and prohibitions about externally disseminating information. Employees should be told who the designated press contact is. When it comes to external breach inquiries, employees should always defer to those authorized to speak about the incident and not provide information themselves.

Internal breach announcements should be timed to avoid conflict with other organizational initiatives and to avoid negative legal exposure. To minimize the chance of leaks, align messaging, and demonstrate transparency, these announcements should also be delivered at the same time as external statements.

A breach may affect an organization's real or perceived financial viability, so the HR team should prepare to address a range of employee concerns. How these concerns should be addressed must be considered in light of a company's legal risks and exposures. If an event has occurred but does not affect employees directly, the following activities may help supplement the internal announcement process:

- Creation, approval and posting of employee-only FAQs

- Response training for HR personnel and call center staff

- Creation, approval and distribution of explanatory letter, email or intranet communications

9.10.3 External Announcements

The creation and release of external communications should be closely coordinated with the call center, in connection, of course, with legal counsel. In addition to notification letters and press releases, other external strategies and tactics may be deployed to announce and manage breach communications. Among the most important of these is to engage a professional crisis management or communications firm (if none are available internally) and designate a senior, media-trained executive as the organization's spokesperson.

Talking points should be developed as quickly as possible, so the spokesperson may confidently address the media. For consistency, foundational message points can be used to create content for press releases, intranets, the organization's website, and FAQ sheets for call centers. A dedicated toll-free number should be secured and routed to the correct call center to properly handle incoming calls.

While there's no single correct way to communicate about a breach, messaging should always be consistent. Potential consequences of inconsistent messaging include public misunderstandings and assumptions, legal liability issues, loss of trust and consumer confidence, and evidence of poor planning. Organizations should also consider call center FAQ review and training, staffing-level assessment to ensure adequate coverage.

9.10.4 Regulator Notifications

Legal counsel should provide guidance on which state, federal or international regulatory agencies require notification in the event of a data breach. In many instances in the United States, it is appropriate to contact the state attorney general and, in some cases, the FTC. In the healthcare industry, the Department of Health and Human Services (DHHS) may need to be notified as well. Notification to these agencies would be determined on a case-by-case basis, depending on the size and scope of the data breach; work with your legal counsel with data breach experience to provide such notices.

9.10.5 Letter Drops

Letters and emails are the most common forms of breach notification. As organizations decide to notify, the need to meet specific deadlines in accordance with applicable laws while working within the constraints of complex production and delivery processes can be unwieldy and difficult to reconcile.

Unlike outputting documents from a computer, industrial-level printing requires a great deal of preparation and quality control. Verifying mailing file completeness, format consistency, and age of mailing list data can add days to the production timeline.

Moreover, changing content during production or delivering assets (e.g., logos, signatures, copy) after specified deadlines can unnecessarily delay notification and burn precious days in an already accelerated schedule.

Here are some time-proven methods for ensuring a more efficient process:

- If appropriate, establish a secure data transfer channel

- Create letter copy and put it into Microsoft Word or another preferred format

- Obtain any necessary content approvals from the compliance and/or legal team

- Send usable data files to the print shop, including a properly formatted logo and electronic signature

- Supply a return address for undeliverable mail

- Review final letter layout for a legible, aesthetically pleasing appearance

When planning letter drops, remember that a data breach may also involve criminal activity and, therefore, law enforcement personnel. If officials determine that the notification will impede their investigation or threaten national security, delays can be expected.

9.10.6 Call Center Launches

Call centers normally in place have the infrastructure, policies and procedures needed to seamlessly switch from providing general customer service to answering breach-related calls. For a switch to be successful, proper preparation for every call center component is required. Adequately staffing the incident response team is one particularly critical consideration.

To increase headcount, temp agencies or outsourcers may be retained. The next steps are drafting phone scripts (sometimes in multiple languages), conducting call-handling training, and recording a message for the call tree. A dedicated toll-free number should be assigned and a call escalation process identified. Other preparations may include:

- Creating, approving and uploading email templates
- Training the quality assurance team on the details of the initiative
- Pulling and analyzing reports
- Monitoring call levels to determine staffing needs

9.10.7 Remediation Offers

Besides trying to protect incident victims' identities, companies tend to offer remediation services to soften the blow of a breach. If a remediation offer is made, the organization should facilitate the dialog between the parties involved, which typically include the credit-monitoring provider, letter print shop, and call center.

As a best practice, the notification letter should feature a full description of the remediation product, enrollment instructions, and a customer service phone number or email address. An activation code, by which the recipient may redeem the remediation product, should also be included. To assure close collaboration between the three groups, the following steps are highly recommended:

Remediation Organization

- Create one activation code per affected person for inclusion in notification letters
- Provide a full product description to the printer and the call center vendor, along with a toll-free number and an enrollment website URL
- Launch and test the website for enrollments
- Ramp up and train internal call center staff to enable phone enrollments and answer product questions
- Approve the final letter copy as it pertains to the accuracy of the offer details

Print Shop

- Obtain product description and activation codes from the remediation firm
- Merge product copy and activation codes into notification letters
- Print and mail letters according to agreed-upon standards and timelines

Call Center

- Receive product description and, as appropriate, train internal staff on basic product questions

- Determine and institute call transfer procedures between the vendor call center, remediation firm and affected organization

9.10.8 Progress Reporting

There is some debate about the level and type of progress reporting that is needed for an incident. Keep in mind that every situation is different. That said, making sure the incident team is well-informed and moving toward a unified goal is critical.

For complex or large-scale data breaches where notification is required (as determined by legal), there will be a significant number of letters mailed, calls received, and credit-monitoring enrollments. Keeping track of this information and being prepared to report up (or down) is important, and having a strong reporting structure plays a pivotal role in distilling the chaotic flow of reports into a clearer, more manageable stream.

You will need to give different types of reports to different stakeholders based on their need to know. Regardless of audience, progress reporting during the breach recovery period should focus on the question, "What data do they need, and when do they need it?"

During the breach notification period, the incident team may be called upon to provide metrics about how the event is being received by affected individuals, the press, regulators and the public generally. Requests may come from company leadership, the board, impacted departments, or even regulators who are closely watching the company. Typically, stakeholders will want weekly updates, although in some circumstances daily reports are requested.

The type of reporting and frequency should always be customized to each individual event. When putting together a reporting plan, keep in mind who is asking, what they need to know, and legal issues of privilege and risk. The answers to these questions will inform the format of the reporting content and structure.

During the active notification period, mail drops should be reviewed at least daily to ensure alignment with approved delivery deadlines. Additionally, mailing and call center activities should be closely coordinated to ensure response staffing levels are optimal. In situations where victims receive credit activity monitoring or other remediation, it may be beneficial to track enrollments and customer escalations daily for at least the first few weeks.

In the first days or weeks (depending on the severity of the incident), senior management may request briefings on the developments daily. Similarly, the PR group will often track daily breach-related news coverage to confirm that the organization's event narrative is being interpreted as intended. To mitigate public backlash, clarifying responses to inaccuracies or negative press should be prepared and practiced in advance.

Investors and other external stakeholders will naturally want to keep abreast of all breach-related developments. If the organization is publicly traded, a good practice is to update senior management at least weekly for the first few months after breach notification.

Regular reviews should be scheduled to update functional leaders, senior managers and other key stakeholders about the status and impact of the incident response effort. A breach's effects on employee productivity and morale should not be underestimated, so keeping workers informed about how the incident is being handled is always a top priority.

9.11 Recovering from a Breach

9.11.1 Response Evaluation and Modifications

Incident response can be tested with a variety of scenarios. But even a well-written plan can falter when the theory behind it collides with realities on the ground. As teaching tools, real-life breaches are far superior to hypothetical scenarios, so lessons learned from all incidents must afterward be captured, recorded and incorporated into the plan.

Once the initial chaos of a breach has subsided, the affected organization should carefully evaluate its incident response plan. Even the most well-thought-out responses can benefit from the lessons learned after a live event.

Among the most beneficial questions to answer about the response are:

- Which parts of the process clearly worked as intended?

- Which worked only after some modification?

- Which did not work at all?

- What did the team do exceptionally well? What didn't go well?

- Were any unforeseen complications encountered? How could they have been avoided?

- How well was the team prepared for the unexpected?

- How realistic were the plan's response timelines?

- What was the difference between actual and budgeted costs?

- Was the team sufficiently staffed?

- Were all relevant parties part of the team?

- What could be learned and what be improved upon for the next potential breach?

9.11.2 Calculating and Quantifying the Costs

While many breach-related costs can be identified and tallied using actual invoices, others are less apparent. Lost business opportunities and damage to brand equity are examples of costs that may affect the bottom line for years following a breach. Table 9-3 includes typical categories of breach-related expenses in cases where costs can be traced to specific activities.

Table 9-3: Breach-Related Expenses

Expense	Description
Legal Costs	
Punitive Costs	Fines, lawsuits and other penalties stemming from negligence in preventing or improperly responding to the breach
Internal Costs	
Outside Counsel	Legal review of the organization's contractual and regulatory obligations after a breach; may include defense costs if litigation results
Crisis Management/PR	Experts to help the organization craft and deliver cohesive, properly timed and customer-friendly communications about the incident
Forensic Investigators	Specialists to confirm, contain and eliminate the cause of the breach and determine the size, scale and type of records affected
Call Center Support	Staffing, training and support of the customer care team responsible for handling calls and emails related to the incident and its aftermath

Expense	Description
Equipment Replacement and Security Enhancements	Equipment changes, system upgrades and physical security improvements to mitigate the current breach and prevent future incidents
Insurance	Retention (deductible) payments and fee increases associated with the breach
Card Replacement	The cost of issuing new cards (in incidents when credit card numbers have been compromised)
Employee Training	Educational activities intended to improve upon previous programs that facilitated the breach
Remediation Costs	
Victim Notification	Creation and delivery of letters, emails, web pages and other methods/channels to notify affected individuals about the incident
Remediation Offers	Provision of services such as credit monitoring, fraud resolution and identity theft insurance to breach victims
Victim Damages	Costs related to correcting damages incurred by breach victims
Intangible Costs	
Customer Retention	Marketing campaigns designed to prevent customer attrition and win back lost business following an incident
Lost Revenue and Stock Value	Reductions in stock price, lost customers and other revenue decreases directly related to the loss
Opportunity Costs	Lost productivity and revenues, as employees suspend regularly assigned tasks to assist with breach response

According to the Ponemon Institute, the probability of a data breach in a 24-month period is almost 28 percent.[13] The numbers shown in Table 9-4 can be helpful when a privacy manager is attempting to conduct a cost-benefit analysis or get buy-in or budget from organizational leadership for breach preparedness measures. Several factors can affect the per-capita cost of a data breach—both positively and negatively. Knowing this can help organizations prioritize their spending to mitigate potential costs of a breach.

Table 9-4: Average Cost Saved per Record in the Event of a Breach[14]

Incident response team	+$14.00
Extensive use of encryption	+$13.10
Employee training	+$9.30
Business continuity management (BCM) involvement	+$9.30
Participation in threat-sharing	+$8.70
Artificial intelligence platform	+$8.20
Use of security analytics	+$6.90
Extensive use of data loss protection (DLP)	+$6.80
Board-level involvement	+$6.50
CISO appointed	+$6.50
Data classification schema	+$5.10
Insurance protection	+$4.80
CPO appointed	+$1.80
Provision of ID protection	-$1.20
Consultants engaged	-$3.70
Rush to notify	-$4.90
Extensive use of internet-of-things (IoT) devices	-$5.40
Lost or stolen devices	-$6.50
Extensive use of mobile platforms	-$10.00
Compliance failures	-$11.90
Extensive cloud migration	-$11.90
Third-party involvement	-$13.40

NOTE: These figures indicate money saved; e.g., having an employee training program saves, on average, $9.30 per record in the event of a data breach.[15]

9.12 Benefiting from a Breach

While no organization would choose to experience a data breach, failures breed opportunity for organizational change and growth. How can you ensure you walk away from a breach better prepared for the future? Be sure to conduct a breach or incident response review, or a post-incident assessment. At minimum, review these items:

- Staffing and resourcing
- Containment, including timing and processes

- The C-suite commitment, including signoff on new measures and allocation of resources
- Clarity of roles of the response team and others
- The notification process for individuals, regulatory bodies and others

Your organization's objectives for breach management will likely change after an incident. Take this time to renew your funding, focus and commitment.

9.13 Summary

A proper breach response plan provides guidance for meeting legal compliance, planning for incident response, and handling privacy incidents. An organization needs to be prepared to respond to its internal and external stakeholders—including regulators. The privacy professional and related team members need to be prepared to respond appropriately to each incoming request to reduce organizational risk and bolster compliance with regulations.

Endnotes

1 Ponemon Institute, *2018 Cost of Data Breach Study*, p. 3, July 2018, https://public.dhe.ibm.com/common/ssi/ecm/55/en/55017055usen/2018-global-codb-report_06271811_55017055USEN.pdf (accessed November 2018).

2 *Id.*, p. 19.

3 *Id.*

4 U.S. Department of Labor, Bureau of Labor Statistics (2017), https://www.bls.gov/news.release/archives/union2_01192018.pdf (accessed November 2018).

5 AFL-CIO, www.aflcio.org/About/AFL-CIO-Unions (accessed November 2018).

6 *State of the Phish Report*, p. 3, Wombat Security, https://www.wombatsecurity.com/blog/2018-state-of-the-phish-phishing-data-insights-and-advice (accessed November 2018).

7 *Id.*, p. 6.

8 *Id.*, p. 7.

9 *The 2016 Continuity Insights and KPMG LLP: Global Business Continuity Management (BCM) Program Benchmarking Study*, p. 10, https://assets.kpmg.com/content/dam/kpmg/kz/pdf/2016-CI-KPMG-Report.pdf (accessed November 2018).

10 *Id.*

11 *Id.*

12 *Id.*, p.13.

13 Ponemon Institute, *2018 Cost of Data Breach Study*, IBM, p. 1, July 2018, https://public.dhe.ibm.com/common/ssi/ecm/55/en/55017055usen/2018-global-codb-report_06271811_55017055USEN.pdf (accessed November 2018).

14 *Id.*, p. 22.

15 *Id.*, p.22.

CHAPTER 10

Monitoring and Auditing Program Performance

Tracy Kosa

10.1 Metrics

This section will assist the privacy professional with general best practices for identifying, defining, selecting, collecting and analyzing metrics specific to privacy.

With advances in technology and the corresponding legal obligations, organizations must ensure proper protections are in place and functioning optimally. Tracking and benchmarking through performance measurement is critical to ensure both currency and value. Products, services and systems that cannot provide value or protect data must change; otherwise, loss of information through breaches, noncompliance with regulatory requirements, and/or data misuse may result in loss of consumer and investor confidence as well as financial and reputational harm.

Performance measurement is used by organizations to inform different audiences (e.g., leadership, management, employees) about operations. Measurement systems must be easy to understand, repeatable, and reflective of relevant indicators. A metric is a unit of measurement that should be as objective as possible. Metrics can provide data that helps to answer specific questions. As a basic rule, a metric must add value by accurately reflecting the state of business objectives and goals. The same logic applies to privacy programs and operations: An objective can be broad-based, but a goal should be structured in a way that is measurable. For example, an objective could be to develop privacy notices, while a goal could be to provide privacy notices to 100 percent of the customer base within a specific time frame. Metrics like these have the added benefit of helping to increase the understanding of necessary protections to meet privacy obligations.

While metrics assist leaders with tracking specific privacy objectives and goals, there are other ways they help the entire organization understand and implement effective privacy policies. First, by normalizing privacy, metrics help conversations about the privacy regime be meaningful to key stakeholders, who may not be familiar with the concept or profession. Second, the use of metrics can help eliminate terminology and jargon, making it easier for decisions to be made at the program and operational level with colleagues in different roles and specializations. Third, metrics consider but are not based on a specific technology or application (e.g., iPhone versus Android, or Facebook versus Twitter). Fourth, using metrics advances the maturity of privacy programs and operations, which is critical now as regulations and expectations are on the rise. To be beneficial, metrics must be described clearly; otherwise, they may not represent similar value throughout an organization. Generic privacy metrics should be developed for different processes, e.g., collection, responses to data subject inquiries, use, retention, disclosure, incidents, training, review coverage, risk and assessments. Once defined, that data should be captured regularly to enable trending-over-time analysis. It can also help demonstrate the return on investment (ROI) of the privacy program, overall program maturity, and privacy resource utilization—and thus feed in to overall business resiliency metrics.

That said, more metrics do not equate to more value. Metric identification is difficult and must be done in consideration of what is both sustainable and scalable. Making informed decisions on the investment and application of privacy-enhancing technology and process improvements (e.g., automated reviews) is a challenge. Using the right metrics as key performance indicators (KPIs) can help the organization set and track multiple objectives and goals.

Start with identifying which metrics are critical to your organization, and why. For example, does X metric reflect your organization's need to adhere to new regulatory guidance? Or does it address a risk around vendor management? Consideration should include all layers of the organization to encourage the overall success and usefulness of any metric beyond the needs of the privacy professional, with group consensus for management and use.

10.1.1 Intended Audience

There are different audiences for different metrics. Relevant stakeholders are generally those who will use the data to view, discuss and make strategic decisions—or some combination of all three. There are no limits to both internal and external audiences, particularly in consideration of reporting requirements. For example, one metric may be useful for a board of directors, another for external auditors.

The difference in audience is based on level of interest, influence and responsibility for privacy as specified by the business objectives, laws and regulations, or ownership. Primary audiences generally include legal and privacy officers, including a data protection officer (DPO) as prescribed under the General Data Protection Regulation (GDPR), senior leadership, chief information officer (CIO), chief security officer (CSO), program managers, information system owner, information security officer (ISO), others considered users, and managers. Secondary audiences include the chief financial officer (CFO), training organizations, human resources (HR), inspectors general and Health Insurance Portability and Accountability Act (HIPAA) security officials. Tertiary audiences may include external watchdog groups, sponsors and shareholders. In healthcare, for example, audiences may include a HIPAA privacy officer, medical interdisciplinary readiness team (MIRT), senior executive staff, and covered entity workforce.

10.1.2 Metric Owner

Since metrics continue to change as the business objectives and goals evolve, an individual should be assigned to both champion and own the metric. A metric owner must be able to evangelize the purpose and intent of that metric to the organization. As a best practice, it is highly recommended that a person with privacy knowledge, training and experience perform this role to limit possible errors in interpretation of privacy-related laws, regulations and practices. It is not necessary that the metric owner be responsible for data collection or measurement.

The metric owner is its champion. They should know what is critical about the metric and how it fits in to the business objective. They should be responsible for monitoring process performance. In addition, the owner is accountable for keeping process documentation up to date, minimizing variance, and undertaking visualizations (e.g., flowcharts, graphs). Finally, the owner is responsible for performing regular reviews to determine if the metric is still effective and provides value, as well ensuring improvements are incorporated and maintained in the process.

10.1.3 Analysis

Once metrics have been collected, data analysis is conducted. Statistical methods ensure data is interpreted correctly. This step sometimes takes the most time due to the potentially large data set. Where possible, the privacy professional should consider use of automated tools or methods to gather, sort and report. Many software applications perform statistical and financial functions; some are open source, in the public domain, or freeware. There are also a number of commercial solutions for small to large organizations. Selection and use of any tool should always be based on organization requirements, budget or direction.

10.1.3.1 Trend Analysis

Trending, or trend analysis, is one of the easiest statistical methods to use for reporting data. This approach attempts to spot a pattern in the information as viewed over a period of time. There are many different statistical trending methods, including simple data patterns, fitting a trend (i.e., least-squares), trends in random data (i.e., data as a trend plus noise, or a noisy time series), and the goodness of fit (i.e., R-squared). Without going into formal statistics (i.e., defining mean, standard deviation, variance, linear trend, sample, population, signal and noise), the privacy professional can focus on looking for data patterns. For example, time series analysis shows trends in an upward or downward tendency, as in number of privacy breaches over time.

A second form of analysis is called cyclical component, which shows data over a time period focused on regular fluctuations. Measuring the number of privacy breaches in the month after an organization rolls out new privacy training, this analysis is focused on explaining any changes in the number reported as the distance from training increases.

Third is a type of analysis called irregular component, or noise. This analysis focuses on what is left over when the other components of the series (time and cyclical) have been accounted for. It is the most difficult to detect—an example would be the absence of privacy breaches.

10.1.3.2 Return on Investment

ROI is an indicator used to measure the financial gain or loss of a project or program in relation to its cost. Financial gains and losses are defined by the organization's leadership but can come from any of the stakeholders or data owners.

ROI analysis provides the quantitative measurement of benefits and costs, strengths and weaknesses of the organization's privacy controls. The data can be fixed or variable and represent a best attempt to form an economical risk assessment to determine the probability of a loss as well as the probable economic consequences, with the goal of maximizing the benefits of investments that generally do not generate revenue; rather, they prevent loss.

There are two considerations in developing the metric. First, the ROI of a given function must be related to the reason for implementing that function. Second, the value of the asset must be defined. In assessing value of an information asset, the privacy professional should consider how that changes over time—for example, the costs of producing (and reproducing) information, repercussions if the information is not available, and other factors such as harm to reputation or loss of confidence.

10.1.3.3 Business Resiliency

To the privacy professional, business resiliency is measured through metrics associated with data privacy, system outages and other factors as defined by the business case and organization objectives. If it exists, the organization's business continuity or disaster recovery office should be contacted to assist in the selection and use of data for this metric type, as it is the expert in this data type and organizational objectives.

Focusing solely on disasters will lead an organization to be defensive, but using a proactive approach enables the organization to "respond to an unexpected event more quickly and more cost effectively. In addition to disaster situations, a strong business resilience program can help your organization prepare for audits and demonstrate compliance with regulatory requirements."[1]

10.1.3.4 Program Maturity

The Privacy Maturity Model (PMM) is a well-established model that sets out maturity levels for privacy programs and operations.[2] Maturity is a useful metric because it focuses on a scale as opposed to an endpoint. For example, acceptable data privacy protections may be in place without being the "most mature." PMM uses five maturity levels described in Figure 10-1.

Figure 10-1: Privacy Maturity Levels[3]

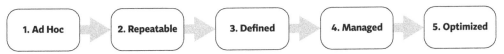

Maturity level one, "ad hoc," is used to describe a situation where the procedures or processes are generally informal, incomplete and inconsistently applied. "Repeatable," or maturity level two, similarly has procedures and processes, but they are not fully documented and do not cover all relevant aspects. Third, the "defined" level indicates that procedures and processes are fully documented, implemented and cover all relevant aspects. "Managed," or maturity level four, indicates that reviews are conducted to assess the effectiveness of the controls in place. The fifth and final level, "optimized," represents a level at which regular review and feedback are used to ensure continual improvement toward optimization of a given process. Each level builds on the previous one; for example, to reach maturity level three, all the requirements for levels one and two must have been met.

The PMM can be customized in many ways, and the authors provide a structure to identify where to start and what to document. Key startup activities include identifying a sponsor (e.g., the privacy officer), assigning responsibility for the project, and considering stakeholders/the oversight committee with nonprivacy representation (e.g., legal, audit, risk management). Once assessment of maturity has begun, it is important to be transparent about the process and results to ensure that identifiable risk and compliance issues are appropriately escalated.

An initial assessment can identify strengths and reveal weaknesses. Once the baseline assessment has been established, the organization can decide at which level of maturity it ultimately wants or needs to operate. Ideal maturity levels can be challenging to pinpoint. Note that "In developing the PMM, it was recognized that each organization's personal information privacy practices may be at various levels, whether due to legislative requirements, corporate policies or the status of the organization's privacy initiatives. It was also recognized that, based on an organization's approach to risk, not all privacy initiatives would need to reach the highest level on the maturity model."[4]

10.1.4 Metrics in Action: Reporting to the Board

A number of factors have contributed to the elevation of the privacy professional in organizations around the world, but perhaps none have been as influential as the GDPR and its "mandatory DPO." Suddenly, organizations processing large amounts of personal data not only must employ a DPO but ensure those DPOs report to "the highest management level" of the organizations.

For many organizations, that means the DPO must report to the board of directors itself—and if not to the board, then to the C-suite, which must then transfer that information up the corporate ladder.

In fact, in the 2018 *IAPP-EY Privacy Governance Report*, 78 percent of organizations said they report privacy matters to the board, and the privacy leader does the reporting themselves 37 percent of the time. The most common topic reported to the board, identified by 83 percent of respondents, is "status of compliance with the GDPR."

This is where metrics are vital to the privacy program. How can the DPO or other privacy leader demonstrate the status of compliance?

To answer this question, the IAPP undertook, in late 2018, the exercise of creating a template for a DPO report. To do this, it identified all the activities the GDPR mandates for the DPO and created metrics for demonstrating compliance.

The PowerPoint template is available at iapp.org/resources.

Of course, some of the metrics in the report are fairly basic: number of privacy staff, total privacy budget, number of products or services utilizing personal data, total number of data subjects about whom data is held, number of processors, and so forth. But it's important to be as granular as possible. What is the ratio of employees in compliance to those in legal, or the ratio of either to the number of employees as a whole? How many business processes use consumer data versus employee data?

While the board may not need this granularity, it's better to have it than not.

The GDPR also mandates operational activities that can be measured. How many data protection impact assessments have been conducted? How many data subject access requests have been received? How many complaints have been received? How many data security incidents have been discovered or reported? How many of those were elevated to notification of the data protection authority (DPA) or to notification of data subjects?

These activities might be tracked by month or by quarter so the organization can identify and demonstrate trends. A rising number of complaints could indicate a poorly performing program—or a need for more staff and budget. For many of these tasks, space is provided for documenting the amount of time and human resources needed to comply so that it can be easier to advocate for more help.

If data subject access requests are increasing, perhaps there's a trust issue with the business—and so public relations (PR) and marketing need to be more closely involved. While a DPO is independent from the business, it's still important that they advise the business about the amount of resources and activity needed from the business to comply with the GDPR.

The template can be adapted to any business; more or less emphasis can be placed on different data elements as they are more and less important to the business. For some organizations, data portability requests will be quite rare. Other such requests will need to be closely tracked as a potential threat to the bottom line.

Obviously, a DPO report is just one way to look at a privacy program and its performance, but it may be a useful way to assess what a DPO report might look like at your organization, whether or not you have a DPO mandated by the GDPR.

10.2 Monitor

This section refers to ongoing activities organizations undertake to control, manage and report risk associated with privacy management practices. Monitoring should be done to ensure that the organization is actually doing what they say they are doing—and what they are supposed to be doing. Monitoring should be continual, based on the organization's risk goals, and executed through defined roles and responsibilities that may include privacy, audit, risk and security personnel. Typical outcomes include compliance, increased awareness, transparency and credibility.

The privacy professional should identify the business-as-usual rhythms of the organization to understand how monitoring practices are used and maintained for privacy management and to validate that programs are being implemented in a manner consistent with the organization's privacy policies and standards. Without a formal process for monitoring privacy requirements, the organization cannot be reasonably assured that personal information is handled appropriately and aligned with the organization, compliance expectations, and policy requirements. A few other general benefits of monitoring include ensuring privacy program goals are achieved, detecting privacy failures early, and obtaining feedback for privacy program improvement.

10.2.1 Types of Monitoring

There are different types of monitoring for different business purposes.

10.2.1.1 Compliance

Compliance monitoring is focused on the collection, use and retention of personal information to ensure necessary polices and controls are in place for compliance. The degree of monitoring an organization needs depends on the sensitivity of the information collected, compliance risk factors, and industry requirements. There are four common approaches: self-monitoring, audit management, security/system management, and risk management. Compliance monitoring is essential for detecting and correcting violations, supporting enforcement actions and evaluating progress.

10.2.1.2 Regulation

Laws, regulations and requirements are constantly changing, so there is a need to monitor the changes and update policies accordingly. Defined roles and responsibilities will determine who owns which tasks, when updates can or should occur, and how to communicate them broadly.

Based on the size of the organization or the scope of regulatory activities, subscription services can be purchased to conduct this type of monitoring externally.

10.2.1.3 Environment

Internal and external environmental monitoring focus on vulnerabilities, which may include physical concerns, such as building access or visitor activities. It may address programmatic concerns, for example, a lack of awareness or training. Finally, it may address insider threats, such as sabotaging, modifying or stealing information for personal gain, or cybersecurity threats to information technology (IT) assets.

10.2.2 Forms of Monitoring

Use of different or multiple forms of monitoring should be considered for each organization and their program goals.

10.2.2.1 Tools

Active scanning tools for network and storage can be used to identify risks to personal information and to monitor for compliance with internal policies and procedures. For example, a scan result may find files with personal information are incorrectly stored on a network that is publicly accessible, thus proactively identifying a potential privacy breach.

10.2.2.2 Audit

Audits include internal and external reviews of people, processes, technology, finances and many other aspects of business functions. This topic will be further reviewed in Section 10.3.

10.2.2.3 Breaches

As discussed in Chapter 9, breach management practices are more important than ever before, driven by the laws and regulations of countries, states or provinces.[5] Tracking (particularly over time) the type of breach, severity and time to remediation is an important type of monitoring to determine if both training activities and program processes are sufficient.

10.2.2.4 Complaints

Complaint-monitoring processes track, report, document and provide resolutions of customer, consumer, patient, employee, supplier and other complaints. Tracking details about the type and origin (location) of complaints can provide early indicators of the potential for regulatory activity. (This topic is discussed further in Chapters 2, 6 and 9.)

10.2.2.5 Data Retention

Records management and data retention should meet legal and business needs for privacy, security and data archiving. In monitoring, looking for potential areas for risk present in retention schedules or practices, such as excessive collection, inadequate controls (access and use), or undue disclosure practices.[6]

10.2.2.6 Controls

Relying on an established set of privacy controls at the operational and program level, this type of monitoring is about assessing the design and efficacy of a given control set. Some governance, risk and compliance (GRC) tools may provide automated means to undertake some or all of these checks, right through to tracking remediation activity.

10.2.2.7 Human Resources

Human resources (HR) is responsible for ensuring privacy protections are in place for employee personal information across HR processes. Multinational organizations are required to meet local regulations and the privacy expectations of their employees in all countries in which they operate. While the employment contract provides overall employee consent for certain work-related activities, some workplace monitoring will require additional privacy considerations. For monitoring purposes, investigations related to compliance with security and privacy practices are of particular interest. (This topic is covered further in Chapter 2 and 9.)

10.2.2.8 Suppliers

Outsourcing of operations to suppliers (e.g., subcontractors, third parties) and the use of technology providers (e.g., cloud services) are guided by agreements, which should contain monitoring protection procedures. Supplier monitoring should include appropriate privacy and security requirements, as well as provider performance, to ensure compliance to contract specifications, laws and policies. In addition, you should monitor the security of mobile devices to confirm that personal information contained in those devices is adequately protected. (This topic is covered further in Chapter 4.)

10.3 Audit

Audits are an ongoing process of evaluating the effectiveness of controls throughout the organization's operations, systems and processes. While typically associated with accounting or finance, audits are now commonplace in IT. Generally concerned with process and technical improvements, audits can be used to identify the risks posed by vulnerabilities and weaknesses and provide opportunities to strengthen the organization.

Elements of the audit process in respect of privacy may happen simultaneously or in separate components depending on organizational requirements.

10.3.1 Definition

The purpose of a privacy audit is to determine the degree to which technology, processes and people comply with privacy policies and practices. Privacy audits help measure efficacy of privacy procedures, demonstrate compliance, increase the level of general privacy awareness, reveal gaps, and provide a basis for remediation planning.[7] Audits differ from assessments in that they are evidence-based. For more on assessments, see Chapter 4.

10.3.2 Rationale

Audits may be conducted either regularly, ad hoc, or on demand, depending on the purpose. Privacy audits provide evidence regarding whether privacy operations are doing what they were designed to do and whether privacy controls are correctly managed.

However, there are other reasons to perform audits. Audits are conducted when change occurs—whether that's policy degradation, system updates or maintenance, or some kind of security (or other) event. They are also triggered by user errors or accidents, security or privacy breaches, or requests from regulators, leadership or media. Other factors may include new categories of customers or acquisitions of new lines of business, changing priorities, new suppliers, new countries of operations, or risks identified through other business processes.

10.3.3 Phases

The auditor must have full authority to perform duties; otherwise, the tasks and actions may be challenged and delay the work. Stakeholders and corresponding roles and responsibilities should be defined before the audit begins. Stakeholders may include executive leadership, those who have related functional duties (security officer), and/or regulators.

Scoping the audit is critical to determine the types of personnel (e.g., employees, contractors, third parties) who are permitted to handle personal information. Once scoping is complete, the five-phase audit approach begins, as illustrated in Figure 10-2.[8]

Figure 10-2: Audit Lifecycle

The audit planning phase generally involves conducting a risk assessment, setting a schedule, selecting the right auditor, completing a pre-audit questionnaire, hosting an introductory meeting to prepare for the audit, and compiling a checklist. Once complete, the preparation phase requires confirming the schedule, preparing any additional checklists and sampling criteria, and finalizing the audit plan. The actual audit takes place in phase three, including meeting with stakeholders and business process owners and executing the functional goals of the audit.

Reporting is phase four: recording and reporting on noncompliance (providing records, categorizing instances as major or minor), drafting a formal audit report, and hosting a close-out meeting. Copies of the audit report should be distributed as appropriate. Specific report formats will vary, based on organization requirements, auditing methodologies, privacy framework and other factors. Ideally, the report will be a formal record of what was audited and when, insight into areas that comply (or do not), details to support the findings, and suggested corrective action and work estimates, among other topics.[9] Instances of noncompliance should be sufficiently documented to include facts and evidence. Findings should be communicated to all stakeholders along with risks, remediation plans and associated costs.

The final audit phase involves confirmation of the scope of remediation activities, scheduling those activities, and addressing any requirements around methodology. Once completed, the audit can be closed out entirely.

10.3.4 Types

There are three types of audits: first-party (internal), second-party (supplier) and third-party (independent). The frequency and type will vary based on resources, organizational culture, risk tolerance and demand.

First-party audits are generally used to support self-certifications; scope is based on resources and the current state of compliance. The self-certification process can provide the relevant facts, data, documentation and standards necessary to reflect consistent, standardized and valid privacy management that aligns to a particular privacy standard, guideline or policy. Like other audits, first-party audits will consider the organization's risk management culture, identify privacy risk factors, and evaluate control design and implementation.

Second-party audits reference the notion of supplier audits (covered in Chapter 4). When a data collector outsources activities related to personal information management, accountability for compliance is retained. Contract language should include specific privacy protections and regulatory requirements and be mapped to service-level agreements as if the supplier were part of the organization. The entity outsourcing must have the right to audit the supplier for evidence of these protections. To summarize, the purpose of the contract is to surface the requirements; the audit function provides evidence of that compliance.

Third-party audits are conducted by independent outside sources, typically under consent decree or regulatory request. They may align to various regional or industry frameworks such as the National Institute of Standards and Technology (NIST) or International Organization for Standardization (ISO). There are some advantages to these kinds of audits—they identify weaknesses of internal controls, make first-party audits more credible, and provide a level of expert recommendations. There are also a few disadvantages, mostly related to bringing in external parties: cost, scheduling, and the time it takes to get up to speed. Ultimately, when an independent authority attests to the efficacy of privacy controls, there is increased confidence that the organization's practices are an accurate reflection of its claims.

10.3.5 Review

The activities described in this section are not useful without time to analyze results. The audit process should have a trigger to signal the privacy officer to step back and evaluate the program, or (ideally), specific pieces of it.

10.4 Summary

This chapter started with a discussion of metrics and outlines how they can provide a baseline for evaluating projects and gauging their contribution over time as privacy technologies, processes and programs evolve. Metrics help privacy professionals communicate the value they add to the organization.

Yet metrics are just part of the puzzle; active ongoing monitoring helps to identify any gaps in privacy program function and provides a mechanism for program and policy optimization and scale. Auditing (whether first-, second- or third-party) can assess how well the program and controls are working together. Finally, communication about metrics, monitoring and audit activities combined helps to create greater awareness of the privacy program (internally and externally) and ensures flexibility to respond to environmental changes.

10.5 Glossary

Performance measurement: The process of formulating or selecting metrics to evaluate implementation, efficiency or effectiveness; the gathering of data and production of quantifiable output that describes performance.

Metrics: Tools that facilitate decision making and accountability through collection, analysis and reporting of data. They must be measurable, meaningful, clearly defined (with boundaries), and able to indicate progress and answer a specific question to be valuable and practical.

Metrics lifecycle: The processes and methods to sustain a metric to match the ever-changing needs of an organization.

Metric audience: Primary, secondary and tertiary stakeholders who obtain value from a metric.

Metrics owner: Process owner, champion, advocate and evangelist responsible for management of the metric throughout the metric lifecycle.

Endnotes

1 IBM, "Business Resilience: The Best Defense is a Good Offense," p. 3, January 2009, https://www-935.ibm.com/services/uk/en/it-services/Business_resilience_the_best_defence_is_a_good_offence.pdf (accessed November 2018).

2 AICPA/CICA, Privacy Maturity Model, March 2011, https://iapp.org/media/pdf/resource_center/aicpa_cica_privacy_maturity_model_final-2011.pdf (accessed November 2018).

3 *Id.*

4 *Id.*

5 Theodore J. Kobus III, "Data Breach Response: A Year in Review," December 27, 2011, *Data Privacy Monitor*, BakerHostetler, https://www.dataprivacymonitor.com/breach-notification/data-breach-response-a-year-in-review/ (accessed November 2018).

6 Ulrich Hahn, Ken Askelson and Robert Stiles, "Global Technology Audit Guide: Managing and Auditing Privacy Risks," Institute of Internal Auditors, p. 4, June 2006, https://www.interniaudit.cz/download/ippf/GTAG/gtag_5_managing_and_auditing_privacy_risks.pdf (accessed November 2018).

7 Bruce J. Bakis, "Mitre: How to conduct a privacy audit," June 6, 2007, Presentation for the 2007 New York State Cyber Security Conference, https://www.mitre.org/sites/default/files/pdf/HowToConductPrivacyAudit.pdf (accessed November 2018).

8 UK Information Commissioner's Office, A guide to ICO audits, September 2018, https://ico.org.uk/media/for-organisations/documents/2787/guide-to-data-protection-audits.pdf (accessed November 2018).

9 *Id.*

About the Contributors

Executive Editor and Contributor

Russell Densmore, CIPP/E, CIPP/US, CIPM, CIPT, FIP
Russell Densmore is the global privacy compliance program manager for Raytheon. He brings a multidisciplinary understanding to cybersecurity, digital forensics, enterprise risk management and privacy compliance with his more than 30 years of experience.

He is renowned for information security, cyber-forensic investigations, privacy program management, and physical security. He has been recognized by the U.S. attorney general and the Federal Bureau of Investigation for support against cybercriminals. He is a proven professional with a record of establishing and managing multiple cross-functional cybersecurity and privacy teams.

Densmore holds a BS from Regis University, where he graduated *magna cum laude* in computer information systems with a minor in computer networks. He has earned accreditation as a Certified Information Systems Security Professional (CISSP) and is currently obtaining a master of engineering degree in cybersecurity from George Washington University.

Contributors

Susan Bandi, CIPP/US, CIPM, CIPT, FIP
Susan Bandi serves as the global chief privacy officer and data protection lead for Monsanto/Bayer. With more than 25 years' IT experience, she has served in multiple leadership and executive roles responsible for application development, infrastructure, and information security. For the past 16 years, her focus has been on IT security, privacy, business continuity/disaster recovery and data governance. Prior to her work at Monsanto/Bayer, Bandi was the assistant vice president and chief information security officer (CISO)/chief privacy officer (CPO) for Enterprise Holdings, Inc.

She is experienced in providing thought leadership and implementing effective, comprehensive global solutions in the areas of enterprise risk management, data governance, data privacy, IT security and business continuity. She also serves as an adjunct professor in the Cybersecurity Master's Program at Washington University in St. Louis.

She is an active member of the IAPP, Executive Women in Privacy, Chief Privacy Council Board, The Future of Privacy Forum, ISACA, CISO Coalition and the FBI Citizen Academy. She also serves on the executive leadership team for the American Heart Association "Go Red" for Women Campaign.

João Torres Barreiro, CIPP/E, CIPP/US

João Torres Barreiro is global chief privacy officer for Willis Towers Watson based in London. He is a member of the European Advisory Board of the IAPP and a keynote speaker at universities and several privacy symposiums. Recently, Torres Barreiro was awarded the 2018 Data Leader Award on Data Protection and Information Management by *Information Age* magazine.

Before joining Willis Towers Watson, he was HCL Technologies chief privacy officer (CPO) and practiced as an attorney in law firms and as legal counsel at Celgene (Switzerland), IBM (Ireland), the European Medicines Agency (UK), and the Portuguese Ministry of Health (Portugal).

Torres Barreiro holds CIPP/US and CIPP/E certifications and has postgraduate qualifications in intellectual property law and pharma law.

Ron De Jesus, CIPP/A, CIPP/C, CIPP/E, CIPP/US, CIPM, CIPT, FIP

Ron De Jesus leads the privacy function at Tinder, Inc. and was responsible for operationalizing Tinder's GDPR strategy. He also manages the privacy program of all American dating apps at Match Group, including Tinder, Match.com, OKCupid, PlentyOfFish and Hinge.

Prior to Tinder, De Jesus served as the global privacy director for Tapestry, Inc., where he developed and implemented its first-ever global privacy program and led privacy compliance efforts for all Tapestry brands, including Coach, Stuart Weitzman and Kate Spade.

In 2013, he helped establish PwC's Data Protection & Privacy Practice in New York and consulted to major financial, retail, pharmaceutical and telecommunications clients nationwide. Before PwC, he consulted with Deloitte, where he conducted dozens of EU/Swiss-U.S. Safe Harbor assessments and privacy readiness reviews, designed functional privacy controls and managed registrations with EU data protection authorities (DPAs) for global clients. In his early career, Ron consulted for Anzen, Inc., a boutique

Canadian privacy consulting firm, where he led numerous privacy impact assessments for large health IT system implementations across Canada.

De Jesus was also privacy director for American Express Global Network Services, where he developed its privacy program, led its strategy to comply with the EU e-Privacy Directive, and served on the Amex Privacy Board.

Jonathan Fox, CIPP/US, CIPM

Jonathan Fox, director of privacy engineering and strategy and planning, is a member of Cisco's chief privacy office and coauthor of *The Privacy Engineer's Manifesto: Getting from Policy to Code to QA to Value* (ApressOpen, 2014).

With more than 17 years of privacy experience, Fox's principal areas of focus have been product development, government relations, mergers and acquisitions, and training. He is a CIPP/US and CIPM, and was a Certified Information Security manager (CISM).

Prior to Cisco, Fox was senior privacy engineer at Intel. His previous roles include director of data privacy, McAfee; director of privacy, eBay; deputy chief privacy officer for Sun Microsystems; and editor-in-chief of sun.com.

Fox frequently speaks at industry events and is a member of the IEEE P7002 Personal Data Privacy Working Group, the IAPP Privacy Engineering Section Forum Advisory Board, and the U.S. Technical Advisory Group for ISO/PC 317 Consumer protection: privacy by design for consumer goods and services.

Tracy Kosa

Dr. Tracy Ann Kosa is currently teaching privacy at Seattle University, conducting research at Stanford University, working in security at Google, and serving as the ombudsman for the AI Ethics Board for Axon. Kosa has previously held a number of privacy leadership roles at Microsoft, the Government of Ontario, and related technology agencies, where she has helped multiple teams pioneer measurement and assessment programs across their organizations as key components of corporatewide privacy functions.

Kosa has been active in technology ethics, privacy, and user trust across healthcare, education, finance and law enforcement sectors for 20 years. She specializes in interdisciplinary approaches to developing models, systems and processes that capture human values for computational purposes. She has specialized in privacy programs, technical solution design, privacy product development, incident response and breach notification with a focus on automation.

Kosa has been awarded degrees in computer science (PhD), ethics (MA), public policy (MA) and political science (Hons.BA).

Jon Neiditz, CIPP/E, CIPP/US, CIPM

Jon Neiditz co-leads the cybersecurity, privacy and data governance practice at Kilpatrick Townsend & Stockton LLP, which specializes in knowledge asset protection law.

Neiditz has been named a Cybersecurity Trailblazer by the *National Law Journal* and a Ponemon Fellow. He is listed as one of the Best Lawyers in America® both in information management law and in privacy and data security law and is recognized by Twitter as a person of influence in the world of data security.

One of the first lawyers to focus broadly on data governance and knowledge asset protection, Neiditz helps clients anticipate and obviate information risks, appropriately monetize information, comply with information laws, contain incidents and maximize recoveries and resilience. He has managed responses to multiple data breaches and information security incidents as well as helped design and implement strategic and compliance initiatives in the areas of privacy, cybersecurity and information management. He received his JD from Yale Law School and a BA, *magna cum laude*, from Dartmouth College.

Chris Pahl, CIPP/C, CIPP/E, CIPP/G, CIPP/US, CIPM, CIPT, FIP

As a privacy professional, Chris Pahl has worked within legal and compliance departments to develop overarching enterprise privacy programs while providing ongoing advisory services. He works with business units including customer service, information technology, human resources, sales, marketing, legal, and procurement to determine compliance with ethical and regulatory requirements for the collection, protection, use and transfer of personally identifiable information. He is responsible for privacy-related activities on matters such as privacy impact assessments, regulatory audits and company due diligence encompassing five million customers and 20,000 employees and retirees.

Pahl chairs the multidisciplinary privacy incident response teams at Southern California Edison, investigating potential privacy incidents and managing remediation actions. He has built and operationalized privacy compliance programs, completing multiple privacy assessments in the areas of enterprise data transfers and customer and employee support systems. In addition, he has worked on supporting system inventories and audits, data encryption, and implementation of data loss prevention (DLP) applications in live operating environments and implemented DLP solutions.

Pahl holds a doctoral degree in strategic leadership, actively writes for industry publications, and is a recipient of Southern California Edison's prestigious Edison Award based on his experience developing large-scale privacy programs from the ground up.

Tajma Rahimic

Tajma Rahimic is a privacy and data security associate on the global sourcing and technology team at Kilpatrick Townsend & Stockton LLP, focusing her practice on cybersecurity and data privacy.

Prior to joining the firm, Rahimic was an associate in the Washington, D.C. office of an international law firm specializing in telecommunications regulatory law in addition to privacy and security issues.

While attending law school, she served as a public policy intern at Comcast, government affairs legal intern at the Wireless Infrastructure Association, legal intern at the Federal Communications Commission in the Office of Commissioner Ajit Pai, legal intern at the International Trade Administration in the Department of Commerce, and law clerk at the Office of Overseas Prosecutorial Development Assistance and Training in the Department of Justice. Rahimic has also served as a member of the George Washington International Law Review.

Liisa Thomas

Liisa Thomas is a partner in Sheppard Mullin's Chicago and London offices and co-chair of its privacy and cybersecurity team, providing thoughtful legal analysis combined with real-world practical advice.

Thomas is the author of the definitive treatise on data breach, *Thomas on Data Breach: A Practical Guide to Handling Worldwide Data Breach Notification*, described as "a no-nonsense roadmap for in-house and external practitioners alike."

As an industry leader in the privacy and data security space, she has been recognized by Leading Lawyers Network, Chambers and The Legal 500 for her depth of privacy knowledge.

Thomas was named to *Cybersecurity Docket*'s "Incident Response 30," recognized as 2017 Data Protection Lawyer of the Year–USA by *Global 100*, 2017 U.S. Data Protection Lawyer of the Year by *Finance Monthly*, and a Leading Woman Lawyer by *Crain's* in 2018.

Thomas received her JD from the University of Chicago, is admitted to the bar in Illinois and the District of Columbia, and is an adjunct professor of privacy law at Northwestern University.

Amanda Witt, CIPP/E, CIPP/US

Amanda Witt is a partner at Kilpatrick Townsend & Stockton LLP and co-leader of the firm's cybersecurity, global privacy and data governance team. She is a CIPP/US and CIPP/E.

Witt advises clients on U.S., EU, and global privacy; cybersecurity; technology transactions; e-commerce; outsourcing; licensing and procurement; intellectual property protection; strategic alliances; software and mobile app development, licensing and global manufacturing; and distribution agreements relating to internet-connected devices.

Witt currently teaches cyber law and privacy as an adjunct professor at Georgia State's College of Law. She is a frequent presenter on topics related to EU and global privacy as well as technology-related topics such as blockchain, and has published articles on cybersecurity, privacy, cloud computing, electronic signatures, security laws, outsourcing and media.

Witt earned her LLM in international intellectual property, *magna cum laude*, from Catholic University at Leuven, Belgium and her JD, *cum laude*, from Emory University School of Law. She earned a bachelor of arts, *magna cum laude*, from the University of Florida, where she was inducted into *Phi Beta Kappa*.

Edward Yakabovicz, CIPP/G, CIPM, CIPT

Edward Yakabovicz is a cybersecurity architect and technical fellow for Northrop Grumman's cyber and intelligence mission solutions division, a leading global provider of advanced cyber solutions for defense, intelligence, civil agency and commercial customers.

Yakabovicz has more than 30 years' experience in cybersecurity, information security management, privacy management and engineering and is an experienced speaker who has given recent presentations at the NATO Cyber Resiliency Conference in 2017 and the COSAC and SABSA World Congress 2018. He currently chairs the National Defense Industrial Association(NDIA) Privacy Subcommittee and has held board positions with several colleges and universities and with the Information Systems Security Association and the IAPP.

Yakabovicz is currently a doctoral candidate in cybersecurity with a specialization in cyber workforce. His focus is to address the current human capital crisis in cybersecurity within government, defense and intelligence, and the problems facing international customers trying to meet complex, evolving cyber threats.

He coauthored the first edition of *Privacy Program Management: Tools for Managing Privacy Within Your Organization* textbook and contributed to many cybersecurity and privacy publications, both in print and online. In addition to his Certified Information Systems Security Professional (CISSP) accreditation, Yakabovicz holds numerous certifications across security and privacy industries and has received numerous awards for leadership, excellence and innovation.

Index

C

Federal laws. *See* Data subject rights in the
  United States
Federal Privacy Act of 1974, 40
Federal Trade Commission (FTC), 139, 149
  Children's Online Privacy Protection Rule
    (COPPA), 18
  DNC Registry and, 112
  privacy-related laws enforced by, 40, 41
  unfair and deceptive trade patterns and, 106
Federal Trade Commission Act, 106
Federal Trade Commission Act (Section 5) of
  1914, 41
Final audit phase, in audit lifecycle, 228
Finance stakeholders
  planning role, for data breach, 182–183
  role of, during an incident, 196–197
Financial privacy-related concerns, 42
Fines, 73
First-party audits, 228
First responders, 31
Forensic firms, 199–200, 204
Fox, Jonathan, 149–171, 233
*Framework for Improving Critical Infrastructure
  Cybersecurity Version 1.1* (NIST), 21
Frameworks, for building the privacy program
  awareness-raising and, 138
  defined, 19
  emerging, 19
  importance and purpose of, 19
  laws, regulations and programs, 20
  management solutions, 21–22
  objectives, 21–22
  principles and standards, 19–20
  rationalizing requirements, 22–23
France
  guidance on legal frameworks, 20
  privacy impact assessment guidelines, 77
Freedom of Information Act (FOIA), 113–114
Functional groups, understanding needed by, 5

G

Gap analysis, 67

GDPR (General Data Protection Regulation)
  appropriate technical and organizational
    measures, 152–153
  BCR requirements, 20
  breaches, responses to, 173
  compliance with, 1
  creation of, 46
  data protection by design and by default,
    151–152
  data protection officers (DPOs) required
    under, 33–34
  DPIA features set out in, 76
  electronic consent, 109
  fines for violations, 52
  framework for data protection and
    organizational obligations, 20
  as general privacy law, 39
  as global standard for data protection, 46
  on handling personal information, 15
  material scope, 47
  metrics for demonstrating compliance and,
    222–223
  noncompliance with DPIA requirements, 73
  overview, 46–49
  principles and standards, 19
  privacy as default, 149
  privacy notices and, 108
  privacy notices to children, 110–111
  records of processing activities under, 67–69
  subject-matter and objectives, 47
  territorial scope, 48–49
  vendor assessment under, 82
  what consumers can do, 48
  what organizations must do, 49
  what regulators can do, 49
  See also Data subject rights in the United
    States
General commercial liability (GCL), 197
General Data Protection Regulation (GDPR).
  See GDPR (General Data Protection
  Regulation)
Generally Accepted Privacy Principles (GAPP),
  20

Points of contact, in employee policies, 95
Policies. *See* Privacy policies
Policy or administrative controls, 158, 167-168
Ponemon Institute, 174, 213
Preparation phase, in audit lifecycle, 228
President/CEO
    planning role, for data breach, 183
    role of, during an incident, 201
Preventive controls, 158
Print vendors, 200
Privacy
    across the organization, 5–8
Privacy Act of 1974, 113
Privacy assessment, measuring compliance and, 69
Privacy by design (PbD)
    diagramming, 154–156
    dictates of, 149
    facilitated by a PIA, 69
    foundational concepts, 149
    foundational principles, 149–150
    illustrated, 150
    paradigm of, 150–151
    privacy engineering and, 154
    purpose and approach of, 21
Privacy champion, 26
Privacy checkpoints, 83
Privacy committee, 8
Privacy dashboard, 108
Privacy-enabling technologies (PETs), 163
Privacy engineering, 154, 168
Privacy-first mindset, 187
Privacy governance
    components of, listed, 11
    framework development and
        implementation, 19
    frameworks, 19–23
    governance, risk and compliance (GRC)
        tools and, 24
    governance models, 28–30
    organizational model, responsibilities and
        reporting structure, 30–34
    privacy strategy development, 24–27
    privacy team, structure of, 28

privacy vision and mission statement,
    creating, for organizations, 11–14
program scope, 14–18
See also entries for individual topics
Privacy impact assessment (PIA)
    accomplish early, 70
    defined, 69
    International Organization for
        Standardization (ISO) and, 72–73
    privacy professionals and, 71
    requirements regarding, 69
    triggering events, 70
    in the United States, 71–72
    uses of, 69, 70–71
    See also Data protection impact assessments
        (DPIA)
Privacy incidents, leveraging, 138–139
Privacy leaders
    educational and professional backgrounds
        of, 32
    titles used for, 31–32
Privacy Maturity Model (PMM), 221–222
Privacy mission statement, 11
Privacy notices
    communication considerations and
        re-evaluation of the fair information
        practice principles, 108–109
    defined, 92, 105–106
    design challenges and solutions, 106–108
    effectiveness of, 108
    elements of, 106
    goal of, 107
    illusion of control of, 108
    just-in-time, 107
    privacy policies versus, 91–92, 105–106
    providing, approaches to, 107
Privacy policies
    acceptable use policies (AUP), 96–97
    cloud computing acceptable use, 99
    communication of, within the organization,
        92–93
    compliance issues of, 91
    components of, 90–91